# THE DEVIL'S RICHES

## SPEKTRUM: *Publications of the German Studies Association*

Series editor: David M. Luebke, University of Oregon

Published under the auspices of the German Studies Association, *Spektrum* offers current perspectives on culture, society, and political life in the German-speaking lands of central Europe—Austria, Switzerland, and the Federal Republic—from the late Middle Ages to the present day. Its titles and themes reflect the composition of the GSA and the work of its members within and across the disciplines to which they belong—literary criticism, history, cultural studies, political science, and anthropology.

# The Devil's Riches

## A Modern History of Greed

JARED POLEY

berghahn
NEW YORK · OXFORD
www.berghahnbooks.com

Published in 2016 by

Berghahn Books

www.berghahnbooks.com

**Library of Congress Cataloging-in-Publication Data**

Poley, Jared, 1970–
    The devil's riches : a modern history of greed / Jared Poley.
        pages cm. — (Spektrum : publications of the German Studies Association ; Volume 11)
    Includes bibliographical references and index.
    ISBN 978-1-78533-126-8 (hardback : alk. paper) — ISBN 978-1-78533-127-5
    1. Avarice—History. I. Title.
    BJ1535.A8P65 2016
    178—dc23

                                                                        2015034839


**British Library Cataloguing in Publication Data**

A catalogue record for this book is available from the British Library


ISBN 978-1-78533-126-8 hardback
ISBN 978-1-78533-127-5 ebook

But he who loves riches sits on a shaky limb; a little breeze comes—and it enters his head to steal, to practise usury, to drive hard bargains, and other such evil practices, all of which serve him only to acquire the riches of the devil and not those of God.

—Paracelsus, *Liber prologi in vitam beatam* (1533)

Terms gradually die when the functions and experiences in the actual life of society cease to be bound up with them. At times, too, they only sleep, or sleep in certain respects, and acquire a new existential value from a new social situation. They are recalled then because something in the present state of society finds expression in the crystallization of the past embodied in the words.

—Norbert Elias, *The History of Manners*

# ❧ CONTENTS ❧

# ᐱ PREFACE ᐯ

I was struck during a trip to the Florida Panhandle in March 2009 by the visual indications of financial collapse. Miles of beachfront property stretched out along Highway 30a, each house with a "for sale" sign. Other houses had been framed but the construction halted, and they were being reclaimed by nature; wind and sand tore away the house wrap and pitted the wood. Standpipe memorials to acquisition slowly crumbled. To be clear, this was not Detroit, or Stockton, or even Atlanta, cities demolished by the fallout of the economic neutron bomb of 2008. Highway 30a was in theory something different, a kind of monument to American real estate fantasy, one populated by vacation rentals, investment properties, and luxurious getaways. Even Karl Rove owned a house there, in Rosemary Beach. I remember thinking at the time—naively, in hindsight—that the detritus of the housing bubble strewn along this stretch of the beach surely indicated some permanent change in the operations of unrestrained capitalism, the wreckage clear evidence that the machinery of desire had stripped its gears. Even my friend the banker seemed concerned.

That dire assessment was not entirely accurate, of course, but that is beside the point. Our collective anxiety about the origins of the financial crisis was quite real, fueled by the responses to the role that greed played in economic downfall. *The Devil's Riches* (which takes its title from a passage written by Paracelsus in 1533) is about the history of greed in the modern period. One part history of emotions and one part intellectual history, the volume examines how greed has been represented, understood, and analyzed since roughly 1450. It is oriented around three central themes: religion, economics, and health. Each of these areas of intellectual life was concerned with producing knowledge about, and channeling the power of, financial desire.

The volume shows how ideas about greed and avarice, never simply static or natural, helped formulate core elements of the modern experience. As discourses about religion, economics, and health underwent periods of dramatic change, greed was there to assist people make sense of those changes. Those undertaking an analysis of greed both clarified and advanced the self-interrogation and argument that constitutes the Western intellectual tradition. This book tells that story.

\* \* \*

I have incurred many debts—intellectual and otherwise—in the course of writing this book. The research was supported by the Georgia State University

History Department, by the College of Arts and Sciences, and by the GSU Research Foundation. I express my gratitude to David Warren Sabean, Mary Lindemann, Jason Coy, Ben Marschke, Claudia Verhoeven, Mike Sauter, Barry Trachtenberg, Merry Wiesner-Hanks, Ali Garbarini, Britta McEwen, Janet Ward, David Barclay, Charles Lansing, Roman Lach, Alexander Schunka, Wolfgang Breul, and Duane Corpis. The participants in the Southeast German Studies Workshop—who patiently offered their collective criticism of this project at various stages—have been extremely helpful, and the friendships I have made through this remarkable constellation of academics have been particularly meaningful. Monica Black, Tom Lekan, Eric Kurlander, Doug McGetchin, Tony Steinhoff, and Bryan Ganaway deserve special notice. There is a long list of people, geniuses all, to thank in my department at GSU: David Sehat, Nick Wilding, Jake Selwood, Marni Davis, Greg Moore, Denis Gainty, Julia Gaffield, Hugh Hudson, Jeff Young, Alex Cummings, and Isa Blumi, but most especially Rob Baker, Denise Davidson, and Michelle Brattain. I also call attention to those in our wonderful community in Decatur: David Davis, Odile Ferroussier, Reagan Koski, Geoff Koski, David Naugle, Rachel Ibarra, Lisa Armistead, Dan Kidder, Lyn Jellison, Jim Jellison, Joey Pate, Laurie Pate, Michele Hillegass, Aaron Hillegass, Grant Eager, Ginger Eager, Christi Wiltse, Justin Wiltse, John Ellis, Duran Dodson, Miguel Alandete, and Joy Pope as well as all of their great kids. Robert and Martha Poley—my parents—and James and Sylvia Carruth—my in-laws—are uniquely loving and supportive. James: you are missed.

I am especially grateful to the editor of the Spektrum series, David M. Luebke, for his collegiality, warmth, and intelligence; to Marion Berghahn for her support; to Chris Chappell for his editorial work; and to the anonymous reviewers for selflessly providing such useful critiques of the manuscript. Of course, all the errors that remain are my own.

I dedicate this book, with love, to Laura, Felix, and Vivian.

# The Devil's Riches
## A Modern History of Greed

Poggio Bracciolini's dialogue "On Avarice," written in the 1420s, depicts a conversation between three men at a dinner party. The discussion is a wide-ranging one, and the three conversationalists cover a number of themes: the importance of religion to understanding the establishment of power and social relations; the centrality of the profit motive to commerce; and the danger that avarice poses to one's spiritual health. Poggio's position on the issue of avarice is clear from the outset. Quoting Cicero, he suggests that avarice is the "main vice from which 'all crimes and misdeeds derive,'" and indeed the function of the dialogue is to suggest the many ways that covetousness disrupted not only the internal qualities of a person but also the social fabric.[1] One of the men, the host Bartolomeo da Montepulciano, argues that avarice is worse even than lust. A rebuttal is provided by one of the guests, Antonio Loschi, who appreciates what could be termed the "collateral benefits of greed." A final critique of acquisitiveness and a rebuttal of Loschi's arguments are provided by another guest, Andrea of Constantinople, who reaffirms da Montepulciano's attack by suggesting that greed is unnatural, effeminizing, and even a form of self-enslavement.

Poggio (1380–1459) is typically seen as a classic example of the Renaissance humanist courtier. He served the Papal Curia and was patronized by the rulers of Florence. He was known not only for the lucidity of his rhetoric but also as a renowned book hunter who could sniff out lost texts for his patron's collections with incredible capability. Poggio's text on avarice is well known, and the positions that his speakers lay down have been understood as defining the range of possibilities informing the moral universe of the late medieval understanding of acquisitiveness. The dialogue poses a traditional view of avarice as the worst of all vices (a position established in the dialogue by Bartolomeo da Montepulciano) against what historian Richard Newhauser characterizes as a "utilitarian, even modern" vision of greed that includes an "open acknowledgement of what is positive in the urge to acquire possessions" voiced by Antonio

Loschi.[2] Indeed, Newhauser argues that by the time Poggio's text was written in the 1420s the "boundaries of the definition of avarice as a vice" were set.[3]

The task of this book is to examine how greed, perhaps momentarily crystallized into a particular form in the 1420s, enjoyed a robust historical development over the subsequent centuries. Those changes are evident in the three areas covered by this text: religion, economics, and health. Intellectual historians have not treated the modern history of greed with quite the same energy as other topics. This book offers a multilayered treatment of the problem of what happened to greed over the course of the past five hundred years, considering how it was experienced, shaped, and feared. Greed, the evidence shows, was something we learned to feel in our moral centers and was expressed in the ways we rationalized and made sense of an unjust world.

The writing of this book coincided with much of the recent economic upheaval and social dislocation adhering to the Great Recession. I drafted the first chapters in the fall of 2008, other sections were written as the Occupy movement sought to generate a conversation about income inequality and the exercise of political power, and the book is being concluded as Thomas Piketty's *Capital in the Twenty-First Century* generates a renewed interest in similar themes.[4] It is fair to say that the events of the past five or six years have led to the idea that greed has been a way of framing all sorts of flaws in our system; greed has taken on a power of its own to articulate a set of morally inflected criticisms. Indeed, we see the word used more than 1,100 times in the pages of the *New York Times* opinion section since September 2008.

This book aims to uncover the understandings of avarice and greed in the early modern and modern worlds, locating greed within the history of ideas and within differing political economies. If we understand "covetousness" to be the lynchpin or organizing principle of the modern capitalist economy then we must investigate the roles that religion and religious categories have had in the creation and critique of this economy. By locating greed in various historical and theoretical contexts, it becomes possible to make a significant contribution to our understanding of the basic categories of human behavior over the course of the past five centuries. Greed is about more than money. It offers us a lens through which to glimpse the ways that human behaviors, codes of conduct, and intellectual, emotional, and cultural systems have changed over time. The history of greed is intimately bound up with histories of desire, of the emotions, and of passion. Greed allows us to investigate anew the relationships forged by humans between the material, the cultural, and the social. I begin with the assumption that acquisitiveness and covetousness are not "natural" but instead are deeply historical and the products of the human intellect. Humans have drawn the line between legitimate consumption and illegitimate desires differently at different times; we have determined in radically different ways the differences between need and luxury. As such, a history of greed offers us the opportunity to investigate some of the most human of the humanities: the ways that desires have been produced and understood, defended and attacked, denied and repressed.

Because the focus of the present work is on human ideas and how these ideas have changed over time, the project is situated in such a way that humans and their interactions with the material world and with each other are the central area of focus. The work historicizes essential aspects of the human experience and allows us to understand exchange more broadly than the merely financial. The study contributes to the humanities as an organized field of knowledge by generating the language required to understand acquisition and its perceived moral failures and constructing a historical grammar within which these issues may be narrated.

My approach to the broader problem of the history of greed is situated at the intersection of the history of emotions and the history of ideas. Historians have been interested in emotions at least since the publication of Johan Huizinga's *Autumn of the Middle Ages* in 1919.[5] The field of study acquired a theoretical foundation with the publication of Carol Stearns and Peter Stearns's 1985 essay in the *American Historical Review* in which they coined the term "emotionology" to describe the social scientific study of emotions and their histories.[6] William Reddy's 2001 book *The Navigation of Feeling* introduced another important principle to the problem: the integration of emotions, history, and practices.[7] Monique Scheer follows Reddy's insight by indicating how the social and the emotional might intersect by applying a Bourdieuian approach to "emotional capital" as a way to probe larger social structures.[8] It is also important to note that the field has not been limited to the work of American and French historians. A 2009 special issue of *Geschichte und Gesellschaft* demonstrates how German scholars have approached these problems. The German Studies Association has sponsored a network on emotions for several years; dozens of sessions have been included in the annual conference.

While this book is usefully looked at alongside other "history of emotions" texts, it may be equally helpful to consider its approach as a more traditional exercise in the history of ideas. Looking at how ideas about avarice and greed have changed, we can see better how we might approach a larger history of desire. In that spirit, this book addresses a "bedrock" category within the Western experience and may be situated alongside allied histories. While it does not approach a similar chronological or temporal complexity, I hope that my book will remind readers of Darrin M. McMahon's *Happiness: A History*, which traces the history of a feeling through an analysis of ideas.[9] Other works on the history of greed have not typically followed this path. Richard Newhauser's work stands out for its emphasis on ideas and his savvy reading of early religious texts.[10] Anthropologist A.F. Robertson approaches the subject from that disciplinary standpoint, while economist Nancy Folbre considers the importance of gender to the development of economic thinking in her 2009 book *Greed, Lust, & Gender: A History of Economic Ideas*.[11] Other significant entries in the field include Phyllis Tickle's *Greed: The Seven Deadly Sins*, which provides a lively popular analysis of the problem.[12]

This book differs in important ways from previous analyses of the topic. It embraces a different chronological perspective, examining the topic from the late medieval to the twentieth century. Like Newhauser, who argues that discourse on greed was frozen by the time of Poggio's *Dialogue* in 1429, this study notes the similarities between Poggio's understanding of greed and our own. But more importantly, it seeks to trace the wide perambulations of the category since the fifteenth century. Poggio's understanding of greed was not identical to our own. Poggio's description of greed is recognizable—genetically similar, I suppose, to our contemporary understanding of the topic—but it is a cousin, not a progenitor, of our ways of framing the vice. While mindful of Barbara Rosenwein's critique that the medieval often presents a useful foil to historians of the modern period, the argument of this book is not as concerned with the intellectual foundations of modernity as it is with tracing historical contours of the modern experience.[13] It is not the case, as Rosenwein cautions, that the premodern period should be seen as emotionally childlike and transparent, when feelings were felt roughly and intensely, unlike the restrained and suppressed modern period.[14] Greed demonstrates, if nothing else, the connecting points across temporal periods. To employ a hoary image: emotions flowed—perhaps with differing intensities at different times, but certainly within different channels depending on historical context.

The book, although following a generally chronological framework, traces three particular themes: religion, economics, and health. Each of these topics has been characteristically significant in the historical trajectories that we will consider in the course of the book. The focus on religion allows us to take up the question of how old religious precepts worked, and were reworked, over a period of acute religious upheaval and "secularization" and in the construction of new forms of spirituality. Tracing a period from just prior to the Reformation to the creation of "new spiritualities" in the nineteenth and twentieth centuries, we see the continuing effects of religion on a set of critical behaviors. When we consider economics, we wrestle with the larger problem of how desires and consumerist behaviors intersected with the elaboration and proliferation of capitalist and industrial economies. We also examine health, considering the transformations from an alchemical discourse on desire and well-being from the early modern period to a psychological and psychoanalytic one produced in the early twentieth century.

Blaise Pascal writes in the *Pensées* (which was published posthumously in 1669), "Concupiscence has become natural for us and has become our second nature. There are therefore two natures in us: one good, the other bad. Where is God? Where you are not. *And the kingdom of God is within you.*"[15] We see in this passage a hint of several themes that animate our study of how religion and the history of greed have intersected in the Western tradition over the course of the past six hundred years. Pascal wrestled with the nature of desire, seeking to understand where desire originated and how desire produced a type of force field within which social relations and individual moral claims to understand good and evil unfolded. Understanding greed was a central thrust in larger Western projects of defining social justice, orienting people to the correct direction of God, and justifying both individuality and communal power structures alike.

We will see as the book unfolds how older religious beliefs inherited from antiquity were reimagined and given a new importance. Martin Luther and the Protestant Reformation, in tandem with the Catholic Reformation of the sixteenth century, sought new ways to understand and to mobilize financial desires. Luther's understanding of "honorable wealth" or Erasmus's attack on princes who merely seek "new ways to squeeze money out of citizens" indicate some of the perambulations upon which greed embarked in the early modern period.[16] We also consider the ways that new theological positions on wealth, money, and riches informed the penetration of confessionally determined "emotional regimes" centered on money. Taking Jean Calvin's analyses of covetousness as a foundation, we consider the ways that confession and confessionalization helped forge new ways of financial being.

Religion—and its apprehension of greed and avarice—also promoted certain visions of the proper communal and social relations, although, as we will see, there were many different valuations of thrift and economy that were produced on a religious foundation. As Pascal wrote, "And God himself is the enemy of those whose covetousness he disturbs."[17] Concepts like duty and charity, filtered through the prescriptions of the Church, were expressed in a language hostile to greed. Visions of a functioning religious community, then, sought to place new limits on acquisition and retention. As Pascal claimed in the *Pensées*, "For there are two principles which divide man's will: cupidity and charity. It is not that cupidity is incompatible with faith in God, and that charity is incompatible with earthly benefits. But cupidity makes use of God and delights in the world, whereas charity does the opposite."[18]

We trace in later chapters of the book new ways of thinking about greed and money as they were expressed in heterodox, underground, or historically novel religious movements. We consider the ways that late nineteenth-century Satanism, for instance, imagined financial desire. We examine how theosophy—with its orientalized language of astral planes, oneiric transport, and harmonious communal connection—envisioned greedy souls and their auras. We connect the early modern occult to the modern variety, probing the ways that magic and money functioned in the midst of rational, progressive, bourgeois life.

It is nearly impossible to divorce a study of the history of greed from an analysis of how it blossomed within various religious contexts. The same is true for economics, yet one is struck by the many ways that religious ideals continuously informed economic ones. Since the publication of Albert Hirschman's *The Passions and the Interests* in 1977, scholars have been attuned to the ways that economics has borrowed key principles from other areas of human life.[19] We trace in this book aspects of how economics, in its search for the best ways to husband resources, has wrestled with the problem of desire—linking it to various moral conditions and seeking to understand how to mobilize it in the name of human progress.

Writing in 1930, John Maynard Keynes noted the ways that money, greed, and morality were entwined, and he posited a central role for historical change in his analysis of these problems:

> When the accumulation of wealth is no longer of high social importance, there will be great changes in the code of morals. We shall be able to rid ourselves of many of the pseudo-moral principles which have hag-ridden us for two hundred years, by which we have exalted some of the most distasteful of human qualities into the position of the highest virtues. We shall be able to afford to dare to assess the money-motive at its true value. The love of money as a possession—as distinguished from the love of money as a means to the enjoyments and realities of life—will be recognized for what it is, a somewhat disgusting morbidity, one of those semi-criminal, semi-pathological propensities which one hands over with a shudder to the specialists in mental disease.[20]

The passage continues, and Keynes's reader is reminded anew of the importance of morality to economic functioning:

> I see us free, therefore, to return to some of the most sure and certain principles of religion and traditional virtue—that avarice is a vice, that the exaction of usury is a misdemeanour, and the love of money is detestable, that those walk most truly in the paths of virtue and sane wisdom who take least thought for the morrow.... But beware! The time for all this is not yet.... Avarice and usury and precaution must be our gods for a little longer still. For only they can lead us out of the tunnel of economic necessity into daylight.[21]

Writing from the vantage point of 1930, and imagining the future of greed and the "economic possibilities" for his grandchildren, Keynes embraced a moral critique of acquisition and retention that echoed earlier ones. Keynes, of course, was only one voice in this chorus. Commenting nearly at the same time as Keynes was writing, Ludwig von Mises took a predictably different approach to the problem of the "moral economy." Noting the ways that "classical economics" had leveled a devastating blow to the idea that behaviors should be conditioned by anything other than the logic of self-interest, von Mises writes in 1933:

Price rises, increases in the rate of interest, and wage reductions, which were formerly attributed to the greed and heartlessness of the rich, are now traced back by this theory to quite natural reactions of the market to changes in supply and demand. Moreover, it shows that the division of labor in the social order based on private property would be utterly impossible without these adjustments by the market. What was condemned as a moral injustice—indeed, as a punishable offense—is here looked upon as, so to speak, a natural occurrence. Capitalists, entrepreneurs, and speculators no longer appear as parasites and exploiters, but as members of the system of social organization whose function is absolutely indispensable. The application of pseudomoral standards to market phenomena loses every semblance of justification. The concepts of usury, profiteering, and exploitation are stripped of their ethical import and thus become absolutely meaningless.[22]

By 1945, the stakes had become even more sharply defined for von Mises, who reaffirmed the utterly world-changing nature of Smithian economics, a position that was no doubt correct. He argued in one presentation:

From the point of view of "natural law," the only just state of affairs is equality of income. The unfathomable decrees of Heaven have brought about inequality. It would be tantamount to a rebellion against divine and human law for the underprivileged to resort to violence in order to abolish this injustice. By such methods they could profit on earth, but they would imperil their spiritual salvation. On the other hand, the rich have only one means to atone for their questionable riches. They must make the proper use of their wealth, that is, they must be charitable and must subordinate their greed to justice and fairness.... Utilitarianism and classical economics have entirely overthrown this philosophy.[23]

We see in these passages a diversity of opinion about the meaning and significance not only of the eighteenth-century invention of classical economics but also of the place of morality in economic thinking. Over the course of the book we consider these themes in some detail, tracing how Lutheran positions on commerce helped shape ideas about the "instrumentality of money" by secular thinkers like Michel de Montaigne. We consider the role played by discussions of miserly behavior in grounding debates about exchange and circulation, take up questions related to law and empire, the place of property and property rights, and the idea of profligacy, which in some eras was castigated and in others celebrated for its economic impacts. In later chapters we consider the importance of the category of greed to the place of "moral sentiments" as they conditioned economic behaviors and probe the centrality of greed to the founding of key social sciences in the nineteenth century. Taking on larger questions about the relationships between money and society, we also consider the ways that money—and how people treated and used it—could serve as a foundation for several "philosophies" of money in the nineteenth and twentieth centuries.

These philosophies of money—to which an analysis of greed and desire remained central elements—were often backward looking, taking inspiration and emphasis from previous historical epochs. As Keynes wrote in 1930 in an essay titled "Auri Sacra Fames" (The Accursed Hunger for Gold):

> [Gold] no longer passes from hand to hand, and the touch of the metal has been taken away from men's greedy palms. The little household gods, who dwelt in purses and stockings and tin boxes, have been swallowed by a single golden image in each country, which lives underground and is not seen. Gold is out of sight—gone back again into the soil. But when gods are no longer seen in a yellow panoply walking the earth, we begin to rationalise them; and it is not long before there is nothing left.... It is not a far step from this to the beginning of arrangements between Central Banks by which, without ever formally renouncing the rule of gold, the quantity of metal actually buried in their vaults may come to stand, by a modern alchemy, for what they please, and its value for what they choose.[24]

Keynes's reference to what he called a "modern alchemy" recalls the third theme of the book: medicine and health. Alchemy—as it was conceived in the early modern period and reworked in the nineteenth century—sought not only to transform the base into the noble but also to align and balance the humors and the elements for optimal health. Alchemy was thus concerned with understanding and regulating the connections between internal and external, isolating blockages and removing them. Health was as much a part of alchemical discourse as the transformation of metals. And alchemy, as we will see, also sought answers to the questions plaguing early modern people: How should society be regulated? What duties did the social body have to its constituent elements? How should inequality be understood? How could humans understand the fabric of God's creation? Answers to these questions could be located in an analysis of the health of a body—whether it was social or individual.

Alchemists sought to relate exterior signs to internal conditions. Later medical discourse operated in similar fashion, and again greed and avarice produced valuable symptoms that could be read by a trained eye. One seventeenth-century text identifies the physiognomic signs for which to watch: "Of the Covetous. His Face, Members and Eyes are little; his Complexion somewhat Ruddy, hath a crook'd Back, and a sharp piercing querulous voice."[25] Another from the same period counseled men to be on the lookout for "Great plenty of hair in a woman," which "doth shew boisterousness and covetousness."[26]

In both these cases we see how greed—covetousness in this case—related body to soul, connecting one's inner character to a range of bodily signs. The close connection between bodily health and spiritual health that we see in these examples was replicated in later periods in descriptions of the miser's body, which was typically depicted as unhealthy. It is useful to note, however, that some writers chalked up the existence of a healthy body to the degree of avarice animating one's behavior: "The passion called avarice…tends rather to preserve than to destroy the physical health," wrote Martyn Westcott at the turn of the twentieth century. "The hoarding of money, to be carried out successfully, implies the exercise of several qualities which are in themselves excellent. A large proportion of disease among us at the present day is doubtless the result of our luxury and pampering. The miser by his extreme economy, denies himself all luxuries because they are so expensive, and so he runs little risk of the disorders due to excesses in eating and drinking."[27]

Greed, as we will see, was depicted by other writers as the etiology of a set of mental disorders peculiar to modernity. Some fixated on the lack of calm and spiritual restlessness associated with the tortures of a desire spun out of control; others commented on the role of the "passions" in driving humans to strange behaviors on account of their desire for money. The consumer revolution brought about its own set of disorders—*Affekten* as one seventeenth-century German called them—associated with greed, elements of which one may see demonstrated in later psychological descriptions of "oniomania": the passion for buying things one does not really need.

Sigmund Freud, as we will see in later chapters, placed greed as a primary expression of the "anal personality type," thus embodying avarice in novel ways in the early twentieth century. His followers, impressed by Freud's extension of individual qualities into character traits affecting large numbers of the population, used his method of characterology to apply psychoanalytic insights about the origins of greedy behavior to entire groups of people. In short, the evidence that we will consider demonstrates that greed and avarice were intimately bound up with ideas about health—not just spiritual, but also physical and mental—since the sixteenth century.

These arguments about the role of avarice and greed in larger debates about religion, economics, and health unfold over seven chapters. We begin by examining the problem of greed before absolutism, looking carefully at Poggio's dialogue, Martin Luther's ruminations on a range of topics including commerce and honor, and the writings of the alchemist Paracelsus, before taking up the question of how Latin terms like *avaritia* and *cupiditas* were transmitted into vernacular languages in the sixteenth century. We turn in Chapter Two to the question of confessionalization of greed as an emotion, looking at Catholic reformers, Jean Calvin, and the humanist Michel de Montaigne as examples of the process in the sixteenth century. Chapter Three considers the problem of greed in international and natural law of the seventeenth century, using Hugo Grotius, Samuel von Pufendorf, John Locke, and François Fénelon to probe the issue.

In Chapter Four we expand the discussion into the eighteenth century, looking into how academics like Christian Thomasius and Christian Wolff; authors like Bernard Mandeville, Jonathan Swift, and Thomas Fielding; leaders like Frederick the Great; and thinkers like Jean-Jacques Rousseau, Adam Smith, and Jeremy Bentham incorporated greed and avarice into their respective disciplines. In Chapter Five we take on the topic of liberalism and socialism and the ways that each treated the problem of greed as a foundation of human economic behavior. In the course of the discussion we look at William Godwin, Thomas Malthus, and Jean-Baptiste Say before considering a range of bourgeois novels from the nineteenth century to understand the popular stakes involved. The chapter concludes with an analysis of how greed was included in socialist thought by intellectuals John Stuart Mill, Karl Marx, and William Morris.

Chapter Six takes up the issue of "new spiritualities," probing how theosophists like Helena Blavatsky and Rudolf Steiner understood greed, how decadent writers worked with the category, and how religious analysts like Marcel Mauss employed the term. The chapter also considers ways of using anthropology and social theory to understand the incorporation of greed into "occult" theologies. The book concludes by examining the inclusion of greed and avarice in psychological and psychoanalytic thought by considering aspects of the work of, among others, Max Nordau, Georg Simmel, Sigmund Freud, and Sándor Ferenczi.

In short: greed has a history. This book tells it.

## Notes

1. Poggio Bracciolini, "On Avarice," in *The Earthly Republic: Italian Humanists on Government and Society*, ed. Benjamin G. Kohl and Ronald G. Witt (Philadelphia: University of Pennsylvania Press, 1978), 242.
2. Richard Newhauser, *The Early History of Greed: The Sin of Avarice in Early Medieval Thought and Literature* (New York: Cambridge University Press, 2000), xii.
3. Newhauser, *Early History of Greed*, xii.
4. Thomas Piketty, *Capital in the Twenty-First Century* (Cambridge, MA: Harvard University Press, 2014).
5. See Barbara H. Rosenwein, "Worrying about Emotions in History," *The American Historical Review* 107, no. 3 (2002): 821–45 for an overview of the historiographical landscape.
6. Peter N. Stearns and Carol Z. Stearns, "Emotionology: Clarifying the History of Emotions and Emotional Standards," *The American Historical Review* 90, no. 4 (1985): 813–36.
7. William M. Reddy, *The Navigation of Feeling: A Framework for the History of Emotions* (New York: Cambridge University Press, 2001).
8. Monique Scheer, "Are Emotions a Kind of Practice (And Is That What Makes Them Have a History)? A Bourdieuian Approach to Understanding Emotion," *History and Theory* 51, no. 2 (2012): 193–220.
9. Darrin M. McMahon, *Happiness: A History* (New York: Grove Press, 2006).
10. Newhauser, *Early History of Greed*; Newhauser, ed., *In the Garden of Evil: The Vices and Culture in the Middle Ages*, Papers in Mediaeval Studies 18 (Toronto: Pontifical Institute of Mediaeval Studies, 2005); Newhauser, *Sin: Essays on the Moral Tradition in the Western Middle Ages* (Aldershot: Ashgate/Variorum, 2007).

11. A.F. Robertson, *Greed: Gut Feelings, Growth, and History* (Cambridge: Polity Press, 2001); Nancy Folbre, *Greed, Lust & Gender: A History of Economic Ideas* (Oxford: Oxford University Press, 2009).
12. Phyllis Tickle, *Greed: The Seven Deadly Sins* (New York: New York Public Library, 2004).
13. Rosenwein, "Worrying about Emotions," 828.
14. Ibid., 827.
15. Blaise Pascal, *Pensées and Other Writings*, trans. Honor Levi (Oxford: Oxford University Press, 2008), 122. Pascal practiced Jansenism, a variant of Catholicism practiced mainly in France that promoted the usefulness of grace, predestination, and the centrality of the Fall to an understanding of the depraved condition of humanity.
16. Martin Luther, *Works of Martin Luther: With Introductions and Notes*, Philadelphia ed, vol. IV (Philadelphia: Muhlenberg Press, 1930), 166; Desiderius Erasmus, *The Praise of Folly and Other Writings: A New Translation with Critical Commentary* (New York: Norton, 1989), 67.
17. Pascal, *Pensées and Other Writings*, 176.
18. Ibid.
19. Albert O. Hirschman, *The Passions and the Interests: Political Arguments for Capitalism before Its Triumph* (Princeton: Princeton University Press, 1977).
20. John Maynard Keynes, "Economic Possibilities for Our Grandchildren," in *Essays in Persuasion* (Harcourt, Brace, 1932), 369.
21. Ibid., 371–72.
22. Ludwig von Mises, *Epistemological Problems of Economics* (Auburn: Ludwig von Mises Institute, 1976), 209.
23. Ludwig von Mises, *Economic Freedom and Interventionism: An Anthology of Articles and Essays by Ludwig von Mises* (Indianapolis: Liberty Fund, 2007), 254.
24. John Maynard Keynes, "Auri Sacra Fames," in *Essays in Persuasion* (Harcourt, Brace and Company, 1932), 183–85.
25. Frederick Hendrick van Hove, *Oniropolus, or Dreams Interpreter. Being Several Aphorisms upon the Physiognomy of Dreams Made into Verse. Some of Which Receive a General Interpretation: And Others of Them Have Respect to the Course of the Moon in the Zodiack. To Which Is Added Several Physiognomical Characters of Persons of Different Humours and Inclinations. After Which Follows the Praise of Ale. And Lastly, the Wheel of Fortune, or Pithagoras Wheel.* (London: Tho. Dawkes, 1680), 67.
26. William Lilly, *A Groats Worth of Wit for a Penny, Or, The Interpretation of Dreams ... by Mr. Lilly*, Early English Books, 1641–1700/1152:46 (London: Printed for W.T. and sold by Ionah Deacon ..., [1670?], 1670), 13.
27. Martyn Westcott, "On the Influence of the Passions on Our Health," *Womanhood: The Magazine of Woman's Progress and Interests, Political, Legal, Social, and Intellectual, and of Health and Beauty Culture* 5, no. 27 (1901): 177.

# Bibliography

Bracciolini, Poggio. "On Avarice." In *The Earthly Republic: Italian Humanists on Government and Society*, edited by Benjamin G. Kohl and Ronald G. Witt, 241–89. Philadelphia: University of Pennsylvania Press, 1978.
Erasmus, Desiderius. *The Praise of Folly and Other Writings: A New Translation with Critical Commentary*. New York: Norton, 1989.

Folbre, Nancy. *Greed, Lust & Gender: A History of Economic Ideas.* Oxford: Oxford University Press, 2009.

Hirschman, Albert O. *The Passions and the Interests: Political Arguments for Capitalism before Its Triumph.* Princeton: Princeton University Press, 1977.

Hove, Frederick Hendrick van. *Oniropolus, or Dreams Interpreter. Being Several Aphorisms upon the Physiognomy of Dreams Made into Verse. Some of Which Receive a General Interpretation: And Others of Them Have Respect to the Course of the Moon in the Zodiack. To Which Is Added Several Physiognomical Characters of Persons of Different Humours and Inclinations. After Which Follows the Praise of Ale. And Lastly, the Wheel of Fortune, or Pithagoras Wheel.* London: Tho. Dawkes, 1680.

Keynes, John Maynard. "Auri Sacra Fames." In *Essays in Persuasion,* 181–85. New York: Harcourt, Brace, 1932.

———. "Economic Possibilities for Our Grandchildren." In *Essays in Persuasion,* 358–73. New York: Harcourt, Brace, 1932.

Lilly, William. *A Groats Worth of Wit for a Penny, Or, The Interpretation of Dreams ... by Mr. Lilly.* Early English Books, 1641–1700 / 1152:46. London: Printed for W.T. and sold by Ionah Deacon ... , [1670?], 1670.

Luther, Martin. *Works of Martin Luther: With Introductions and Notes.* Philadelphia ed. Vol. IV. Philadelphia: Muhlenberg Press, 1930.

McMahon, Darrin M. *Happiness: A History.* New York: Grove Press, 2006.

Mises, Ludwig von. *Economic Freedom and Interventionism: An Anthology of Articles and Essays by Ludwig von Mises.* Indianapolis: Liberty Fund, 2007.

———. *Epistemological Problems of Economics.* Auburn: Ludwig von Mises Institute, 1976.

Newhauser, Richard. *The Early History of Greed: The Sin of Avarice in Early Medieval Thought and Literature.* New York: Cambridge University Press, 2000.

———, ed. *In the Garden of Evil: The Vices and Culture in the Middle Ages.* Papers in Mediaeval Studies 18. Toronto: Pontifical Institute of Mediaeval Studies, 2005.

———. *Sin: Essays on the Moral Tradition in the Western Middle Ages.* Aldershot: Ashgate/ Variorum, 2007.

Pascal, Blaise. *Pensées and Other Writings.* Translated by Honor Levi. Oxford: Oxford University Press, 2008.

Piketty, Thomas. *Capital in the Twenty-First Century.* Cambridge, MA: Harvard University Press, 2014.

Reddy, William M. *The Navigation of Feeling: A Framework for the History of Emotions.* New York: Cambridge University Press, 2001.

Robertson, A.F. *Greed: Gut Feelings, Growth, and History.* Cambridge: Polity Press, 2001.

Rosenwein, Barbara H. "Worrying about Emotions in History." *The American Historical Review* 107, no. 3 (2002): 821–45.

Scheer, Monique. "Are Emotions a Kind of Practice (And Is That What Makes Them Have a History)? A Bourdieuian Approach to Understanding Emotion." *History and Theory* 51, no. 2 (2012): 193–220.

Stearns, Peter N. and Carol Z. Stearns. "Emotionology: Clarifying the History of Emotions and Emotional Standards." *The American Historical Review* 90, no. 4 (1985): 813–36.

Tickle, Phyllis. *Greed: The Seven Deadly Sins.* New York: New York Public Library, 2004.

Westcott, Martyn. "On the Influence of the Passions on Our Health." *Womanhood: The Magazine of Woman's Progress and Interests, Political, Legal, Social, and Intellectual, and of Health and Beauty Culture* 5, no. 27 (1901): 177–78.

# CHAPTER ONE

# Greed and Avarice
# before Absolutism

In Poggio Bracciolini's 1429 dialogue "On Avarice" Bartolomeo da Montepulciano begins his critique of greed with a thought problem, a comparison of the "two cruelest plagues [to] infect the human race," lust and avarice.[1] The vices, "so pernicious that it's difficult to remain unaffected by them," attack mercilessly and widely. Da Montepulciano, echoing the medieval tradition of constructing hierarchies of sin, places avarice and lust in a primary position: "Avarice and lust are, as it were, the seat and foundation of all evils."[2] Lust, da Montepulciano argues, may be dismissed as truly perilous because "it can be, in a sense, a kind of pleasant evil that is involved in the procreation of children. It is harmful to itself alone and not to others, and it is related to the continuance of the human race."[3]

Avarice, on the other hand, caused demonstrable social chaos: "Avarice is a despicable crime, harming everyone, and aimed at the subjugation of all mortals. It is harmful to all, injurious to everyone, and hostile to everyone. It is joined to nothing that is praise-worthy or honorable. It is a horrible, dreadful monster born to ruin people, to destroy fellowship among men. You can believe me that nothing is more loathsome, nothing baser, nothing more horrible than avarice."[4] The twin problems posed by the ruin of the individual and the collapse of "fellowship" indicated close connections between internal conditions and external ones that could be revealed and made known through the close study of avarice.

In his classic assessment of the late medieval period, *Autumn of the Middle Ages*, Johan Huizinga argued that greed, once the younger twin of pride, had risen to prominence in an age dedicated to market relations. "Pride," Huizinga wrote, "is the sin of the feudal and hierarchic period during which possessions and wealth circulate very little."[5] With the early modern period, however, a great change overtook the ranking of sins, and avarice took on renewed importance. The evidence, drawn here from sources that range across the Italian- and

German-speaking territories as well as Britain from the 1420s to the 1560s, indicates the contours of an emotion that was thought capable of forging relationships between individuals and God, between individuals and their communities, between rich and poor, and between producers and consumers.

Talking about avarice, greed, covetousness, or desires inappropriately spun out of control provided a language through which morality, nature, economic exchange, divinity, social conditions, power relations, and gender codes could be articulated. The source material that we will consider is drawn from social elites, all of them men, so it is important to remember that while there is considerable richness to and diversity within the discourse on covetousness from this time, the evidence reflects the values of the social core, not the periphery. Our aim is to indicate the axes upon which discourse on greed traveled during this period and not to give an exhaustive survey of every mention.

We begin by considering avarice in Italian humanism, examining in detail Poggio Bracciolini's dialogue "On Avarice" for what it tells us about social crime, nature, and covetousness; the positive outcomes of inappropriate desire; and the perceived duality of the sin. Following the discussion of Poggio's dialogue, we turn to an analysis of the ways that Martin Luther understood avarice in terms of honor and sin, looking especially at his descriptions of honorable wealth and profit taking in order to probe how these issues were understood in the sixteenth-century German lands. We turn next to consider alchemy and the ways that health, society, and spirituality were intertwined in the thought of another German: the alchemist Paracelsus.[6] Finally, we consider the ways that *avaritia* and *cupiditas* were deployed in early modern Bibles in order to understand the religious precepts that ordered ideas about covetousness in the sixteenth century.

The suggestion raised in the passage beginning this chapter is that avarice is an emotion that incorporated a social crime into itself—a crime that not only ruins a person but also could destroy community—indicates the seriousness and multiple valences that avarice carried in the fifteenth century. In the dialogue Poggio advances three central definitions of avarice. One of his speakers, the critic of avarice da Montepulciano, provides one definition that focuses on how financial qualities have become critical markers of identity. He defines avarice as a "boundless desire to possess, or better still, a kind of hunger to accumulate wealth," but this definition stems from a broader discussion of avaricious behaviors that allow the categorization of humanity according to wealth.[7]

Poggio writes that there are people who "are desirous of gold, silver, or bronze, who put all their effort into amassing wealth, who are always seeking it, always wanting it, who are reluctant to spend money and despise no means to satisfy their desire for profit, who judge everything from the standpoint of their own benefit and reckon success always in terms of money—these persons are rightly called avaricious."[8] This striking emphasis on individuality, self-promotion, and "reckoning success" through financial criteria is usefully placed within the context of the humanist project, but it is also important to remember that Poggio and his proxy da Montepulciano are offering a critique of such methods.

Antonio Loschi and Andrea of Constantinople are less explicit in their definitions of avarice and even include some positive evaluations of the category. Loschi argues that to his mind "lust is always harmful, while avarice, sometimes, is beneficial."[9] In a different passage, Loschi subscribes to the definition of avarice provided by St. Augustine: "Saint Augustine … [has] written: 'Avarice is the desire to have more than enough.'"[10] Andrea is even less helpful, in part because he seems to disassociate merely possessing wealth from the emotional life of the avaricious person. Andrea argues, "If you wish to become rich, you can obtain wealth quicker and more easily by despising it than by lusting after it."[11] While Loschi and Andrea had a difficult time providing a concrete definition of avarice that matched the one provided by da Montepulciano, Poggio had them each devote significant effort in placing avarice within the realm of, or fundamentally opposed to, nature itself.

Da Montepulciano initiated this line of argumentation in the dialogue by claiming that avarice "is the enemy of nature."[12] Loschi was unconvinced, and in the context of his halfhearted celebration of avarice, he attempted to naturalize avarice as a way of defusing the claim that the emotion was a poisonous one. Loschi begins this argument by locating avarice within the terms of normal financial exchange:

> In fact, everything we undertake is for the sake of money, and we are all led by desire for gain, and not a small profit either. If you were to remove that profit, all business and work would entirely cease, for whoever undertakes anything without hope of it? The more evident the profit, the more willingly we enter into the enterprise. All follow gain, all desire it. Whether you consider the military profession, or business, or agriculture, or the arts, both liberal and mercenary, the desire for money is innate in everyone. Everything we treat, work at, or undertake is directed at getting as much profit as possible. For its sake we undertake hazards and run risks. The more we profit, the more we rejoice, and those profits are almost always measured by money. Therefore, everything is done for money, that is, because of avarice.[13]

If avarice and normal profit seeking were one and the same, the attacks on avarice provided by da Montepulciano could be revealed as mere hyperbole.

Loschi continues to naturalize avarice by suggesting that the desire for money and the desire for "food and drink and the other things with which we sustain life" were functionally identical because "nature has instilled an instinct for survival in all living creatures; for this reason, we seek food and whatever else is necessary for the care and nurture of the body."[14] This line of attack reveals the possibility that avarice was merely a form of natural desire that could be satisfied through money. If these desires were natural, as Loschi suggests, then it is made more difficult to challenge the emotion on moral grounds. Loschi in fact argues based on this logic: "Avarice is not against nature but instilled in us and imprinted on us by nature itself, just like the other desires with which we were born. Moreover, what exists in us by nature should not be criticized in any way. Hence, you must acknowledge that the desire for money is present in all men by their very nature."[15]

Loschi backs this argument linking desire and an avaricious excess of desire, placing both as entirely natural. Loschi says, "What everyone wants must be thought to emanate from nature and result from its influence. And indeed you will find no one who does not desire more than is sufficient; there is no one who does not wish to have an excess. Therefore, avarice is a natural thing."[16] Because desires, and even excess desires, are completely natural, humans must stop trying to deny its existence. They must instead learn how these desires could prove beneficial, even useful. Because "avarice is not only natural, it is useful and necessary," acquisitiveness could even possess a utilitarian purpose: "It also teaches to provide for themselves those things that they know are necessary for sustaining the frailty of human life and avoiding many troubles."[17]

Loschi's impulse to naturalize avarice means that the behavior is value-free; the sin of avarice is in reality a product of other evil behaviors. Avarice itself is blameless; the stupidity and evil of some humans and the "malignant nature" they possess are not: "There are many men whom even I criticize, not as avaricious, but as doltish, stupid, foolish, wretched, troublesome, stubborn. These are the worst dregs of humanity, who derive their harsh and cruel ways not from avarice but from a malignant nature."[18] Avarice possesses a type of duality, and therefore cannot unreservedly be identified as a moral catastrophe. Loschi remakes the point about the evil characters of some people and then figures avarice as a tool for both good and evil, explicitly linked to other natural forces, like fire and water.[19] "What," Loschi asks, "do we have that is more beneficial than fire and water? Nonetheless, have we not heard of regions devastated by floods and many fine cities consumed by fire?"[20] Desire is merely a natural force, one that is tended by humans and a part of the human experience and that only devolves to malignancy when cultivated in the mind of a person of evil character.

Andrea of Constantinople also envisions avarice as a natural thing but refuses to see positive elements in it, preferring instead to promote a vision of avarice's duality that focuses attention on the role of human agency and choice. Andrea argues, "There are certain natural appetites, which are free from blame" such as for food and clothing, which promote human dignity.[21] The key for Andrea was the notion of temperance: "There is nothing reprehensible in such measured and temperate desire [for necessary items and charitable contributions] that you would not be mistaken in calling natural." As people moderated their desires, separating out the legitimate (and the good, such as wanting money in order to "support the needy") from the illegitimate, it was possible to avoid avarice.

Acquisition was not inherently troubling, but an unnatural desire, or one that was oversatisfied, could spell trouble. Andrea says, "There is another immense desire, an insatiable lust for having more than is proper, more than is necessary; this is a violent desire that exceeds measure, and when there is a thirst for stealing and piling up, when there is a zeal for money and an anxious state of mind, then there is avarice—and the larger it grows the more despicable it becomes."[22] The point of this argument consists in Andrea's challenge to the naturalness of desire as Loschi posits it. If avarice is found in the illegitimate satisfaction of immense desire, Andrea indicates that there are important differences between natural desires that may be legitimately satisfied and unnatural ones characterized by a "despicable" avarice.

Avarice, according to Poggio's Andrea, is the antithesis of nature. Nature is inherently charitable; nature gives and never takes, and therefore avarice cannot be natural. "Avarice is entirely opposed to and quite removed from nature. Nature gives and bestows; avarice robs and steals.... It can be rightly said that everything *but* avarice operates according to nature."[23] If avarice was unnatural it could never be considered an innate characteristic of a human. "If avarice," Andrea argues, "were a product of nature, everyone would be born avaricious. For natural instincts come into the world with us, once they are implanted no training can remove them; no instrument can destroy them."[24] Avarice is a product of human decisions and agency: "A few men are avaricious, but they are not born that way; they become so out of distorted opinion."[25]

Poggio's dialogue also illustrates the ways that avarice allowed a critical evaluation of social conditions. Avarice provided a lens through which Poggio's speakers commented on the connections between individuals and larger social units. Da Montepulciano characterized the avaricious in ways that made clear that the one "seized by avarice" had withdrawn into a type of internal exile. The avaricious person, da Montepulciano says, "possesses nothing that is good. He is utterly stripped of every virtue; he is completely devoid of friendship, benevolence, and charity. He is filled with hatred, fraud, malevolence, impiety—making him a monstrous and cruel criminal instead of a man, so that all the other vices are united in him."[26] The warped personality of the *avarus* renders one so totally turned inward that he or she is friendless, incapable of social interaction.

Antonio Loschi, predictably, promotes a vision of all the social benefits that are fostered through avarice. Loschi never offers a direct critique of consumption, but he does imply a kind of second tier of benefits that are to be derived from acquisition in which wealth is thought to facilitate charitable giving. Loschi employs a thought experiment to make this point, imagining a world in which people consumed only enough to satisfy their own desires and never anything further. Such an economy would result in "total confusion," in part because people would be "deprived of fine virtues such as mercy and charity, for undoubtedly no one could be generous and liberal in those circumstances. After all, what can anyone give away if he has nothing in excess to give? How can anyone be munificent who has only enough for himself? Every splendor, every refinement, every ornament would be lacking."[27]

Assuming a charitable impulse exists in people, Loschi imagined that the avaricious drive to collect riches would translate into a type of a trickle-down economy. Such a vision stands in stark contrast to the typical image of the miserly hoarder, the person so obsessed with savings that he or she spends nothing. Loschi also moves to suggest that avarice is really merely a subsidiary vice to the sin of individualism, pride, suggesting that the remedy to the perverted nature of the avaricious would be to "expel ambition instead of avarice?"[28]

Loschi continues to promote the perceived social benefits of avarice in another section of the dialogue when he argues that even those who are "desirous of wealth beyond the norm" are responsible not only for charitable giving but also for the health and strength of state institutions.[29] "For when money abounds the sick and wretched may be helped, many in dire straits may be benefited, and both private citizens and the state may be aided."[30] Even more directly, greed ensures good government. "Money," Loschi says, "is necessary as the sinews that maintain the state. Hence, where many are avaricious, they must be considered its basis and foundation."[31]

Loschi's theory that state and society are in fact aided by avarice rather than undermined by it illuminates in fascinating ways that what Poggio imagined as covetousness was in fact a permeable barrier between public and private. While we are used to imagining the development of a separate public and private as a nineteenth-century phenomenon, the financial characteristics of fifteenth-century Italy allow us to examine the history of morality as a problem of private and public. Da Montepulciano argues early in the dialogue that "He [the avaricious person] will be a slave to his own private interests and mold himself to them in thought, word, and deed, attentive only to his own affairs, unmindful of public duties."[32] The issue of slavery is an important one, and we will return to it soon, but instead we investigate now the paired antithesis of "private interests" and "public duties."

An excessive but privately felt desire prevents the exercise of a public persona; private emotions of greed were thought to have public ramifications. The divergences between private and public translated into social calamity. Da Montepulciano says, "The avaricious man, who is dedicated only to himself and looks out only for himself, not only deserts but even opposes the public welfare and is its enemy. In the interest of his own profit, he never brings benefits to many but hurts everyone. It is certain that, just like a traitor to humanity, he departs from the law of nature itself; for avarice is distant from nature's law and opposed to public good, for whose protection and preservation we exist."[33] Recalling earlier arguments about the unnaturalness of avarice, Poggio critiques the interior withdrawal of the *avarus*.

The danger to the public good was made clear again and again by da Montepulciano. The miser is a "public enemy to all" who "deserves our common hatred."[34] The avaricious person should be excluded from society, because "in no way is it fitting that we should love someone who, leaving aside everything, takes from us love and kindness, the two bonds of human society without which no public or private undertaking can endure."[35] The miser is truly despicable, a catastrophe wrapped in human skin: "What else is the purpose of the miser except to destroy the very foundation of the human race?"[36] Even worse, there is in da Montepulciano's argument the figure of that "terrible monster," the "public plunderer" who "burning with desire, ... always devotes himself to making money, yearns for gold, shuns no profit; he strives, seizes, extorts, destroys. He lives in insatiable longing, piling up money without respite, and, once gotten, he guards it with extreme anxiety."[37]

For da Montepulciano, the solution to a private crime was public punishment: "But the avaricious man should himself be destroyed and be outlawed since he is useless to the city and ruinous to the state."[38] Exile was perhaps too soft a punishment, and Poggio's speaker proclaims, "You will judge the avaricious [to be] monsters of the human race, who should be removed from among us and dispersed elsewhere like the filthiest refuse of the cities, so that they will neither sicken us with the stench nor infect us with their contagion."[39] We see in this rich language a secular analysis of avarice; there is no discussion here of avarice as a crime against God.

Antonio Loschi was unconvinced by these arguments and explains in his section of the dialogue that there are important differences between what could be called an individual form of avarice and a collective or corporate one. He poses "one greedy man" against the "whole citizen-body" when he makes this distinction.[40] But more importantly, Loschi suggests that within the financial world of fifteenth-century Italy, individual cases of overacquisition had lost the ability to shock the conscience of the social collective.

Loschi argues, "Wherever you turn your inquiring mind, you will find not unworthy examples of public and private avarice so that if you think that the avaricious ought to be censured, then the whole world should be censured, and all mankind should change its ways and adopt other rules for living. Desire for money has grown, so that avarice is not considered a vice but a virtue; the richer a man is, the more he is honored."[41] Public celebrations of a private and trivial vice demanded a reconsideration of the social dimensions of avarice. When an entire society celebrates the achievements of the avaricious, it becomes impossible to say that avarice is crime against society and humanity.

Andrea of Constantinople rejects this line of argumentation by advancing an image of the avaricious sovereign. The connection between public harm and private sin is perhaps most clear when examining such a figure, and Andrea suggests that the "avaricious king or prince is like a monster, for nothing harsher, nothing more perverted, nothing more criminal can be imagined than the avarice of sovereigns, which becomes the source of all evils."[42] The moral condition of the ruler could be a critical indication of public health, and an attack on a sovereign's moral status was a clear method of political critique.

Andrea elevated the moral status of the ruler above that of the ruled, arguing, "Private men can attribute their crime of avarice to fear of scarcity, and say that they are afraid they will starve and have to go begging in the future. But this same fear cannot arise in princes or kings in whose care, control, and protection are placed all the possession of their subjects."[43] The moral status of the ruler helped shape the moral status of his or her subjects, and the example set by the ruler was an indication of the health and welfare of the entire public community.

The ways that public and private were mobilized by these different speakers within the dialogue explain much about self and other in the fifteenth century. Referencing public and private, conceptualizing morality in those categories, Poggio set out one axis upon which avarice and moral conditions could be arranged. Other categories—individual and society or person and community—could have been employed but were not. Within the web of financial transactions that characterized the capitalist economy of the fifteenth-century Mediterranean, Poggio's use of conceptual categories like public and private help explain how economics, profit motivations, and exchange were related to larger cultural and moral communities.

If public and private were not accidentally chosen concepts for Poggio, an analysis of the figurative terms that appear in the essay suggest that independence and slavery as well as masculinity and femininity were also important elements of the discourse on avarice. Each of the speakers in the dialogue who attack avarice sought to link it to a type of servitude or slavery. Bartolomeo da Montepulciano suggests that the person afflicted with avarice is a "slave to money" whose "thirst for gain is never quenched."[44] He is "a slave to his own private interests."[45] Andrea of Constantinople argues, "He who is afflicted with the love of money will never use it. He is the slave of money, not its master; its guardian, not its dispenser. A miser wants to accumulate money, but he never lets it leave his hands; he never lets go."[46] The *avarus* "submits freely to the servitude of concupiscence and becomes the slave and obedient servant of someone who he has made his own master."[47] "He who serves avarice is not a lord but a most contemptible and abject slave."[48]

Even worse, the miser "is afflicted in this life with the miserable slavery in which he is bound, and his soul will be handed over to the torments of the devil" after his death.[49] Andrea also provides a long analysis of Ephesians 5:5 centering on the claim there that "a miser is a slave."[50] Written in the context of the medieval Mediterranean slave trade Poggio provides a provocative take on the character of the slave in a commercial economy, made even more distressing because the condition of slavery seems to be self-imposed. The problem with slavery, of course, is that slaves find themselves in a condition of dependence. Poggio seems to suggest that the thing that makes a person dependent—a weak slave—is money, the item that would seem to hold out the hope of complete independence.

If the figure of the slave was one way to attach a world of signification to the moral question of avarice, Poggio's employment of gendered language is equally significant. Each of the three speakers raises the question of greed's effeminizing power. Da Montepulciano equates the avaricious person to the mythical figure of the Harpy: "the avaricious man surpasses the deformity of any monster. So that you may truly see the face and likeness of the avaricious, I would like to refer to those famous lines of Vergil where he described the Harpies, for these lines depict the very nature and shape of greed.... ['winged things with maiden's countenance, bellies dropping filth, and clawed hands and faces ever wan with hunger (Aeneid 3.216–18)']"[51]

The miser is gendered through this comparison, and his features apparently compound his moral debasement. Loschi also raises the specter of people becoming "foolish, effeminate, and cowardly," of desires that "reduce ... a man into a woman" but is happy to lay blame for such gender chaos at the door of lust rather than avarice.[52] Andrea of Constantinople also brings up the issue, wondering whether one could "find any courage in the man who said this since avarice has so corrupted his mind and manly body."[53] Avarice, like lust, emasculates.

Poggio is an important marker of historical change who gives us an encapsulated vision of late medieval thought on greed. In this short dialogue one can see a range of issues that the evidence will show continued to populate the imaginations of people for the next century. Poggio addressed the question of profit and basic economic motivations and the role that religion could or should play in the economy. He broached the question of public and private (which will inform some of the contrasts that developed in the early sixteenth century regarding individual and community). Poggio also took up the question of the "nature" or the naturalness of greed—and the intensely humanistic theory that our desires make us who we are.

The debate about whether greed was entirely evil or not—and the presumed "modernity" of an argument that could posit the existence of positive attributes to acquisitiveness also developed over the course of Poggio's dialogue. Poggio established a definition of avarice as the oversatisfaction of legitimate desires; he contemplated how people reached a breaking point of feverish consumption that was against both nature and God, and he advanced a theory of avarice as crime both private and public. He located avarice in dependence and slavery; he characterized the desire to possess more than necessary as feminine.

Poggio's Antonio Loschi offered a theory of avarice that promoted its positive or beneficial offshoots (only, it is important to add, to be defeated in the dialogue). For whatever other faults Loschi's arguments may have held in the 1420s, his suggestion that the social connections and the web of economic exchanges that he imagined forming the background to his analysis of greed remained for other critics a helpful way to imagine the banks within which the emotional currents of desire continued to flow in the sixteenth century. Loschi offered a tangentially secular vision of the social benefits that accrued as a result of avaritial behavior: charity, a stronger state, care of the poor, beautiful churches and civic landscapes, and libraries all were promoted by the avarice of the rich.

His opponents da Montepulciano and Andrea of Constantinople were unconvinced by this argument, and they promoted an image of avarice as both an individually moral and a social catastrophe. This financial and economic context within which Poggio wrote—the economic mastery of Florence and the close connections throughout the Mediterranean wrought by the city-states of Renaissance Italy—suggest that capitalist exchanges were beginning to shape the ways that thinkers like Poggio imagined social relations. Poggio's intimation that it was possible (if not necessarily desirable) to "reckon success always in terms of money" is a remarkable indication of the extent that financial conditions and economic exchanges were able to mark out social hierarchies.

It is thus important to remember that even (especially?) during the Renaissance, nothing succeeded like success. Equally remarkable is the way that these financial considerations and the importance of financial markers infiltrated other sectors of life. When one looks at a variety of texts from Martin Luther (1483–1546), written between 90 and 110 years after Poggio's dialogue "On Avarice," we see the extent to which avarice and desire remained critical mechanisms for discussing the moral and political economies. Poggio's text provides a summary statement of the late medieval understanding of greed. As that world collapsed in the sixteenth century, only to be replaced by an early modern one focused on religious conformity and schism, state formation, individual discipline, and so on, we see how greed provided an intellectual matrix through which that new world was made sensible to its inhabitants.

Luther scholar Charles Jacobs believes that Luther's early texts on wealth, greed, and trade—those dating from the late 1510s and early 1520s—indicate the persistence of a medieval view of money. Jacobs writes, "Nummus non paret nummum (Money does not produce money), was for him [Luther] ... a fixed principle. Any effort to make money productive seemed to him to be sinful, contrary to the law of nature, and a violation of the laws of God, contained in the Old and the New Testaments. It had its roots in avarice, and the fruit of av-arice is usury."[54] Writing a "Treatise on Usury" in 1519, Luther understood eco-nomic conditions as having undergone a recent and radical transformation.[55] He suggested that by the late 1510s, "it should be known that in our times ... avarice and usury have not only taken a mighty hold in all the world, but have undertaken to seek certain cloaks under which they would be considered right and could thus practice their wickedness freely, and things have gone almost so far that we hold the holy Gospel as of no value."[56]

Luther's assertion that he was living in a time peculiarly conditioned by avarice was a recurring complaint in the early modern period. Erasmus sug-gested in *In Praise of Folly* (written in 1509), when laying out the precursors of madness, that the Furies could "stir the passions of men to warlike hatred or rouse them to insatiable thirst for gold," thus leading to manifold crimes and becoming wretched examples of humanity. The mad were prone to "illicit and forbidden lust, to parricide, incest, sacrilege, and other such hateful actions."[57] What makes Luther's suggestion different from other critics, however, was his willingness to interpret avarice as a personal and a social sin alike. "A Treatise on Usury" (written in 1519, a decade after Erasmus's text) begins with a long celebration of charity and maintains the virtue of not being overly impressed with "temporal goods" in favor of "eternal" ones.

Cautioning his readers and listeners not to get caught up in the never-ending pursuit of material possessions, he demanded a wide range of selfless Christian charity instead. Luther counsels his audience to give away things to the needy; should they give to the rich, especially if under the condition of an implied quid pro quo, they would miss the point. Luther suggests, "There is neither measure nor limit to the entertaining, the high living, the eating, drinking, giving, pre-senting; and yet they are all called good people and Christians, and nothing comes out of it except that giving to the needy is forgotten. O what a horrible judgment will fall upon these carefree spirits, when it is asked, at the Last Day, to whom they have given and done good!"[58]

While avarice was certainly a topical concern, the real issue that Luther addressed in the essay was the question of usury. Continuing to validate the old ban on lending for profit, Luther takes up the question of what is called *Zinskauf* for much of the essay. *Zinskauf* was a financial practice established to skirt the ban on moneylending at interest by substituting a transaction fee in place of an interest rate and, in that sense, provide an interesting Chris-tian corollary to Islamic loans, which also were forbidden to charge interest. While critiquing the practice of *Zinskauf*, Luther provides a larger criticism of what could be called capital formation. "I do not think it is permissible," Luther wrote, "to act as do some avaricious fellows (*Geytzige blasen*), who collect their incomes at stated times, and quickly invest it again in income—so that the one income always drives the other along, as water drives the millwheel. This is such open and shameless avarice that no man, however stupid, can deny that it is avarice; and yet all that is held to be right."[59]

Luther was attracted again to the topic of usury and its relationships to trade in an essay published in June 1524 called "On Trading and Usury" that opened by examining the differences between foreign and domestic trade. Luther conceded that trade was necessary but attacked foreign trade—and the connections that linked the German states to the global economy of the early sixteenth century—as especially ruinous due to its emphasis on luxury. Luther critiqued these global entanglements by arguing that "foreign trade, which brings from Calcutta, India, and such places, wares like costly silks, gold-work and spices, which minister only to luxury and serve no useful purpose, and which drains away the wealth of land and people,—this trade ought not to be permitted, if we had government and princes.... It will have to stop of itself when we have not more money. Until then neither writing nor teaching will do any good. We must first feel the pinch of want and poverty."[60] The theological ramifications of this trade in luxury items, and the mercantilist critique of economic exchange that Luther anticipates, are made clear in a second passage from the essay. "God has cast us Germans off," Luther worried:

> We have to throw our gold and silver into foreign lands and make the whole world rich while we ourselves remain beggars. England would have less gold if Germany let it keep its cloth, and the king of Portugal, too, would have less if we let him keep his spices. Count up how much gold is taken out of Germany, without need or reason, from a single Frankfurt fair, and you will wonder how it happens that there is a heller left in German lands. Frankfurt is the gold and silver hole through which everything that springs and grows, is minted or coined here, flows out of Germany. If that hole were stopped up we should not now have to listen to the complaint that there are debts everywhere and no money; that all lands and cities are burdened with taxes and ruined with interest payments.[61]

The cumulative results of many small sinful practices were both worldly and widely felt. Trade should be enacted on individual bases, merchants and consumers meeting and working together toward a common goal. By this logic, the development of trading combinations, of "companies," was beyond all forms of evil, and the practice left Luther uncharacteristically silent: "Of the companies I ought to say much, but that whole subject is such a bottomless abyss of avarice and wrong that there is nothing in it that can be discussed with a clear conscience."[62]

Luther may have initiated a study of trade by contemplating the range of newly crafted revived global connections that linked German-speaking cities like Frankfurt to Calcutta, but the theological dimensions of trade—and the desires that fueled trade—remained a topic of critical importance. Luther accepted the basic virtue of trade and he recognized the necessity of exchange, but he disliked the notion of profit, writing, "Merchants have among themselves one common rule, which is their chief maxim and the basis of all their sharp practices. They say: I may sell my goods as dear as I can. This they think their right. Lo, that is giving place to avarice and opening every door and window to hell."[63] Luther identified the problem with profit taking within the nexus of local social relations. Luther suggested that profits gained through trade placed the merchant in a mental state in which the individual existed as a social category but was so abhorrent to the continued functioning of the community that it needed to be condemned.

Because profit taking violated the social bonds of the secular and Christian communities and helped establish individual desires and demands as the constituent social unit, it served as the vehicle through which new social pressures were both identified and challenged. Luther imagined the voice of the desiring individual merchant: "'I care nothing about my neighbor; so long as I have my profit and satisfy my greed, what affair is it of mine if it does my neighbor ten injuries at once?' There you see how shamelessly this maxim flies squarely in the face not only of Christian love, but of natural law. Now what good is there in trade? How can it be without sin when such injustice is the chief maxim and the rule of the whole business? On this basis trade can be nothing else than robbing and stealing other people's property."[64]

In a longer passage, Luther reiterates the claim that profit motives are unabashedly immoral. He indicates first that the ability of the merchant to judge the desires of others, and not his own inconvenience, is the root of the problem. Luther writes, "For when this rogue's eye and greedy belly of a merchant finds that people must have his wares, or that the buyer is poor and needs them, he takes advantage of him and raises the price. He considers, not the value of the goods or what he has earned by his trouble and risk, but only the other man's need; not that he may relieve it, but that he may use it for his own profit, to raise the price of goods, which he would not have raised if it had not been for his neighbor's need."[65] The space between satisfying the need of another and exploiting it is the mental geography of greed, the contours within with desires were defined and quantified.

What is particularly important in the understanding of greed that Luther provides here is the inherently social aspect of the emotion. The merchant's greed is only made known by the way he or she helped others satisfy their own desires. The merchant is not greedy because he himself consumes—or consumes too much—but because of how he facilitates or prevents consumption by other people. This is made clear as Luther completes a section of this argument on the social dynamics of trade:

> Because of his [the merchant's] greed, therefore, the wares must have a price proportioned to his neighbor's need for them, and his neighbor's need, like his own wares, must have a valuation. Pray, is not that unchristian and inhuman conduct?

Is not that selling a poor man his own poverty? If, because of his need, he has to buy his wares so much the dearer, it is just the same as if he had to buy his own need; for what is sold is not the wares as they are, but the wares plus the fact that he must have them. This and like abominations are the necessary consequence when the rule is: I may sell my wares as dear as I can.[66]

Luther promoted a moral economy rather than an abstracted set of market forces, suggesting, "The rule ought to be, not: I may sell my wares as dear as I can or will, but: I may sell my wares as dear as I ought, or as is right and proper."[67] This indicates a radical departure from other understandings of the profit motive, for instance those promoted by Poggio through the voice of Antonio Loschi, who suggested that trade was inherently profit driven. Luther completely departed from this conception of exchange crafted in the context of the Mediterranean world by arguing that any profit taking derived by an assessment of the buyer's desire whatsoever indicated avarice on the part of the merchant, and so was by its very nature sinful.

Luther included in his attack on profit a critique of price gouging, suggesting that those who "raise the price of their wares for no other reason than because they know that there is no more of that commodity in the country, or that the supply will shortly cease, and people must have it" were basely immoral.[68] "That is a very rogue's eye of greed," he continued, "which sees only one's neighbor's need, not to relieve it but to make the most of it and grow rich on one's neighbor's losses. All such people are manifest thieves, robbers and usurers."[69] Luther's position on profit did not rule out accumulation, however. Some retention was unproblematic, and in fact saving could be considered virtuous in some cases. Luther grounded this argument in his analysis of Joseph's ability to stockpile grain for lean years, suggesting this was an appropriate role for hoarding, in part because the stores were for communal use. Luther wrote:

> Accumulation of this kind is not self-interest, or monopoly, but a really good Christian providence for the community and for the good of others. It is not practiced in such a way that they seize everything for themselves alone, like these merchants, but out of the yield of the common market, or the yearly income which everyone has, they set aside a treasury, while others either cannot or will not accumulate, but get out of it only their daily support. Moreover the Scriptures do not tell us that Joseph gathered the grain to sell it as dear as he would, for the text clearly says that he did it not for greed's sake, but in order that land and people might not be ruined. But the merchant, in his greed, sells it as dear as he can, seeking only his own profit, caring nothing whether land and people are ruined by it.[70]

Profits themselves were not inherently sinful. Luther was careful to allow space for a merchant to profit but only insofar as the profit realistically reflected "his trouble, his labor, and his risk."[71] To ensure the honesty of merchants and to help them protect their moral conditions, Luther urged the creation of local commissions that would set fair prices. But in the absence of price setting, Luther reminds merchants to "lay it upon your conscience to be careful and not overcharge your neighbor, and seek not avaricious gain, but only an honest living.... Therefore you must make up your minds to seek in your trading only your honest living, count your costs, trouble, labor and risk on that basis, and then fix, raise, or lower the price of your goods, so that you are repaid for your trouble and labor."[72] The burden is on the individual to use "good conscience" to come to a fair price, to avoid temptation to avarice.[73]

Luther's use of conscience is a fascinating problem here, and the status of a person of good conscience was a critical way to evaluate the existence of avarice. In his study of the Western conscience and its relation to subjectivity, Edward Andrew argues that the category of the conscience was a central aspect of Christianity after Luther. Andrew writes, "Christian conscience presents the capacity for choice as the definitive feature of human beings. Nothing is more important for Christians than moral choices; their ultimate destiny depends on avoiding those sins that will consign one to damnation."[74] Luther raises the issue of conscience and its relation to avarice in a passage of "On Trading and Usury" that revolves around the question of accidental, but still excessive, profit. Luther dismissed small profits of 2 to 3 percent as "another of those inevitable sins that cleave to all of us. It is not selfishness or greed that forces you to this mistake, but the very nature of your occupation."[75]

Indeed, Luther compared this accidental profit with the marginally sinful pleasures of the marital bed, suggesting, "Just as the marriage duty is not performed without sin, and yet because of its necessity God winks at it, for it cannot be otherwise."[76] Motives, desires, and behaviors were all joined together. The person of good conscience who worked diligently to minimize exposure to sinful thoughts, who carried out his duties without an eye toward personal profit and pleasure but to maintaining the health of the larger communal structure could be excused for engaging in a set of accidental sins. That the conscience, as an internalized form of discipline, could be used as a form of social control is an obvious predicament for those that see the interiority of conscience to be an escape valve for the crafting of an internal and private sphere of autonomous individuality.[77]

While Luther encouraged exchanges that operated independently of a profit motive, the larger issue of how to motivate people to work remained a significant question. Without financial incentives to encourage people to work, other structures had to be imagined, and Luther was quite comfortable with the idea that force could be applied to compel labor. He writes in "On Trading and Usury":

> I have often taught that the world ought not and cannot be ruled according to the Gospel and Christian love, but only by strict laws, with sword and force,

because the world is evil and accepts neither Gospel nor love, but lives and acts according to its own will unless it is compelled by force. Otherwise, if only love were applied, everyone would eat, drink and live at ease on someone else's goods, and nobody would work; nay, everyone would take from another that which was his, and there would be such a state of affairs that no one could live because of the others.[78]

Luther wrote the passage just in advance of the Swabian uprisings and the larger tremors caused by the Peasants Revolt of 1525. Responding to the Twelve Articles circulated by peasants in the spring of 1525 (in which peasants, wrongly believing that Luther would side with them in their attempts to circumvent feudal control, articulated a set of demands to the nobility), Luther published in May 1525 "An Admonition to Peace: A Reply to the Twelve Articles of the Peasants of Swabia." While he generally dismissed the claims of the peasants, and he certainly critiqued their uprising, Luther did credit some of the articles with validity. Most notably he suggests to the lords that their squeezing of the peasants was entirely inconsistent with their roles as secular leaders. Luther deemed some of the articles, such as the one attacking the hated "death tax" collected by the nobility upon the demise of a subject, to be legitimate. "For rulers are not instituted in order that they may seek their own profit and self-will," Luther argued in this text, "but in order to provide for the best interests of their subjects."[79]

Luther continued the critique of noble misapplication of power with an image drawn from peasant livelihood: "Flaying and extortion are, in the long run, intolerable. What good would it do if a peasant's field bore as many gulden as stalks or grains of wheat, if that only meant that the rulers would take all the more, and make their splendor all the greater, and squander the property on clothing, eating, drinking, building, and the like as though it were chaff? The splendor would have to be checked and the expenditure stopped, so that a poor man too could keep something."[80] Luther's critique here stems from the greed of social elites that is based on a transgression of the moral economy and inappropriate expenditure.

Luther visited the theme of honor and its relationship to financial desire in "A Sermon on Keeping Children in School" from 1530. In this essay Luther discussed the differences between honorable and dishonorable wealth and promoted the virtue of education and the production of scholars as eminently honorable pursuits. He advanced this argument by contrasting the scholar and his honorable production of knowledge to the avaricious man. The *avarus*, unlike the dedicated scholar who goes on to a useful profession, "earns his wealth with spite (even though his works are not Godless and sinful) and with hateful works, about which he cannot have a glad conscience, and cannot say that he is serving God with them. For my part, I would rather earn ten gulden by a work that is a service of God, than a thousand gulden by a work that is not a service of God, but only of my own profit and of Mammon."[81]

Keeping children in school and encouraging young men to academic pursuit was a way of ensuring their suitability and honorableness for the professions. Overwhelming desire provided an unnatural limit to a person's honor. Luther asserts that wealth gained through a profession and through careful attention to avoid unnecessary profits culminates in an honorable persona, suggesting that "with this honorable wealth honor also goes."[82]

The connection that Luther paints between wealth and honor, between individualized behaviors and one's standing in a community, reveals the multiple ways that wealth, when decoupled from older forms of social hierarchy based on blood, allowed social relations in German-speaking areas of Europe to be reconfigured just as they had been in Poggio's Florence. That both wealth and honor were reshaped in light of the larger transformations adhering to the Reformation is not entirely surprising. What is novel is the degree to which the professions were equated in seemingly original ways with a type of honor that was predicated upon an antithesis between order and barbarism that was defined in part by the extent to which avarice penetrated into a population.

Having argued that "with this honorable wealth honor also goes," Luther discusses a range of occupations that were defined by their honor and their ability to contribute to the rule of law. Honor came with serving diligently in an occupation, and Luther presented it as a contrast to the "greedy-belly … and his Mammon," who "comes to no such honor, and dirties himself the while with his rust-eaten money."[83] Luther indicated the extent of the problem when he suggested that honorable men "recognize that the soul is more than the belly, and that the belly may easily have enough and be obliged to leave behind that which is more than enough. But they that seek riches will take all their goods with them; how can that fail?"[84]

Luther demanded that people be allowed to study law, which leads to all sorts of positive conditions because he imagined government—and the lawyers who served it—as an institution divinely created to maintain peace, justice, property rights, family autonomy, and safety. Government was the thing that allowed humans to rise above the level of beasts. Denying children the ability to study (most notably the law) translated into a crime not only against humanity but also against God and was directly related to the perpetuation of a binary contrast between peaceful orderliness and beastly, gluttonous avarice.

There is further evidence for this argument in a passage from this text in which Luther argues, "It is a shameful despising of God that we do not grant this glorious and divine work to our children, and only stick them into the service of the belly and of avarice, and do not let them study except to seek a living, like hogs, wallowing forever with noses in the filth, and do not train them to so worthy a rank and duty. Certainly we must either be crazy, or without love for our children."[85] While the animals might find themselves stuck in a perpetual condition of avarice, humans must aspire to a greater position, and by denying the demands of the mute body's desires, a human being could silence the whispered urge to sin. The social implications were even more dire, however.

The social chaos that would inevitably develop in the absence of a lawyer class was deeply troubling, leading Luther to argue, "All this [social chaos] you assuredly are doing, especially if you are knowingly keeping your son out of this wholesome office for the belly's sake."[86] Luther continues, attacking what he believed was the avarice of parents who were unwilling to support the years of scholarship necessary to the production of lawyers who could be counted on to provide security for all:

> Now are you not a fine, useful man in the world? Every day you use the empire and its peace, and by way of thanks you rob it of your son and stick him into the service of avarice, and thus you strive with all diligence that there may be no one to help maintain the empire and law and peace, but that everything may go to destruction, provided only that by this empire you may have and keep your own body and life, property and honor.... And yet you want to make a daily use of the empire's protection, peace, and law, and to have the preaching office and the Word of God ready for you and at your service, so that God may serve you free of charge both with preaching and with worldly government, in order that, without any worry, you may take your son away from Him and teach him to serve only Mammon. Do you not think that God will some day say such a Benedicite over your avarice and belly-care as will ruin you, both here and hereafter, with your son and all that you have? Dear fellow, is not your heart terrified at the abominable abomination?[87]

In this passage we see hints of the ways that Luther hoped Christians would delay their own pleasures, avoiding wealth in the short term so that their children could move up the social ladder and provide a useful—and absolutely necessary—service to the state. Avoiding the quick gains derived from employing children in order to educate them provided a vital safety net for the social structure of the Empire as whole. Without lawyers to preserve peace, the entire Christian community was threatened.

The evidence here indicates that Luther, as he envisioned avarice and how it affected people, moved beyond the well-known problem of usury. While lending at interest remained a problem for him, he was also concerned with how producers and consumers met within the terms of the marketplace. Only by setting fair prices (whether done of one's own volition or through communal commissions) could a merchant be free of the temptation to avarice. Not only was avarice a problem developed or flouted through "internal" conversations with the conscience, but it also was defined through relationships with others. While Luther saw the community, the individual, and the market all as spaces

within which passionate desires could spring into existence, he was not particularly unique in this position. Indeed, medicine was yet another forum within
which a discourse on avarice, individual, and community was established, and we
turn now to the ways covetousness was apprehended in the work of Paracelsus.

Luther and the alchemist Paracelsus were contemporaries who died within
five years of one another. Paracelsus, the name adopted by Philippus Aureolus
Theophrastus Bombastus von Hohenheim, was born at Einseidln (near Zu-
rich) the year after Columbus's first voyage, 1493. His father was a physician,
and he arranged an apprenticeship for his son in the Fugger mines at Villach (in
Carinthia) after the family moved there around 1500. Before 1510, Paracelsus
left home to begin his studies, possibly earning a medical degree at Ferrara,
although his later membership in the grain merchant's guild (and not the sur-
geon's guild) suggests that this educational background may have been a fiction.

Paracelsus traveled throughout central Europe in the 1510s and 1520s,
stopping his peripatetic lifestyle for a short time in 1527, when he was ap-
pointed to the position of "municipal physician" at Basel, only to be chased out
of town within a short period of time due to the controversial nature of his
teachings. While in Basel he befriended Erasmus of Rotterdam. Paracelsus was
summoned to Salzburg in 1541 by the suffragan bishop Ernest of Wittelsbach
and died soon after. Paracelsus wrote constantly during his life, but the historian of science Allen Debus shows that his texts were mainly published only
after his death. After 1550 his texts were in high demand, and by 1600 they
had been republished in several editions with commentaries.[88]

Paracelsus (1493–1541) embraced the hermetic tradition—the attempt
to suss out the mystical relationships between things—and he also sought to
understand how people and social relations expressed these hidden, inner relationships. It is useful, in other words, to consider Paracelsus, and Paracelsian thought, as a way into late medieval and Renaissance theories of exchange
and economy. Paracelsus is famous, of course, for having promoted himself as
someone who could construct the philosopher's stone and who was privy to the
alchemical secrets that would yield gold. To later generations, Paracelsian fantasies of the creation of gold from lead would represent a stripped-down road
to wealth, one that was denuded of the rich conceptual world of the sixteenth
century and fit uncomfortably into nineteenth-century notions of instrumental
wealth.

Paracelsus was a significant thinker in the late sixteenth century. Despite, or
maybe because of, his Catholicism, Paracelsus had a wide intellectual influence.
Even the physician to the Danish king, Peter Severinus, embraced paracelsian-
ism for its blend of neo-Platonism and hermeticism.[89] Paracelsian thought ap-
pealed to other thinkers as well. Robert Fludd applied Paracelsian theories in
Protestant England, and Robert Boyle's great *Skeptical Chymist* was deeply informed by Paracelsian alchemy; Jean-Baptiste van Helmont spread Paracelsian

ideas in France. Together, Paracelsians represented a third way between the Aristotelians who controlled the universities and the mechanists like Galileo and Descartes.

It is useful to consider some of the broader contexts within which Paracelsus worked and wrote. The political turmoil of the Holy Roman Empire, while certainly offering radicals like Martin Luther spaces within which his critiques could develop a social life, offered intellectuals like Paracelsus the same opportunities. Even in the wake of the Reformation and the first wave of social turmoil that developed from it, the catholic Paracelsus was not subject to the types of confessionalization—the attempt to enforce consistency of belief within a particular religious context—that would characterize the second half of the sixteenth century. His ideas, in other words, developed during a time of ferment and freedom that political, intellectual, and religious officials could not completely contain.

Paracelsus inhabited a world with a lush understanding of human relationships and financial interactions. As the individual was linked to others in a society, bodies too were rich homologues of the heavens. "Everything," Paracelsus writes in a medical text completed around 1520, "that astronomical theory has profoundly fathomed by studying the planetary aspects and the stars … can also be applied to the firmament of the body."[90] These links between the body and the soul, between the material and immaterial, were important because they allowed careful observers to understand how another person might be placed within social networks and hierarchies. Paracelsus writes in his *Paramirum* (written between 1531 and 1535), "Since the body is the dwelling place of the soul, the two are connected and the one must open access to the other."[91] These lush homologies between the internal and the external worlds provided rich conduits of information. Greed and desire played special roles in this understanding of the world, because desire was a mechanism by which inner and outer worlds were brought into relationship with one another.

Emotions like greed or desire provided the realm within which homologies were formed, expressed, and then sent out to populate the dual worlds of the Renaissance naturalist. Paracelsus expressed this notion in the following way, directly linking the circulation of the cosmos to a set of bodily desires, including the inappropriate extension of desire into greed. He suggested in his 1537–38 *Astronomia Magna*:

> The light of nature in man comes from the stars, and his flesh and blood belong to the material elements. Thus two influences operate in man. One is that of the firmamental light, which includes wisdom, art, reason. All these are the children of this father.… The second influence emanates from matter, and it includes concupiscence, eating, drinking, and everything that relates to the flesh and blood. Therefore one must not ascribe to the stars that which originates in

the blood and flesh. For heaven does not endow one with concupiscence and greed…. From heaven come only wisdom, art, and reason.[92]

The preceding passage offers a short analysis of the nature of humans, suggesting a type of dualism—the heavenly and the material—that come to be expressed as influences on behavior. Strikingly different from the ideas contained in Poggio's dialogue, good behavior and legitimate actions and thoughts stem from the heavens, while their extension into illegitimacy originated in the base, material worlds.

Paracelsus provided in another passage a broader understanding of the origins of destructive behavior, again drawing conclusions about the ways that human emotions—in this case sexual desires (and it is important that the financial and sexual were linked in his twin condemnation of concupiscence and greed in the previous passage)—stemmed from the animal natures of humans. Paracelsus made this claim in *De fundamento scientiarum sapientiaeque* by suggesting,

> Just as toads and snakes always behave according to their nature, so do men. And just as dogs and cats hate each other, so nations fall into conflicts. All this is rooted in the animal nature. When dogs bark and snap at one another, it is because of envy or greed, because each of them wants to have everything for himself, wants to devour everything himself and begrudges everything to the other; this is the ways of beasts. In this respect, man is the child of dogs. He, too, is burdened with envy and disloyalty, with a violent disposition, and each man grudges the other everything. Just as dogs fight over a bitch, so the courtship of men is doglike in nature. For such behaviour is also found among the beasts, and it is the same among them as among men.[93]

Desire, in other words, could be the lens through which mystical homologies might be discovered, but the emotion and the behavior were clearly derived from basic, animal life that continued to be expressed atavistically in humans. Despite Paracelsus's claims about the naturalness of greed, there is a manifestly different tenor here from what was seen in Poggio's dialogue. Greed might be basic, even natural, but the ability to transcend desires was derived from the "firmamental" components of the human soul.

If behaviors could be reliable guides to moral conditions or to metaphysical realities, then the social networks within which a set of behaviors were expressed became useful fields through which to issue critical claims about power, wealth, and the constitution of the social structure. Paracelsus took up the problem of accumulation in variety of different texts that examined accumulation as a set of behaviors that were based on animal nature. The person who broke the social bond, accumulating beyond what was necessary or even possible to consume, had committed not only a crime against society but also a sin against God.

Paracelsian homologies seemed to equate God and society. Paracelsus included such an argument in a passage in which he dwelled on the interplay between flesh and spirit, good and evil, human and divine. In this passage, Paracelsus comments on what he saw as a divine requirement to maintain control of the body, a topic of concern to serious intellectuals that promoted, among other things, a neostoic response to the chaos and turmoil of the religious wars.[94] God, in this formulation, tested humans by creating situations in which the oversatisfaction of desires could be contemplated; the overaccumulator was figured as a sinner. Paracelsus writes in the *Paramirum*,

> The flesh made out of earth is nature, and is subject to her measure and her justice. But the evil that arises from the flesh does not come from material nature, but springs from the intangible, ethereal body; it is this body which exceeds the measures of nature…. Consequently man has a second, immaterial body; it is the ethereal body, which Adam and Eve acquired in Paradise through eating the apple; it was only by acquiring this body that man became completely human, with knowledge of good and evil. Because he has this body, man can eat more than is required by nature, and drink more than he needs to quench his thirst. God in His benevolence has set before our eyes the things that we desire—good wines, fair women, good food, good money. And this is the test: whether we keep ourselves under strict control, or whether we break and exceed the measure of nature."[95]

Exceeding nature, losing control, consuming more than you need—these unfortunate lapses arose from the soul that made one human. Paracelsus defined a type of moral community that depended upon the ability of people to exercise restraint and discipline. This argument does not recapitulate Protestant discipline codes from the early days of the Reformation. Rather, one sees in this passage something more radical: a hint at a different type of self, one that was both individuated and part of a society, a body that came partially from the earth and partially from original sin. The emphasis on Adam and Eve, and the moment of the Fall is quite important here. Ignoring salvation, Paracelsus instead envisioned a kind of doubled sinfulness: original sin gave humans the knowledge of the test they must pass. Typical Christian narratives of salvation, let alone Lutheran doctrines like *solo fide*, are completely avoided. God's requirement to maintain "control" of the body may be a test, but the Paracelsian difference between desire and the ability to (over)satisfy desire provided a type of countertheology to the Reformation.

Like the "chains of being" that linked the natural and divine worlds, and consistent with a medieval theology that imagined a vertically oriented hierarchy of sins, Paracelsus also arranged behaviors in a pyramid structure. Richard Newhauser illustrates the ways these sin hierarchies functioned for medieval theologians.[96] Newhauser demonstrates that medieval debates about the ordering of sin in these structures was an important method of envisioning the ways that sins were linked together, organized according to certain principles, one perhaps stemming from another.[97] In these formulations, the sin of covetousness was often depicted as a root cause of other sins.

Paracelsus followed in this tradition but included a theory of sin that examined behavior as a social crime as well as a sacred one. Physicians, for instance, were socially bound to practice their trade not for riches but for the social good. The rich doctor has transgressed certain social boundaries just as much as he has committed a sacred crime. Paracelsus writes in book II of *Der Grossen Wundarznei* (1536), "Everyone can judge why a man has become a physician: not out of love for the patient, which should be the physician's first virtue, but for the sake of money. Where money is the goal, envy and hatred, pride and conceit, are sure to appear—and may God protect and preserve us all from such temptations!"[98] Covetousness of money, in Paracelsus's system, not only led into other sinful behaviors like envy and pride but also was implicated in a set of social inauthenticities: quackery. Behaviors like accumulation that could be said to facilitate the individuation of a person within the social body had both sacred and secular ramifications.

The dual nature of sin as a sacred transgression and a secular crime was part of the sixteenth-century legal tradition.[99] The physician Paracelsus also participated in this intellectual effort, but he was especially interested in considering the role of wealth in this system, writing in his *Philosophia Magna*, "Everything has been created to the end that man may not remain idle, but walk in the path of God, that is to say, in His works and not in vice, not in fornication, not in gambling and not in drinking, not in robbing, not in the acquisition of goods, nor in the accumulation of treasures for the worms."[100] With an inverted sin pyramid, Paracelsus here offers a list of social crimes and sins that culminated in perversely useless accumulation. Removing wealth from social circulation through the twin evils of acquisition and accumulation, one fell away from the path of God.

If vice could be figured rhetorically moving down a path from fornication to miserliness, virtue was also, of course, a topic to consider. Paracelsus dwelled on the meaning of happiness in one passage from *De honestis utrisque divitiis*, suggesting, "Happiness does not consist in laziness, or sensual pleasure, or riches, or chattering, or gluttony."[101] While this negative definition of happiness includes a critique of the miser, Paracelsus was also careful to link this critique to the value of labor. The passage continues by arguing that in "labour and in sweat must each man use the gifts that God conferred upon him on earth" in a given realm of work.[102] Peasants, laborers, miners, sailors, physicians, even pastors who "proclaim … the word of God" could find happiness in the course of doing their jobs.[103]

In another passage Paracelsus returned to this argument, writing, "If you are a peasant and have many fields, many possessions, and you have full enjoyment of them—what is enjoyment? After all, you cannot eat everything by yourself! Give one part to your servants and another to those in need. Amass no treasures; the worms, flies, and moths will devour them in any event."[104] Yet a third passage from De honestis utrisque divitiis also illustrates this point. Paracelsus writes,

> If the purpose of your labour is not wealth, but if you confine yourself to daily bread, you are blessed and you will be happy. Then you will not steal, for stealing is done for the sake of riches, and in order to eat one's bread in idleness; you will kill no one, for the purpose of killing is to gain another man's possession or for an insignificant wage to help another to gain them; nor will you bear false witness, for this is done in order to circumvent God. But how blessed you will be and how happy if you are not burdened with any guilt! If you have understood the blessed life that is achieved by confining yourself to the needs of the day, you have properly understood those three commandments of God.[105]

Labor in a calling is virtuous, its practitioners sure to find happiness in ways that the drunkard, gambler, miser, or glutton were doomed to pass by. Wealth derived from labor was fine, but as we saw in our analysis of Luther, the over-accumulation of wealth or riches obtained through nefarious means was dangerous indeed.

In these aspects of Paracelsus's thoughts about happiness and sadness, wealth and work, one is able to glimpse the larger contours that perhaps defined the way a community was imagined to work. Within larger social networks bound together through vertically oriented but reciprocal relations of duty and obligation, wealth and power were central issues that had to be understood and analyzed. Considering the way that Paracelsus dealt with the problem of greed provides a useful way to gauge how greed was conceptualized as functioning within larger networks of social relations and webs of power. Within Paracelsus's writings he envisioned a set of holistic relationships in such a way that social transgressions were also sins. This raises an important question: what type of critique was Paracelsus issuing in these texts?

Writing after the Reformation, but also after the collapse of the Peasant's War of 1525 (which was particularly acute in Swabia and Switzerland, the regions in which Paracelsus lived), Paracelsus tried to negotiate between the more radical claims of peasants to escape manorial control (like Luther, he did not advocate rebellion), but he also indicated that the wealthy needed to fulfill their obligations to the poor. In this sense Paracelsus clearly worked within larger notions of the moral economy and the power relations and obligations binding the high and the low within this community. But other sections of Paracelsus's writings bring another issue into the light: the development of an individuated self and the ways that wealth played a role in that development of personhood, and one way of reading Paracelsus is to consider his work as a set of thought exercises on the ways that equality and difference were generated and perpetuated.

Paracelsus addressed this topic in a conventionally roundabout way, opening the discussion in *De summo et aeterno bono* with a description of the ways people could obtain salvation: "He who loves much is given much. Salvation is the lot of all, but the gifts that spring from love are unequal ... no one may say: God, our Father, has given me more life than you; for He has given an equal share of life to all."[106] While we all might be equal in Heaven, things were of course much different on earth, but the inequality that was to be witnessed here was entirely inappropriate: accumulation could be a serious problem. The passage continues, "And in the exact same measure are the goods of the earth meted out, since the earth belongs to us and to no one else. And since it is ours, we are entitled to possess it all in the same measure, and not in unequal measures. But if a greater share falls to one man than to another, and a lesser to this man than to that man, and thus there is inequality of distributions, the rich man should nevertheless refrain from asserting that he possesses more than the poor man."[107] While it might be socially unacceptable to remind people of inequality, the rich should, in Paracelsus's estimation, work to level social asymmetries: "For if he has more, that much more should he give away, and not eat everything himself, but like the others content himself with an equal share. God metes out many things, this to one man, that to another, to each his own. But the highest good is meted out to all of us equally—and that is the enjoyment of life on this earth. Hence we should act accordingly and help one another. Those who have much should give much to those who have nothing, that they may be found generous in their gifts."[108]

These attacks on financial inequality and the creation of webs of relations based upon them could even branch out into a critique of social hierarchy determined not as much by birth as by worth. Paracelsus writes in *De felici liberalitate*, "If you are a knight, of what use to you are your golden necklaces and your golden spurs and bridles? If you want to be a knight and champion of blessedness, then be a knight through your generosity and not through the shedding of blood."[109] Despite statements like those that suggested that a type of communitarian equality should be created, Paracelsus did identify different forms of individuation although he specifically denied that wealth—financial status—could serve as a basis upon which social gradations could be generated. Indeed, money was forgettable. Paracelsus wrote in *De honestis utrisque divitiis*,

> The wealth that properly belongs to the happy rich man consists not in treasures, which the moths devour, but in his children who stand round his table like the branches of an olive tree, which stand out in a circle round its trunk. This is the divine wealth of the blessed man, it is his share along with his work. The wealth consisting in such work and such children finds favour in the eyes of God and

He delights in it. But the children of the idler will stand round his table as the thorns round a thistle."[110]

Treasures might decay, but reproductive capability—a special type of labor—could be celebrated here. Indeed, the happy rich man is both happy and rich because he was idle neither in the fields or workshops nor in the bedroom.

In many places in Paracelsus's texts, one finds references to treasure, wealth, and gold. Everything is linked back to purity and to treasure, and because gold is the most pure of the metals, it stands as an example of the pure forms to which people aspired. When considering the ways that God's creation was to be fathomed by natural philosophers, Paracelsus employed the rhetorics of the treasure hunt to explain in *Die 9 Bücher de Natura rerum* (1537–41) how humans should come to understand nature: "And even if He did conceal some things, He left nothing unmarked, but provided all things with outward, visible marks, with special traits—just as a man who has buried a treasure marks the spot in order that he may find it again."[111]

A passage from *Astronomia Magna* (1537–38) makes a similar claim: "We men discover everything that lies hidden in the mountains by external signs and correspondences, and thus also do we find all the properties of herbs and everything that is in the stones."[112] The ability to read signs, and the role that wealth plays as a metaphor for knowledge or Heaven in this passage, speaks to larger issues about the role of gold as a sign of purity in the Paracelsian tradition.

It is well known that one point of alchemy was to enact a transformation of base metals into elevated ones, to allow gold to mature from primitive matter, moving up the "ladder of nature." Paracelsus explained alchemy in the following way in *Labryinthus medicorum errantium* (1537–41):

> Nothing has been created as *ultima materia*—in its final state. Everything is at first created in its *prima materia*, its original stuff; whereupon Vulcan comes, and by the art of alchemy develops it into its final substance.... For alchemy means: to carry to its end something that has not yet been completed. To obtain the lead from the ore and to transform it into what it is made for.... Accordingly, you should understand that alchemy is nothing but the art which makes the impure into the pure through fire.... It can separate the useful from the useless, and transmute it into its final substance and its ultimate essence."[113]

Alchemy, by the time Paracelsus wrote in the early sixteenth century, had already had a long history.[114] Paracelsus's texts from the 1530s and those published posthumously beginning in the 1550s illustrate the tight linkages between social and material transformations: as base metals transformed into gold, the social and cultural connotations of wealth and life also were transformed.

When depicting the stages of transformation, Paracelsus initiated his discussion by indicating that the changes were not magical but were included in larger natural progressions that did not pervert the law of God. In his *Die 9 Bücher de Natura rerum* Paracelsus writes, "The transmutation of metals is a great mystery of nature. However laborious and difficult this task may be, whatever impediments and obstacles may lie in the way of its accomplishment, this transmutation does not go counter to nature, nor is it incompatible with the order of God, as is falsely asserted by many persons."[115] As the transformation of the base metals like copper, tin, lead, iron, and quicksilver was carried out, alchemists like Paracelsus imagined the transmutation through a language of purity and cleanliness. Matter, as he describes in the *Archidoxis* (1526–27), is not only transformed or transmuted through alchemy but also purified, cleansed "of its filth" as it developed "fresh young energies."[116]

The tool that enacted this change was the *tinctura*, or the philosopher's stone, which Paracelsus explained was "like the *rebis*—the bisexual creature— which transmutes silver and other metals into gold; it 'tinges,' i.e., it transforms the body, removing its harmful parts, its crudity, its incompleteness, and transforms everything into a pure, noble, and indestructible being."[117] Curiously absent from this list of qualities possessed by noble gold is any discussion of value, worth, or financial capability. The gold produced by an alchemical philosopher's stone might be pure, but it also was not explicitly suggestive of exchange value.

Deborah Valenze has written provocatively on what she calls the "social life of money" in early modern Britain.[118] One of most important aspects of that text is Valenze's suggestion that money is never just money but serves as a marker, a cipher of larger social relations. Valenze's lesson here bears special importance for an analysis of Paracelsus, for whom money acted as a conduit of exchange but also as a type of social glue that bound a community together. In one especially provocative section of Paracelsus's text, he warns the rich against acquisitiveness and encourages them to charity, writing in his *Spital-Buch* of 1529, "The rich are bound to the poor as by a chain.... You, rich men, learn to know this chain, but if you ever break one link of it, you will not only be breaking the chain, but you yourselves will be cast aside like the broken link."[119]

This language of social connectivity, a chain that joins social ranks together into a form of community, was a particularly rich metaphor in light of the larger context of Renaissance homologies between large and small. The connectivities that joined the micro and the macro, lead and gold, body and Heaven, also linked rich to poor in a mutually constitutive set of reciprocities. This moral economy was so significant that Paracelsus argued, "Without the rich, nothing can be accomplished in behalf of the poor."[120]

Greed was a social catastrophe not merely for the poor but also for the well-off. Paracelsus says to the rich in his *Spital-Buch*: "Why do you make yourselves free from the poor and deny them your help? Just as by taking a few links from a chain, you would be making it too short, so without the poor, your path will be too short to lead to Heaven, and you will never attain to the goal that lies at the end of the chain."[121] If rich and poor were considered to form a single continuity, then the conditions of the poor could directly affect those in more fortunate circumstances: "Know, therefore, that all your diseases on earth lie in one single hospital, whether you be rich or poor; and that is the hospital of God. This you must understand well, and consider that death and disease spare you as little as they do the poor."[122] The Paracelsian system, seeking as it did to read the book of nature in the languages of religion and hidden codes, pictured a common human condition. Rich and poor may have been placed on different rungs in a ladder of society, but acquisitiveness was the social crime that threatened to break the ladder altogether. The great crime of the rich was greed.

If Paracelsus could imagine greed not just as a sin but also as a social crime, generosity and charity were its virtuous cognates. Such a pairing of vice and virtue was a common element of Christian theology, of course, but the Paracelsian explanation of charity is notable for its radicalism. Paracelsus urged the wealthy in *De honestis utrisque divitiis* to dispose of their riches; he advocated a type of gift economy that in the early sixteenth century was already anti-utopian: "Therefore let us be free of care and give of your own free will what exceeds our pressing need.... Blessed are those who die in the Lord! These are the poor who have sought no pleasure on earth."[123]

The preceding passage raises a range of complicated issues. One reading of the passage recalls the gift economy described by Marcel Mauss. The emphasis on pleasurable, carefree gift giving stands as a clear alternative to capitalist exchange. But the language of excess also is significant for its implication that Paracelsus imagined a self that was completely individuated within society. There is the recognition that people possess legitimate desires and demands; the ability of a person to "self-regulate," to plan for the future, to save, to understand needs and wants is seemingly included in the suggestion that one has "pressing needs" and then a set of other possessions that exist to oversatisfy these legitimate wants.

The problem is excess, the oversatisfaction of desires, which in a limited economic world, a finite and closed system of exchange—a mercantile worldview that was being fabricated as Paracelsus wrote—meant that when one person oversatisfies his or her desires, he or she also denied someone else. It would seem that there might only be enough to satisfy precisely each individual, never any more. If conditions of excess truly existed, humans would find themselves living in prelapsarian utopia. Paracelsus seems to suggest in this passage that when humans left the Garden, we lost the ability to oversatisfy without hurting someone else. Potlach, the undersatisfaction of your own desires, allows others in the community to exceed the necessary minimum.

Wealth, as indicated earlier, placed a person in spiritual danger as well as indicating a social crime. A cornerstone of late medieval Christian theology, critiques of acquisitiveness as a counter to charity were understood to endanger the afterlife of the wealthy. Based on a reading of Matthew 25:42, which describes the binary separation of the virtuous and the sinners at the Judgment, Paracelsus offered his own critique of the greedy rich. Paracelsus argued in *De felici liberalitate* that the rich were naturally insensitive to those below them: "There are not many rich people endowed by nature with blessed generosity. How many begrudge the poor even food."[124] The solution was a pedagogical one. Take the rich, who "chok[e] with vulgarity, cruelty, and avarice, and [are] utterly lacking in understanding," and teach them "generosity."[125]

Those who resist this education in social comportment take a serious risk: "For those who have no generosity will be eternally damned, and nothing will help them."[126] Paracelsus, taking a cue from Matthew 25, suggests that these people are damned: "Therefore may blessed generosity be praised, that they [rich people] may gain understanding and learn how to give—these stupid, arrogant, proud men, who imagine that there is no God and they themselves are the masters of heaven and earth."[127] As an unstated corollary to the ungenerous, the greed and acquisitiveness demonstrated by the rich not only led first to other sins like sloth and pride but also linked the social and the spiritual in clear ways.

As people sought to satisfy their needs through labor, Paracelsus imagined that that labor would translate into a balanced emotional and spiritual satisfaction that was derived from the experience of labor and not the acquisition of riches. He writes in *De honestis utrisque divitiis*, "Not in riches does our happiness consist, but in our natural needs. For in our needs there is also love; love does not pursue riches, riches defraud the fellow man."[128] As the individual, the social, and the spiritual were all connected and mutually reinforcing entities, the role of wealth in this system was a perverse one. Wealth that was derived from a type of false labor, the result of a fraud, undermined community and was a spiritual dead end. Paracelsus illustrated this point through a brief discussion of the role of labor, wealth, and divine blessing.

Speaking to physicians, he indicates in one passage, "If the patient gives you, physician, what you need and nothing more, then you are both blessed. If you give him health, which is his need, and nothing more than you are both blessed. If you are a potter, then your fellow men who need your work support you by paying you a wage. Let them give you as much as you need, but no riches; riches would bring you only damnation, but poverty will bring you blessedness. For our kingdom is not of this world, but of the life everlasting."[129] Paracelsus provides a fascinating description of the labor and wage markets in this passage.

In a formulation that nineteenth-century liberals would have appreciated, Paracelsus suggests that wages should be set at a level that "supports" workers but allows them to retain a spiritual safety net by avoiding further payments. There is a hint here as well of the ways an individual worker should negotiate the differences between desires and the legitimate acquisition of wages. The role of riches in these social networks and the privileging of poverty allows Paracelsus to link the individual, social, and Christian bodies. While there was little in this formula that appears particularly novel, the continued suggestion that greed—the oversatisfaction of otherwise legitimate needs—could imperil individuals and communities alike indicates the importance of such considerations throughout the sixteenth century.

The importance both to society and to the Christian community that Paracelsus placed on poverty provides an important marker of the ways that notions of community derived from the medieval period continued to inform thinkers after the Reformation. The ability of a person to triumph over desire, to reject acquisitiveness and the oversatisfaction of needs, remained integral to social cohesion and to the more important spiritual journey a person might make. The ascetic tradition was obviously quite old by the time Paracelsus wrote in the early sixteenth century, but his use of asceticism as a type of social critique of early modern power structures retains some importance. For Paracelsus to claim credibly that wealth was a problem and that poverty a virtue, he could no longer rely on traditional images of the ascetic derived from the early medieval period.

Richard Newhauser describes the transformations from an anchoritic (individually ascetic and hermetical) Christian tradition to one based on cenobitic communities that required members to reject acquisitiveness as they were integrated into the monastic Christian community.[130] There is evidence that Paracelsus imagined many different types of communities that could be developed upon the monastic model. Paracelsus argued that the vow of poverty that was a part of many medieval cenobitic communities could also inform the spiritual state of other communities, as well, and that poverty and wealth were two spiritual conditions, one lead to Heaven, the other to damnation.

The lure of riches was so dangerous, and greed was such a strong emotion, that Paracelsus indicates that desires lead to all sorts of other terrible actions. Paracelsus writes in *Liber prologi in vitam beatam*: "Blessed and thrice blessed is the man to whom God gives the grace of poverty.... Therefore the most blessed is he who loves poverty. It rids him of many fetters, frees him from the prison of hell. It does not lead him to practice usury, to steal, to murder, and so on. But he who loves riches sits on a shaky limb; a little breeze comes—and it enters his head to steal, to practice usury, to drive hard bargains, and other such evil practices, all of which serve only to acquire the riches of the devil and not those of God."[131] Being poor, and liking it, provided a way to regulate the desires that if one were to attempt to satisfy would place a person in a spiritually dangerous position. The solution that Paracelsus offers to the problem of greed and untamed desire is a curious one. He avoids a missionary model that would attempt to teach the rich how to restrain themselves and proposes a different model instead: teaching the poor to appreciate their own virtues.

Paracelsus wrote in the same text: "Therefore let the doctrine of the blessed life be taught not to those who love riches, for they will not find pleasure in it, but only to those who delight in poverty, in the community of the poor, in a just life, so that no one may surpass his fellow man in the satisfaction of his needs, but that each may suffer with the other, and help, and rejoice and weep with him. For to be merry with the merry and to grieve with the aggrieved is fair and just."[132] Indeed, poverty could liberate, freeing a person from political and religious authorities alike. Paracelsus commands his reader: "Become poor, indeed, and become poor as a beggar, then the pope will desert you, and the emperor will desert you, and henceforth you will be considered only a fool. But then you will have peace, and your folly will be great wisdom in the eyes of God."[133]

Paracelsus, with his lush interpretations of wealth and charity, avarice and desire, purity and perfectibility, individual and community, gives us an indication of the ways that the burgeoning sciences of body and soul apprehended the problem of financial disparity. The magical, mystical connections that linked individuals together into larger social structures designate the various conduits through which desires flowed. The axes of avarice, more than the perceived moral collapse they were thought to demonstrate, show us something important about the range of directions in which covetousness moved in the early sixteenth century. Paracelsus, sometime theologian and professor and full-time hermeticist, worked like Luther in German. His use of the vernacular to discuss these weighty moral issues raises a significant question: how did the vernacular "language" of avarice flower from its Latin and Greek roots? In the following section, we consider this problem by examining the ways that *avaritia* and *cupiditas* were transmitted into English in this period.

By examining Bibles and the way they were rendered in vernacular languages it becomes possible to chart some aspects of the changes associated with covetousness over time. The evidence here, culled mainly from Chadwyk-Healey's collection of Bibles, indicates how the confessions began to deal with the cross-cultural problem of covetousness in slightly different ways.[134] The history of ideas is encapsulated in linguistic shifts and translations. I emphasize two passages in this analysis. One, Luke 12:15 (rendered now as "And he said to them, 'Take care, and be on your guard against all greed, for one's life does not consist in the abundance of his possessions'") provides a kind of baseline—a sign of inflexibility in language and the relatively unchanged nature of the passage over time suggests a persistent stability.

I Timothy 6:10, on the other hand, was rendered in much more fluid ways, in part because of its fame as a critique of covetousness, and in part because of its long-standing significance to the medieval Church as a foundation upon which the moral questions raised by acquisition could be contemplated. In later chapters I will examine a longer history of these passages and the changes that they underwent, but at the outset I want to narrow the focus to the period ending with the publication of the so-called Bishop's Bible in 1568.

Luke 12:15 immediately precedes the so-called Parable of the Rich Fool, a story detailing a rich farmer who hordes his possessions and follows a life of ease and luxury, only to be critiqued for saving for himself and not for God. In the Vulgate the passage revolves around the term *avaritia*: "Dixitque ad illos videte et cavete ab omni avaritia quia non in abundantia cuiusquam vita eius est ex his quae possidet" (given in the King James Version as "and he said unto them, Take heed, and beware of covetousness: for a man's life consisteth not in the abundance of the things which he possesseth"). Late medieval and early modern Bibles substituted "covetousness" or "avarice" for the Latin term *avaritia*, but the passage remained fairly stable over time. The Wycliffe Bibles from the 1380s and 1390s used *auarice* and *coueytice* in the passage, while the William Tyndale Bible from the 1530s employed "covetousness."

All succeeding English Bibles in the early and mid sixteenth century employed some variant of "covetousness." Miles Coverdale (1535) used "couetousnesse"; the Great Bible (1540) made use of "couetousnes," and the Thomas Matthew Bible (1549) translated *avaratia* as "coueteousnes." The Bishop's Bible of 1568 also used "couetousnes." Luther's Reformation Bibles employ *Habgier* as a way of rendering in German the Latin *avaritia*.

In contrast to this static translation of *avaritia* in Luke as some variant of "covetousness" there is a remarkable range of connotations invoked in translations of I Timothy 6:10. In the Vulgate, the passage appears as *Radix enim onmium malorum est cupiditas* (The root of all evil is *cupiditas*), and Newhauser reminds us that the *cupiditas* at issue comes from the Greek *filargyria*, a love of silver.[135] The passage today is often rendered simply as "money is the root of all evil," a reading of the Latin text that both reduces and shifts the meaning. The earliest renditions of the Bible into English translated the phrase in a much looser fashion.

The John Wycliffe Bible created in the 1380s suggests that the "roote of alle yuelis is coueytise" (the "late" Wycliffe Bible reproduced this as well: "the rote of alle yuelis is coueytise"). This rendering of *cupiditas* as "covetousness" is suggestive of one of the broadest and loosest translations of *cupiditas*. William Tyndale's Bible from the early 1530s retained "covetousness" as the problem, and Miles Coverdale (1535) did the same. The Great Bible of 1540 offered a more specific, and more accurate, rendering of *cupiditas* through the formulation "coueteousnes of money," but Thomas Matthew reversed this in his 1549 Bible by going back to "couetousnes." The Bishop's Bible, appearing in 1568, offered yet another formulation, translating *cupiditas* as the "loue of money." Luther's Bibles of 1522 and 1546 employed *geytz* and *Geitz* as German-language equivalents.

What is illuminated here? The word *cupiditas* can mean many things. Even Latin dictionaries like Charlton Lewis and Charles Short's *A Latin Dictionary* note that when the word is used in a "positive sense" the term suggests "longing, desire." When employed negatively, cupiditas implies an excessive degree of longing, an inflamed but general desire: "a passionate desire, lust, passion, cupidity." Only when particularized does *cupiditas* indicate a targeted desire: "A passionate desire for money or other possessions; avarice, cupidity, covetousness" or a delicately defined "passion of love," or an economic "greediness of gain in trade, usury, overreaching, fraud" that is also linked to "the lust of power, ambition."[136]

The *Oxford English Dictionary* is less helpful. Its nearest definition, "cupidity," claims a connection to "Ardent desire, inordinate longing or lust; covetousness." These feelings may deepen into a more troubling "inordinate desire or appetite" that is only linked to specific object in a subdefinition that examines "Inordinate desire to appropriate wealth or possessions; greed of gain."[137] *Avaritia* has a strikingly similar meaning according to Lewis and Short, who define the term as "*a greedy desire* for possessions, *greediness, avarice, covetousness.*"[138]

This evidence indicates that when confronted with two words with similar meanings, the translators of moral texts in the late fourteenth, fifteenth, and early sixteenth centuries more or less uniformly kept *avaritia* as a static concept easily rendered as covetousness or *Habgier* but had greater difficulty working with *cupiditas*. *Cupiditas* was much more fluid, being translated variously as "covetousness" or limited to a type of love of money or, for Luther, as *Geitz*. It could be that these critics were loath to "read too much" into Christ's utterances and were more willing to play with Paul's letters, but I think that a better way to understand these differences might be to consider that the sixteenth century saw a massive upsurge in the attempts to apprehend, understand, and control the desire for acquisition.

Richard Newhauser argues in his *Early History of Greed* that I Timothy 6:10 and the ways it was interpreted act as a reliable indicator of larger cultural and intellectual attitudes about acquisition and greed. The biblical source material presented here is certainly not exhaustive, but it does offer important insight into larger mental and cognitive structures informing late medieval and early modern theologians: *avaritia* was a solid concept, but *cupiditas* was not. The method follows that set out by Norbert Elias, who wrote, "The more or less sudden emergence of words within languages nearly always points to changes in the lives of people themselves, particularly when the new concepts are destined to become as central and long-lived as these."[139]

The evidence we have considered here indicates that however stultified greed and avarice had become by the "autumn of the middle ages," to borrow Huizinga's memorable phrase and periodization, the early modern history of greed was considerably more vibrant. Our evidence has come from elite men, but their thoughts were formed in both reform and orthodox traditions, both before and after the Reformation; we have considered source material derived from Italian-, German-, and English-language contexts. While there are many other useful materials that could have been examined in the same detail we applied to these texts, a complete catalog of greed references is neither possible nor desirable. Rather, I have sought to demonstrate the ways that a few late medieval and early modern intellectuals used discourse on covetousness to apprehend the new worlds being formed at the time.

A central question raised by the material asks what effects the Reformation had on understandings of certain sins. To address this issue we considered texts from Reformers and Catholics alike. Martin Luther's writing on the issue of covetousness examined not only the moral condition of people beset with feelings of greed but also mercantile desires, relations between merchants and consumers, the legality of desire, and the connections between honor and wealth. The alchemist Paracelsus, who never participated in a Reformed Church, offered us insights into the ways that Renaissance homologies informed critiques of wealth and social standing. His attempts to understand both purity and the transformations of nature enacted by the philosopher's stone indicate how social connections and financial disparities were glimpsed through the lens of desire. We also took up a recurring question of how desire could by "translated" into vernacular languages by considering how Latin words like *avaritia* and *cupiditas* were rendered in English Bibles in the early sixteenth century.

Writing in the first third of the fifteenth century, Poggio provides evidence of Johan Huizinga's famous claim that the late medieval was "more conscious of greed than of any other evil."[140] Huizinga continues, arguing that an emphasis on avarice was peculiar to the late medieval: "It appears that since about the twelfth century, the conviction had gained credence that it was unrestrained greed that ruined the world and thus replaced pride in the minds of the people as the first and most fatal of sins."[141] Poggio's Mediterranean was a kind of intellectual factory for producing knowledge about finances and wealth. The bourgeois fascination with wealth as a marker for all else is transparently depicted in the dialogue, and this again supports Huizinga's assertion that avarice "is the sin of that period of time in which the circulation of money has changed and loosened the conditions for the deployment of power. Judging human worth becomes an arithmetical process."[142]

We have contemplated the ways that Reformation era thinkers approached similar questions, and we will see the same hint of a social crime populating Lutheran and Paracelsian texts. While Newhauser's claims about Poggio's dialogue are intended to establish the virtue of examining what he calls the "early history" of greed (that is, one centered on late antiquity and the very early medieval rather than the late medieval, Renaissance, or the early modern), there is something important in this argument, because even when a century later Luther and Paracelsus pop up to complain again about avarice and to promote a mercantile (Luther) vision or a communal/hermetic vision (Paracelsus), there is still the commercial, acquisitive individual that Poggio and Newhauser indicate. But is it really modern or even utilitarian to suggest that greed—and, more precisely, a profit motive—can be beneficial?

I will argue in later chapters that the really "modern" forms of greed have little to do with individuals and their profit taking but instead with larger institutional settings: doctors, lawyers, Church officials, and economists who lay a kind of disciplinary or institutional foundation to discussions of money. Huizinga made the claim that the Reformation destroyed notions of avarice. After Luther, one "no longer saw the cardinal sins of pride, anger, and greed in the purple full-bloodedness and shameless assertiveness with which they walked among the humanity of the fifteenth century."[143] He goes on, asserting that "Protestantism and the Renaissance have given greed an ethical value, they have legalized it as useful to promote welfare. Its stigma has given way to the degree that the denial of all earthly goods are praised with less conviction. In late medieval times, by contrast, the mind was still able to positively grasp the distinction, not yet lost, between sinful greed versus charity or freely willed poverty."[144]

Perhaps, although it may be more useful to look at thinkers like Luther and Paracelsus as members of a cultural universe that was not yet postmedieval in its orientation. These thinkers nonetheless envisioned an early modern system—with honorable individuals possessing conscience and states sufficiently strong that they could begin to imagine how to enforce discipline in populations—that indicates the cultural work that an analysis of greed could perform. No longer confined to the imagined confines of the medieval worldview revealed in Poggio's dialogue, greed helped construct an early modern consensus about correct behavior and its policing. The evidence has indicated that Luther and unreformed contemporaries like Paracelsus continued to envision avarice in its "direct, passionate, desperate quality" and that avarice remained a vital way to give definition to social relations and to moral conditions alike.[145]

Poggio's Mediterranean world, Luther's Holy Roman Empire, and Paracelsus's permeably bordered natural world each reserved a special place for covetousness as a way to understand larger forces and social dynamics. While a common, uniform language of covetousness did not develop in this period (an argument supported by the differing methods of translating *avaritia* and *cupiditas*), it is helpful to recast some of the salient elements that fell within its boundaries. Neither *avaritia* nor *cupiditas* was an unreservedly individuated category. The *avarus*, unlike the early medieval examples described so well by Newhauser, was not merely a tormented individual wrestling with his own conscience and his failure to live up to the standards set by God. While early modern individuals did face a range of individuated, even private, decisions about how to confront and understand their desires and where those desires should be limited, that dialogue with the conscience was but one aspect of a larger set of concerns.

Poggio's suggestion that covetousness may have social benefits, Luther's fear that the stability of the Empire was imperiled by the greed of parents, and Paracelsus's attack on the uncharitable rich each charted in different ways the radical changes being felt. Individuals in dialogue with themselves, individuals at the market, individuals within their communities, individuals thinking about sin and God—these were the borders within which avarice and desire were unleashed in the early sixteenth century. The conscience, the community, and the marketplace, merchants, parents, and hoarders: covetousness provided a language for connectivity in the sixteenth century. The Reformation had dramatic but uneven effects on the ways that avarice and covetousness were understood. We consider in the following chapter, which covers events in the late fifteenth and sixteenth centuries, the confessionalization of greed, examining how greed functioned in different theological contexts.

## Notes

1. Poggio Bracciolini, "On Avarice," in *The Earthly Republic: Italian Humanists on Government and Society*, ed. Benjamin G. Kohl and Ronald G. Witt (Philadelphia: University of Pennsylvania Press, 1978), 245.
2. Bracciolini, "The Earthly Republic," 246.
3. Ibid.
4. Ibid.
5. Johan Huizinga, *The Autumn of the Middle Ages* (Chicago: University of Chicago Press, 1996), 25.
6. Portions of this chapter dealing with Paracelsus have appeared elsewhere. See Jared Poley, "Paracelsus: Greed, Self, and Community," in *Kinship, Community, and Self: Essays in Honor of David Warren Sabean*, ed. Jason Coy et al., Spektrum: Publications of the German Studies Association 9 (New York: Berghahn Books, 2014), 111–21.
7. Bracciolini, "The Earthly Republic," 250.
8. Ibid., 250–51.
9. Ibid., 256–57.
10. Ibid., 259.
11. Ibid, 286–87.
12. Ibid., 246.
13. Ibid., 257.
14. Ibid., 258–59.
15. Ibid.
16. Ibid., 259.
17. Ibid., 265.
18. Ibid., 263.
19. "If some of the avaricious live evilly in licentiousness, sin, and deceit, it is not to be attributed to avarice but to their own worthlessness, lust, and wrongdoing" (264).
20. Bracciolini, "The Earthly Republic," 264.

21. Ibid., 267.
22. Ibid.
23. Ibid., 268.
24. Ibid.
25. Ibid., 269.
26. Ibid., 247.
27. Ibid., 260.
28. Ibid., 262.
29. Ibid.
30. Ibid.
31. Ibid., 263.
32. Ibid., 251.
33. Ibid.
34. Ibid., 252.
35. Ibid.
36. Ibid.
37. Ibid., 255.
38. Ibid., 252.
39. Ibid., 255.
40. Ibid., 261.
41. Ibid.
42. Ibid., 270.
43. Ibid.
44. Ibid., 251.
45. Ibid.
46. Ibid., 279.
47. Ibid., 268.
48. Ibid., 272.
49. Ibid., 284.
50. Ibid.
51. Ibid., 253.
52. Ibid., 256.
53. Ibid., 280.
54. Martin Luther, *Works of Martin Luther: With Introductions and Notes*, Philadelphia ed, vol. IV (Philadelphia: Muhlenberg Press, 1930), 10. The quotation comes from Charles Jacobs in his introduction to the text.
55. The text was written in the fall of 1519 and completed in December. A revision was undertaken before a published version of the text was disseminated in early 1520.
56. Luther, *Works of Martin Luther*, IV:37.
57. Desiderius Erasmus, *The Praise of Folly and Other Writings: A New Translation with Critical Commentary* (New York: Norton, 1989), 38–39.
58. Luther, *Works of Martin Luther*, IV:45.
59. Ibid., IV:58.
60. Ibid., IV:13.
61. Ibid.
62. Ibid., IV:34.
63. Ibid., IV:14.
64. Ibid.

65. Ibid.
66. Ibid., IV:14–15.
67. Ibid., IV:15.
68. Ibid., IV:26.
69. Ibid.
70. Ibid., IV:27.
71. Ibid., IV:15.
72. Ibid.
73. Ibid., IV:28.
74. Edward Andrew, *Conscience and Its Critics: Protestant Conscience, Enlightenment Reason, and Modern Subjectivity* (Toronto: University of Toronto Press, 2001), 15.
75. Luther, *Works of Martin Luther*, IV: 17.
76. Ibid., IV: 17.
77. Alexander Cowan and Jill Steward, eds., *The City and the Senses: Urban Culture Since 1500* (Burlington, VT: Ashgate, 2007); David Warren Sabean, "Production of the Self during the Age of Confessionalism," *Central European History* 29, no. 1 (1996), 1–18.
78. Luther, *Works of Martin Luther*, IV:28.
79. Ibid., IV:224.
80. Ibid.
81. Ibid., IV:166.
82. Ibid.
83. Ibid.
84. Ibid., IV:157–58.
85. Ibid., IV:163.
86. Ibid., IV:164.
87. Ibid.
88. Allen George Debus, *Man and Nature in the Renaissance* (Cambridge University Press, 1978), 19–21; Richard Westfall, "Paracelsus, Theophrastus Philippus Aureolus Bombastus von," *The Galileo Project*, accessed 24 June 2014, http://galileo.rice.edu/Catalog/NewFiles/paracels.html; Richard S. Westfall, *The Construction of Modern Science: Mechanisms and Mechanics* (Cambridge: Cambridge University Press, 1978), 66–69; Paracelsus, *Selected Writings*, ed. Jolande Székács Jacobi, Bollingen Series, XXVIII (Princeton, NJ: Princeton University Press, 1988), xxxvii–lxxii.
89. Paracelsus, *Selected Writings*, 21.
90. Ibid., 40.
91. Ibid., 68.
92. Ibid., 40–41.
93. Ibid., 34.
94. Gerhard Oestreich, *Neostoicism and the Early Modern State*, Cambridge Studies in Early Modern History (Cambridge: Cambridge University Press, 1982).
95. Paracelsus, *Selected Writings*, 218.
96. Richard Newhauser, *The Early History of Greed: The Sin of Avarice in Early Medieval Thought and Literature* (New York: Cambridge University Press, 2000), 54, 61, 107, 111, 117, 122.
97. Ibid., 54, 61, 107, 111, 117, 122.
98. Paracelsus, *Selected Writings*, 69.

99. Isabel V. Hull, *Sexuality, State, and Civil Society in Germany, 1700–1815* (Ithaca, NY: Cornell University Press, 1996), 9–52, 66–67.
100. Paracelsus, *Selected Writings*, 108–9.
101. Paracelsus, *Selected Writings*, 115.
102. Ibid., 115.
103. Ibid.
104. Ibid., 175.
105. Ibid., 176.
106. Ibid., 167.
107. Ibid., 167–68.
108. Ibid., 168.
109. Ibid., 176.
110. Ibid.
111. Ibid., 120.
112. Ibid.
113. Ibid., 141, 143.
114. See Tara E. Nummedal, *Alchemy and Authority in the Holy Roman Empire* (Chicago: University of Chicago Press, 2007) for a fascinating analysis of alchemy in the early modern period.
115. Paracelsus, *Selected Writings*, 143.
116. Ibid., 148.
117. Ibid.
118. Deborah M. Valenze, *The Social Life of Money in the English Past* (New York: Cambridge University Press, 2006).
119. Paracelsus, *Selected Writings*, 177.
120. Ibid.
121. Ibid.
122. Ibid., 177–78.
123. Ibid., 175–76.
124. Ibid., 176.
125. Ibid.
126. Ibid., 176.
127. Ibid., 177.
128. Ibid.
129. Ibid.
130. Newhauser, *Early History of Greed*, 47–61.
131. Paracelsus, *Selected Writings*, 178.
132. Ibid.
133. Ibid.
134. The passages in this section of the argument are drawn from the searchable texts available from Chadwyck-Healey's database The Bible in English. Many other side-by-side and historical Bibles are available online; see, for instance, biblegateway .com.
135. Newhauser, *Early History of Greed*, xi.
136. http://www.perseus.tufts.edu/cgi-bin/ptext?doc=Perseus%3Atext%3A1999.04.00 59%3Aentry%3D%2311949, accessed 6 December 2005.
137. http://dictionary.oed.com/cgi/entry/50055847, accessed 6 December 2005.

138. http://www.perseus.tufts.edu/hopper/morph.jsp?l=avaritia&la=la#Perseus:tex
t:1999.04.0059:entry=a^va _ri^ti^a-contents, accessed 24 March 2008.
139. Norbert Elias, *The Civilizing Process: Sociogenetic and Psychogenetic Investigations*,
trans. Edmund Jephcott (Oxford: Wiley-Blackwell, 1994), 43.
140. Huizinga, *Autumn of the Middle Ages*, 25.
141. Ibid., 26.
142. Ibid.
143. Ibid., 24.
144. Ibid., 26.
145. Ibid.

# Bibliography

Andrew, Edward. *Conscience and Its Critics: Protestant Conscience, Enlightenment Reason,
and Modern Subjectivity*. Toronto: University of Toronto Press, 2001.
Bracciolini, Poggio. "On Avarice." In *The Earthly Republic: Italian Humanists on Government
and Society*, edited by Benjamin G Kohl and Ronald G Witt, 241–89. Philadelphia:
University of Pennsylvania Press, 1978.
Cowan, Alexander and Jill Steward, eds. *The City and the Senses: Urban Culture Since 1500*.
Burlington, VT: Ashgate, 2007.
Debus, Allen George. *Man and Nature in the Renaissance*. Cambridge: Cambridge University
Press, 1978.
Elias, Norbert. *The Civilizing Process: Sociogenetic and Psychogenetic Investigations*. Translated by Edmund Jephcott. Oxford: Wiley-Blackwell, 1994.
Erasmus, Desiderius. *The Praise of Folly and Other Writings: A New Translation with Critical
Commentary*. New York: Norton, 1989.
Huizinga, Johan. *The Autumn of the Middle Ages*. Chicago: University of Chicago Press,
1996.
Hull, Isabel V. *Sexuality, State, and Civil Society in Germany, 1700–1815*. Ithaca, NY: Cornell University Press, 1996.
Luther, Martin. *Works of Martin Luther: With Introductions and Notes*. Philadelphia ed. Vol.
IV. Philadelphia: Muhlenberg Press, 1930.
Newhauser, Richard. *The Early History of Greed: The Sin of Avarice in Early Medieval
Thought and Literature*. New York: Cambridge University Press, 2000.
Nummedal, Tara E. *Alchemy and Authority in the Holy Roman Empire*. Chicago: University
of Chicago Press, 2007.
Oestreich, Gerhard. *Neostoicism and the Early Modern State*. Cambridge Studies in Early
Modern History. Cambridge: Cambridge University Press, 1982.
Paracelsus. *Selected Writings*. Edited by Jolande Székács Jacobi. Bollingen Series, XXVIII.
Princeton, NJ: Princeton University Press, 1988.
Poley, Jared. "Paracelsus: Greed, Self, and Community." In *Kinship, Community, and Self:
Essays in Honor of David Warren Sabean*, edited by Jason Coy, Benjamin Marschke,
Jared Poley, and Claudia Verhoeven, 111–21. Spektrum: Publications of the German
Studies Association 9. New York: Berghahn Books, 2014.
Sabean, David Warren. "Production of the Self during the Age of Confessionalism." *Central
European History* 29, no. 1 (1996), 1–18.

Valenze, Deborah M. *The Social Life of Money in the English Past.* New York: Cambridge University Press, 2006.

Westfall, Richard. "Paracelsus, Theophrastus Philippus Aureolus Bombastus von." *The Galileo Project.* Accessed 24 June, 2014. http://galileo.rice.edu/Catalog/NewFiles/paracels.html.

Westfall, Richard S. *The Construction of Modern Science: Mechanisms and Mechanics.* Cambridge: Cambridge University Press, 1978.

CHAPTER TWO

# The Confessionalization
# of an Emotion

We saw in the previous chapter the ways that greed could be invoked to describe a religious problem as easily as it could be used to discuss health, honor, and the body, and we noted how changing descriptions of greed were deployed as part of the broader shift from a medieval to an early modern world. The subject of this chapter is the evolution of religious discourses on greed over the course of the sixteenth century. An essential question facing those who produced sacred interpretations of desire in this period of religious transformation was to determine how religion and religious categories shaped the contours of greed. The divergent intellectual traditions centered on greed and avarice that were informed by awareness of religious difference indicate the ways that greed and avarice developed along confessional tracks in the sixteenth century. Examining this unfolding process of differentiation carried out by lay and religious thinkers alike is the task of this chapter.

We begin by considering the intellectual contexts of sacred interpretations of greed in the twenty years before the Lutheran Reformation. From there, we consider the ways that the process of differentiation, and the mental categories of difference that they engendered, developed in the work of Erasmus of Rotterdam, Jean Calvin, and Michel de Montaigne. Examining greed and avarice in the work of these thinkers reveals the extent to which we can see a process by which greed was "confessionalized"—squeezed into theologically distinct frameworks—over the course of the sixteenth century.

We are accustomed to considering the ways that religious transformation produced radically new forms of statecraft, social hierarchy and organization, and cultural and emotional life. Greed should not be excluded from this system, and in fact an analysis of the confessionalization of greed indicates the extent to which religion and confessionalization helped to transform a suite of mental tools as well. Conversion and confessionalization—the process by which religious and indeed theological positions came to be first institutionalized and then to some degree internalized—have been the subjects of a wide-ranging body of historical work.[1] As new forms of religious difference were constructed after the Lutheran Reformation of 1517, temporarily settled by the Peace of Augsburg of 1555, and then both territorially entrenched and globally extended over the last decades of the sixteenth century, confessional differences produced—at least in the hopes of religious leaders—confessionalized ways of thinking and being.[2] One could argue that on a fundamental level, confessional leaders sought to reify religious difference and to remake identities.[3] Those people thus confessionalized interacted with the material and spiritual worlds in radically different ways. The evidence will show that new ways of understanding greed and financial desire were produced through the experience of confessionalization.

In reduced form, this type of confessionalization is a version of the famous Weber thesis, which argues not only that theological principles shaped material practices but also that the confessional identity of Reformed believers produced identifiable characteristics of behavior.[4] Max Weber famously argued that the theological positions of Jean Calvin and the absorption of those ideas into Calvinist populations helped produce new behaviors and practices that cohered into an "ethic" that ultimately transformed entire economies. No matter what one thinks of Weber's insight—and the thesis has certainly had its detractors—the idea remains a source of intrigue.[5] One task of this chapter is to investigate how the Reformed principles so important to Weber's thesis developed in their own historical context; comparing Calvin with lay contemporaries like Montaigne can illustrate confessional differences that adhered to differing theological positions.

We begin by considering the ways that greed was conceptualized by Christian Reformers before the Reformation. It is little surprise that an accusation of greed could be used to delegitimize or to critique authority. Savonarola, for instance, linked the sin of greed to a broader criticism of sacred authority in his call for the renovation of the Church in 1495: "See if Rome is full of pride, lust, avarice, and simony! See if in Rome the wicked are not always multiplying! And then say that the flagellation is near and that the renovation of the Church is near."[6] Savonarola continued this critique in his "The Oratory of Divine Love (1497)," connecting the moral laxity of Church fathers with a propensity for greed and other types of moral collapse. He argues in the section "concerning good customs":

> Your fraternity cannot include men who either publicly or secretly lead an evil life, namely a life of concubinage, usury, injustice, blasphemy, and let no one among you gamble, nor stay to watch dice or cards, nor other prohibited games, nor at other licit ones through cupidity; and when in church divine offices are being sung, let no one of you go walking up and down or seek occasion to converse

with each other more than is necessary in holy and honest places, always giving good example to each other and to whomever may see you.[7]

The convergence of sins—not only expressed in the form of an "evil life" but linked to an anxiety about the moral status of the Church—indicates the historical contexts in which pre-Reformation Reformers articulated and legitimized their desire for moral renewal.

In the period immediately preceding the Reformation of 1517 we see a continued emphasis on greed as a coded argument about the relative inflexibility of the Church hierarchy. In his convocation sermon of 1512, John Colet argued that the "worldly way and manner of living" was linked explicitly to covetousness, and more specifically to an ocular form of desire, the "lust of the eye" that imperiled the legitimacy of the Church as a whole.[8] The convocation, which was addressed to the priesthood, is a call for reform that would be driven by the attempt to reduce the desires that threatened the Church with corruption. To the English priest Colet, covetousness—the "lust of the eye"—was connected to idolatry and had "taken possession of the hearts of nearly all priests, and has so darkened the eyes of their minds, that nowadays we are blind to everything but that alone which seems to be able to bring us gain."[9] Covetousness was destroying the Church from within, according to Colet, who placed greed at the heart of the structure of the Church.

The passage is a useful indication of the ways that a charge of greed could be connected to a larger attack on the daily organization of the Church as a whole. "From thee," Colet argued, "comes all this piling up of benefices one on top of the other; from thee come the great pensions, assigned out of many benefices resigned; from thee quarrels about tithes, about offerings, about mortuaries, about dilapidations, about ecclesiastical right and title, for which we fight as for our very lives!"[10] Worse, covetousness produced a culture of oversight ("burdensome visitations"), legal corruption, and official haughtiness. Greed, the "mother of iniquity," contributed to ambition, contention, and the asymmetrical application of the law. Colet's conclusion was simple: "Every corruption, all the ruin of the Church, all the scandals of the world, come from the covetousness of priests, according to the saying of Paul, which I repeat again, and beat into your ears, "Covetousness is the root of all evil!"[11]

A similar critique of the Church surfaced at the Fifth Lateran Council (1512), when Egidio da Viterbo joined greed to a gender critique, wondering, "When has our life been more effeminate? When has ambition been more unrestrained, greed more burning? When has the license to sin been more shameless?"[12] The Reform bull produced in response in 1514 counseled Church officials to "act cautiously, and with foresight, lest having a greater number than their means, state, and dignity will permit, they can be accused of indulging in luxury and extravagance; while, on the other hand, they will be considered greedy and niggardly if having an abundance they furnish food to very few."[13]

When we consider these texts in association with one another, it is clear not only that covetousness has taken on the possibility of institutional critique, but also that it has ossified into a general description of behaviors that should be avoided. The question to which we now turn is the one of how confession began to draw distinctions within the category of covetousness. How, in other words, was greed adapted to a multiconfessional framework? We trace this dynamic by first considering how the process played out in a Catholic context, examining post-Reform Catholic texts before looking at lay Catholic thinkers like Erasmus of Rotterdam in order to understand how Catholic theology intersected with a larger cultural attack on covetousness.

Church doctrine was theoretically clear on the matter of greed. And this clarity was reinforced after the Reformation. The Capuchin Constitution of 1536, for instance, took on the question of acquisitiveness by forbidding the use of a "procurator" who would act as the agent of one who had taken the orders: "Christ, Our Lord," the order argued, "also said: 'Beware of all covetousness.' Desiring, therefore, to carry out entirely and fully the pious desire of our Father, who was inspired by the Holy Ghost, we ordain that the Friars shall in no way have a Procurator, or any other person—by whatever name he may be called—to receive or hold money for them, either at their instigation, request, or in their name, for whatever interest or cause."[14]

Another section of the text was even more direct in its ban on financial desire, explaining that the "Seraphic Father was accustomed to say that his true Friars ought to value money no more than dust, and to dread it as a venomous serpent. How often our pious and zealous Father, foreseeing in spirit that many, neglecting this pearl of the Gospel, would become lax by accepting legacies, inheritances and superfluous alms, wept over their downfall, saying that the Friar was nigh to perdition who esteemed money more than dirt."[15] The vow of poverty was a critical tool in the war against desire, and the constitution reminds friars that they "cannot possess at the same time both riches and poverty."[16] Temptation was the key problem, and Capuchins were urged to beware the "noon-day devil" who "pamper[s]" victims with "earthly comforts, which were very often the cause of many evils in religion."[17]

On an institutional level, too, an injunction to resist temptation and financial gain was issued by Pope Paul III's Consilium de Emendanda Ecclesia of 1537. Taking up the question of whether clergy should hold multiple sinecures, the Consilium ruled that "this practice [conferring multiple bishoprics on cardinals] is more harmful in the deliberations of the Church, for this license nurtures greed. Besides, the cardinals solicit bishoprics from kings and princes, on whom they are afterwards dependent and about whom they cannot freely pass judgment."[18] Moreover, there was good theological ground to eliminate the holding of multiple offices. Remembering the claim that one could not serve both God and Mammon (e.g., Matthew 6:24), the council advocated ending the practice "if we wish to abandon the servitude to Mammon and serve only Christ."[19]

Inheritances were another problem facing clergy who had taken a vow of poverty, and the council was particularly attuned to the issue of how inheritance and greed worked together: "It has also been the custom to alter the last wills of testators who bequeath a sum of money for pious causes, which amount is transferred by the authority of your Holiness to an heir or legatee because of alleged poverty, etc., but actually because of greed.... We have already spoken often about greed, wherefore we think that this practice should be entirely avoided."[20]

Church officials, stung by the charges brought by the Reformation, imagined greed as a set of practices that could be policed, and they encoded a version of Catholic reform that did not especially change the category of greed but instead sought to control the ways it was manifested. Lay Catholics like Erasmus, however, were not open to the same types of institutional critique as the Catholic Church as a whole, and the evidence shows that outside the framework of the Church—but still conditioned by its cultural and intellectual contexts—lay thinkers undertook a deep and sustained confrontation with the meanings and practices of covetousness.

When we consider the multiple ways that Erasmus of Rotterdam wrote about the problem of covetousness over the first half of the sixteenth century, we gain an insight into the ways that the Reformation and the Church's internal reforms recast what was understood to be a set of practices with both religious and secular effects in entirely new ways. In the *Handbook of the Militant Christian* (1503), for instance, Erasmus associated greed with a particular phase of life: "Some of these passions either slacken or increase with age. For example, in youth there is lust, prodigality, and rashness, while in old age there is niggardliness, moroseness, and avarice."[21] More importantly, vices could be corrected into virtues with the application of reason. "Another person is somewhat grasping," Erasmus suggests in the text, "let him exercise his reason and he will be frugal."[22] Even before the Reformation, Erasmus saw wealth as ethically neutral and he argued that possessing money was not necessarily spiritually dangerous, although the desires promoting acquisitive action potentially was.

Drawing on his humanist inclinations, Erasmus posited that windfall could be useful but only if it did not harm "personal integrity." In the *Handbook of the Militant Christian*, he writes that such a perversion of money's value could only bring dire consequences: "Anyone who actually admires money as the most precious thing in life and rests his security on it to the extent of believing that, as long as he possesses it, he will be happy, has fashioned too many false gods for himself. Too many people put money in the place of Christ, as if it alone has the key to their happiness or unhappiness."[23]

The inner rot that Erasmus envisions in this passage appears in a different way later in the text, when Erasmus begins to suggest that that the interior life, with its secrets and hidden desires, was a dangerous space, one controlled by greedy desire. "Why do you feed the body and starve the soul?" Erasmus asks. "You keep the Sabbath outwardly, but in the secret recesses of your mind you permit all kinds of vices to run rampant. Your body does not commit adultery, but you make your soul to be an adulterer by your greediness."[24] A new form of self-will was one answer to the problem: "Follow the example of the soldier and use temptation as a means to virtue. If your inclinations are to be greedy and selfish, increase your donations to charity."[25]

Arguably in line with a theology based on the importance of good works, Erasmus situated works and desires along a continuum of temptation and re-sistance in the *Handbook of the Militant Christian*. "If poverty or avarice are your temptations," he explained, "remember that God owns all things and that for your sake He became so poor that he did not even have a place to rest His head. If you follow that plan, it will not be painful to resist temptation."[26]

The emphasis in this passage on the ways that temptation could be man-aged through works should not detract from Erasmus's suggestion that avarice perhaps was also of natural—and at times even supernatural—origin. For one whose "nature tends toward avarice," like the person who found that the "Devil tempts you with that sin," Erasmus counseled a course of action that placed humans at the center of the drama: "Put the above rules into action and think of the greatness of your value as a human being and of the end for which you were created and redeemed, because God wants you always to enjoy the high-est good."[27] Erasmus continued this line of thinking by taking up the question of how God's Creation could function for the avaricious as a massive desire-generating matrix, a "vast machine … created to serve your ends."[28]

Such a corrupt vision of the material wealth of Creation was to be upended through a new way of thinking, one that refused to conflate means and ends. Erasmus writes that human views of the wealth of Creation that were "en-tranced with it as an end" were founded on erroneous principles. Wealth, he argues in the passage, was merely a means to promote God's glory, never the end. "What are gold and silver but red and white earth?" Erasmus asks before admonishing his reader to "forget gold and admire something truly great."[29] This argument surfaced in another section of text, when Erasmus argued, "It is not wrong to have money. It only becomes wrong when money is loved as an end instead of looked on as a means."[30] Wealth in fact could undermine a coherent Christian identity. Erasmus explains that a "person who spends his whole life gathering wealth might be a good businessman but he can hardly be a good Christian. His very preoccupation with wealth betrays a lack of trust in Christ, who so liberally provides for the birds of the air."[31]

In the *Handbook* Erasmus identifies avarice as one of a set of vices that could be combatted through particular remedies (lust, ambition, and anger were others). One especially important passage discusses the ways that avarice in particular and wealth more generally was legitimated by Erasmus's Christian contemporaries. Erasmus, speaking in the voice of the avaricious, establishes, "The more money the better. How can you live a good life any other way?"[32] Erasmus's critique, however, was that this attitude was a mere justification, and those who made these arguments had merely "cloaked their desire in necessity."[33]

The real "remedy," of course, was to adopt a set of behaviors more obviously patterned on those of Christ and the apostles, who "carried neither wallet nor moneybag."[34] The problem, as Erasmus identified it, was that avarice modified behavior, conditioning people to "set a limit on what we require on a basis of our own covetousness."[35] In this formulation, wealth's gravitational pull on the consciousness of humans presented a real problem. "Wealth," Erasmus writes, "is supposed to bring with it many good things."[36]

Yet wealth itself undermined elevated emotions and qualities. Erasmus asks, "What does wealth contribute to your intelligence? You cannot say it brings wisdom or intelligence or understanding. Or that it brings health or beauty. You might say it brings honor. But I ask what kind of honor and reputation it brings."[37] Erasmus concludes this section on the remedies to avarice with the simple claim that what "wealth really brings is a host of evils."[38] He reminds readers of the difficulties of rich men getting into Heaven before commenting on the intricate connections of sin and wealth. "Wealth," he writes, "robs one of a sense of value. St. Paul tells us that avarice and idolatry are the same things, while Christ says that we cannot serve God and Mammon at the same time."[39]

Erasmus continued this critique of wealth and avarice in his 1509 text *In Praise of Folly*. Where the relevant sections on greed in *Handbook of the Militant Christian* ended with references to the Church fathers and to long-standing Christian critique of wealth and desire, Erasmus structured his attack on greed in *In Praise of Folly* by referencing a pre-Christian tradition and its humanist legacies. One long passage in the text discusses the Greek figure of Plutus (Plautus in some figurations), the god of riches. Plutus, in Erasmus's estimation, is a powerful figure: "At the mere nod of his head, all institutions both sacred and profane are turned upside down—so it always was and is nowadays. His decision controls wars, truces, conquests, projects, programs, legal decisions, marriage contracts, political alliances, international treaties, edicts, the arts, matters both serious and silly—my breath is giving out—in short, all the public and private business of mortal men is under his control."[40]

What is important about this passage, aside from the description of the awesome power of desire that Erasmus constructs here, is the larger point that when he sought out a language that could be used to articulate how desire shaped behavior, Erasmus returned to the Greek tradition. Configured in this way, Erasmus connected desires in the sixteenth century with this older way of thinking, but he initiated a critical turn away from the context of the classical world, situating Plutus in the context of early modern statecraft, a topic we consider at greater length in later chapters.

*In Praise of Folly*, of course, is a wide-ranging interpretation of the uses of odd behavior. Madness, broadly defined, helps define the limits of acceptable behavior, and Erasmus—even in this celebration of the strange and the mad— connected madness to new forms of desire that he saw in action in the early sixteenth century even as they recalled earlier traditions. There is evidence for this point in one passage of the text in which Erasmus argues, "Madness takes two different shapes, one which the fearful Furies call forth from the underworld when, with snaky locks flying, they stir the passions of men to warlike hatred or rouse them to insatiable thirst for gold, to illicit and forbidden lust, to parricide, incest, sacrilege, and other such hateful actions."[41]

The thirst for gold identified here, connected as it was to other social ills, has one foot in the ancient world, demonstrated through its association with the Furies. Yet there was also a profoundly contemporary understanding of greed that appears in the text. Erasmus continues the argument, locating greed as a function not only of early modern financial systems but also of the early modern expansion of Europe into overseas colonies. "Some people are so busy minding everybody else's business," Erasmus suggests, that "they have no time for their own. There's a broker who fancies himself rich on his client's money, but soon he'll go bankrupt. Another believes in starving himself so that his heir can be rich. The dubious lure of a little gold entices men to cross oceans one after the other, risking amid winds and waves a life for which no amount of money can compensate them."[42] Written just eighteen years after Columbus's first voyage, Erasmus identified the ways that the New World affected the conscious desires of the old.

This argument is supported by other passages in the text where Erasmus takes up the question of what wealth does to people. He first targets "businessmen," who he claims are the "most foolish of fools" as well as the most "sordid." They do the worst sorts of conniving, then "flaunt fat fingers" bejeweled with "gold rings."[43] Courtiers were considered little better: "They suppose they're performing all the duties of a prince if they ride regularly to hounds, keep a stable full of fine horses, sell government offices for their own profit, and think every day of a new way to squeeze money out of the citizens and funnel it into the royal treasury."[44] The countertype could be seen in a figure filling Erasmus's own position: the wise man who, "neglected, rejected, and despised, in poverty and hunger, while fools are rolling in money, governing the state, and, in a word, flourishing like weeds."[45]

Wisdom, for Erasmus, produced a personality absolutely unable to function in the financial world of the sixteenth century. "Suppose you want to make a pile of money," Erasmus proposes, "how will wisdom help you do that? The wise man will shrink from perjury, blush if caught in a lie, and worry himself sick over the scruples thought up by moralists regarding theft and usury. How can anyone make money that way?"[46]

The critique of wealth and power that Erasmus generated in these texts was continued in *Sileni Alcibiadis* (1515) and *Complaint of Peace* (1517). In the first of these, Erasmus produces an image of legitimate religious authority, drawn from the example of Paul, who explained that a "real pontiff" was "sober, blameless, prudent, given to hospitality, apt to teach; not given to wine, no striker, but patient, not a brawler, not greedy of filthy lucre, not a novice."[47] Pagan kings, on the other hand, surpass "everyone in lust, luxury, violence, pomp, pride, riches, and greed."[48]

In another passage on the collapse of moral order in the face of violence, Erasmus asks why religious officials must "have the face to teach the Christian populace that riches are to be despised, when money is the be-all and the end-all of his life?"[49] With this view in mind, Erasmus initiated a critique of secular wealth, writing that it "brings so much trouble with it that it would be better to refuse it even when voluntarily offered."[50] In the *Complaint of Peace*, written two years later, in 1517, Peace's indictment of humanity was contained in her attack on greed and its deleterious effects on community: "Reason wars with inclinations; inclination struggles against inclination; piety goes one way, cupidity another; lust desires one thing, anger another; ambition wants this, covetousness that."[51]

Following the initial phase of the Reformation, Erasmus returned to these themes in two texts that resituated financial desire in a context that began to have a recognizably Catholic sheen. In *Concerning the Immense Mercy of God* (1524), Erasmus began to think about desire in more relative ways. Rather than advancing a complete ban on desire, Erasmus understood that there were times when acquisition was permitted: "The man who, impelled by poverty, steals something from a rich man has not committed the same crime as the man who steals the only tattered garment of another when he himself has enough at home."[52]

Yet despite this concession, the physical and spiritual hazards of life were inborn—a legacy of the Fall. "Each of you who has attained the prime of life," Erasmus wrote, "should think of the perils and diseases you have escaped and give thanks to the divine mercy. On my part I hold that the most serious evils are those whose seeds are implanted within us. From our birth we are prone to wrath, lust, greed, envy, avarice, and rapacity, while other creatures, by nature, keep within their limits. It is a difficult struggle with these remnants of the old Adam. Few are successful."[53]

Even worse, perhaps, was the person who sought salvation while persisting in sin. Erasmus describes the inner struggle, "The sinner should discharge the evil desires that God despises: lust, arrogance, avarice, excess, and anger. When a man persists in sin and asks the Lord's forgiveness, he is like a warrior who asks for peace with a sword and shield in his hand."[54] Even the logic of salvation through works was imperiled by the presence of this core group of sins that included avarice. But there was hope in a specifically Catholic mode. Written in 1533, Erasmus's *On Mending the Peace of the Church* reminds readers that there "are those also who heed the advice of St. Paul and mortify their members. They rise above the things of this life—namely, lust and greed, which battle the spirit—and conquer Satan in a bloody warfare."[55]

Part of the problem with avarice after the Reformation was its connection to social collapse and the avoidance of charity, an argument, as we saw in the previous chapter, that was echoed later in the century by the Catholic Paracelsus. Erasmus indicates this with the claim that "to be born from a father who is a servant is not base, while to be a slave to lust, avarice, and other vices is most base; to beg one's bread when necessity requires is not shameful, but to refuse the necessities to the poor or to live on what has been stolen from them is a contemptible crime."[56]

We see in this discussion of Erasmus's shifting understanding of greed that there was a significant transformation of his thought that developed in response to the Reformation, and we see his attempt to salvage a specifically Catholic position on greed. Before the critiques of the Church that unfolded during the first years of the Reformation, Erasmus described greed as something that could be subverted through reason because wealth was ethically neutral. He employed the tactics of humanist appropriations of antiquity to promote the existence of a self that experienced authentic feelings and could be saved through works (in the case of greed through a deference to charity). In the wake of the Reformation, Erasmus described greed as a type of evil that should be attacked in a direct confrontation with Satan. This novel understanding of greed that developed in Erasmus's works after the Reformation also presented a changing language of desire and new ways to understand crime, while at the same time offering a reinforced dedication to the value of the externalized action of works in relation to salvation.

Erasmus's *On Mending the Peace of the Church* was published the same year that Jean Calvin experienced his calling: 1533. In one richly worded passage from his *Commentaries on the Catholic Epistles* (1551), Calvin mentions the legacies that Erasmus provided him. Commenting on II Peter 2:14, Calvin writes,

> An heart they have exercised with covetous practices, or, with lusts. Erasmus renders the last word, 'rapines.' The word is of a doubtful meaning. I prefer 'lusts.' As he had before condemned incontinence in their eyes, so he now seems to refer

to the vices latent in their hearts. It ought not, however, to be confined to covetousness. By calling them cursed or execrable children, he may be understood to mean, that they were so either actively or passively, that is, that they brought a curse with them wherever they went, or that they deserved a curse.[57]

This issue of translation opens up the question of how a Reformed theology interacted with a cultural landscape that had developed from the pre-Reformation Church. The issue is an important one because it allows us to see how Reformers included and transformed certain cultural forms like the critique of covetousness within their own emerging theology.

We start with an analysis of Calvin's explanation of the Tenth Commandment ("Thou shalt not covet," contained in Exodus 20:17 and Deuteronomy 5:21), which Calvin took apart in his *Commentaries on the Four Last Books of Moses* (1564). In his analysis of the biblical passages, Calvin notes, "This Commandment extends also to those that have preceded it," and he concludes that the reason for this is to "restrain all ungodly desires."[58] The emphasis on restraint of desire is quite significant, and Calvin continues in his explanation by arguing that the point of the Commandment was to demand "the inward purity of the heart," reflected not only externally but also through the ruthless extermination of "secret unchastity" that finds expression in the "unlawful appetite for gain"[59]

God, in Calvin's estimation, produced the Law in order to interact continuously with people's emotions: "It was God's design, by the whole Law, to arouse men's feelings to sincere obedience of it, yet such is their hypocrisy and indifference, that it was necessary to stimulate them more sharply, and to press them more closely, lest they should seek for subterfuges under pretense of the obscurity of the doctrine."[60] This position on the Decalogue allows Calvin to assert, following Paul, that "the whole 'Law is spiritual,'" acting as a preemptive strike against unlawful desires.[61] Calvin writes that the Tenth Commandment is evidence that God "put restraint upon our minds, lest they should desire to do what is unlawful."[62] This definition of covetousness was recalled later in Calvin's *Institutes of the Christian Religion* in the section "On the Christian Life" when he offered his diagnosis of covetousness in the following way: "We have a frenzied desire, an infinite eagerness, to pursue wealth and honour, intrigue for power, accumulate riches, and collect all those frivolities which seem conducive to luxury and splendour."[63]

The argument that the Law is a ban on imagined desires stems from Calvin's understanding of Paul's conversion experience, and Calvin concludes, "When he [Paul] perceived what the Commandment, Thou shalt not covet, meant, the dead Law was raised as it were to life, and he died, i.e., he was convinced he was a transgressor, and saw the sure curse overhanging him."[64] The interior drama of the conversion experience, so often represented as a blindness suddenly crashing into vision, is here configured much differently, and the fact that it was built upon the disciplining of covetousness is an intriguing twist on the familiar tale.

Temptation, desire, and "evil concupiscence" were described by Calvin in his gloss on Exodus 20:17 as "the root from which all evil and corrupt fruits spring forth."[65] Where does this ungodly desire originate? The body. "The flesh," Calvin writes, "often tempts us to wish for this or that, so that the evil concupiscence betrays itself, although consent may not yet be added."[66] The principle of consent remains an important issue, because God could place a "restraint upon evil desires before they prevail" and "before they have gone so far as to arrive at a deliberate purpose."[67] The cycle by which desire produced sin, in other words, could be short-circuited. "I admit," Calvin wrote, "that the corrupt thoughts which arise spontaneously, and so also vanish before they affect the mind, do not come into account before God."[68] The importance of self-discipline surfaced in other sections of Calvin's writing.

In "On the Christian Life," for instance, Calvin argues, "That self-denial which Christ so strongly enforces on his disciples from the very outset, (Matth. xvi. 24,) which, as soon as it takes hold of the mind, leaves no place either, first, for pride, show, and ostentation; or, secondly, for avarice, lust, luxury, effeminacy, or other vices which are engendered by self love."[69] Self-denial, like other forms of self-discipline, could serve as a brake on the maddening qualities of desire. Indeed, obedience to God provided an antidote to vice. When "we faithfully ... obey God and his commandments [and] lay aside private regard to ourselves, [Scripture] not only divests our minds of an excessive longing for wealth, or power, or human favour, but eradicates all ambition and thirst for worldly glory, and other more secret pests."[70]

In "On the Christian Life," Calvin reiterates this point, explaining, when people are "dazzled with the glare of wealth, power, and honours, that they can see no farther. The heart also, engrossed with avarice, ambition, and lust, is weighed down and cannot rise above them. In short, the whole soul, ensnared by the allurements of the flesh, seeks its happiness on the earth. To meet this disease, the Lord makes his people sensible of the vanity of the present life, by a constant proof of its miseries."[71] God's ability to manufacture misery serves Calvin as a constant reminder that torment and misfortune are merely prods to discipline the thoughts of the sinner "dazzled" by wealth.

Calvin's 1556 exegesis *Commentaries on the Epistles to Timothy, Titus and Philemon* includes analysis of I Timothy 6:6–10 (the passage culminating in the famous claim that "money is the root of all evil") that is instructive for the ways it shows how older assumptions about wealth and evil were inflected with Reformed understandings of wealth and desire. In Paul's letters to Timothy it is clear that pecuniary desire is a troubling problem, and this passage has a long history in Christian theology and belief.[72] Calvin's exegesis of verse 7 ("For we brought nothing into the world....") expresses a theoretical underpinning, a definition of covetousness that resonates with other European models about covetousness and the transgression of behavior codes. Calvin argues in this passage, "Our covetousness is an insatiable gulf, if it be not restrained; and the best bridle is, when we desire nothing more than the necessity of this life demands; for the reason why we transgress the bounds, is, that our anxiety extends to a thousand lives which we falsely imagine." [73]

Calvin concludes with a demand for self-sufficiency, "In order, therefore, that we may be satisfied with a sufficiency, let us learn to have our heart so regulated, as to desire nothing but what is necessary for supporting life." [74] The critique resumes with Calvin's discussion of verse 9, and it is here that he distinguishes between the possession of things and the desire to possess: "the cause of the evils … is not riches, but an eager desire of them, even though the person should be poor." [75] Indeed, the desire for wealth was in fact diabolical: "Every man that has resolved to become rich gives himself up as a captive to the devil." [76] Wealth, and the distractions it engenders, distract people from the path of goodness. Calvin writes in relation to the "universal evil" of "mad desire," "they are so maddened by avarice, that they stick at nothing, however foolish, whenever the glitter of gold or silver dazzles their eyes." [77]

This discussion prepares the way for the main course, Calvin's analysis of verse 10: the claim that "avarice is the root of all evil." In his exegesis, Calvin first defines avarice as "covetousness for riches," but he then makes a case for avarice as the ultimate vice because covetousness precedes other flaws. "There is no necessity for being too scrupulous in comparing other vices with this. It is certain that ambition and pride often produce worse fruits than covetousness does; and yet ambition does not proceed from covetousness. The same thing may be said of the sins forbidden by the seventh commandment. But Paul's intention was not to include under covetousness every kind of vices that can be named." [78]

In fact, Calvin argues in the text, "innumerable evils arise from it (covetousness)" and "there is no evil which it does not produce." [79] And then, just to be clear and to ensure that there were no misunderstandings, Calvin added the following reiteration: "And, indeed, we may most truly affirm, as to the base desire of gain, that there is no kind of evils that is not copiously produced by it every day; such as innumerable frauds, falsehoods, perjury, cheating, robbery, cruelty, corruption in judicature, quarrels, hatred, poisonings, murders; and, in short, almost every sort of crime." [80] Avarice, in other words, was a preeminent form of sin.

Calvin also invokes a language of disease and degeneracy in his analysis of the verse, arguing, "The most aggravated of all evils springs from avarice—revolting from the faith; for they who are diseased with this disease are found to degenerate gradually, till they entirely renounce the faith." [81] While avarice was certainly a concern—and could pull someone away from her or his faith—he also fixed his attention on the psychological dimension, commenting on the "sorrows" and the "frightful torments of conscience" that desire generates in people's minds.[82]

What is especially important, however, is that these torments must be seen by Calvinists as divine retribution. Calvin argues as much when he explains that these moments of mental "torment" are produced in part by God "trying covetous men, by making them their own tormentors."[83] God does not punish sinners; sinners learn to punish themselves. This internalization of God's rule and a disciplined approach to covetousness is especially evocative in light of Weber's claims about the ways that a Calvinist's mechanisms of conscience were particularly important to the development of an approach to the world and to money governed by religious categories.

I Timothy 6:6–10 is a key passage in the Christian understanding of desire, and Calvin's explanation of the passage does much to illuminate the ways that the verse could yield confessionally specific mental categories, behaviors, and cultures. Other elements of the Christian tradition yield equally important insights into the confessionalization of greed. We turn now to examine Calvin's 1555 interpretation of Matthew 6:22–24 and Luke 11:34–36 and 16:13 (in *Commentary on a Harmony of the Evangelists, Matthew, Mark, and Luke*), which contain Christ's announcement that "no man can serve two masters: he will hate the one, and love the other, or he will hold to one, and neglect the other. You cannot serve God and mammon." The passage is often interpreted in fairly straightforward ways: a love of money—greed—impairs a person's ability to participate in the Christian community.

Calvin took a slightly different approach, commenting first on the ways that "Papists" interpreted the passage in such a way as to suggest that humans had free will and the ability to reason and therefore could choose a variety of paths meandering between virtue and vice. Calvin rejected this claim by arguing that sin made it impossible to employ reason correctly: "I confess, indeed, that men naturally possess reason, to distinguish between vices and virtues; but I say that it is so corrupted by sin, that it fails at every step."[84] Furthermore, Calvin's predestination precluded such an interpretative model, and the idea of predestination must be seen as a theological key to understanding the larger dimension of Calvinist attitudes toward money and possession.

The origin of this psychical makeup could be found in the moral dynamics of the Fall. The light of reason, nearly extinguished by the Fall, is maintained in a diminished and pathetic condition. Calvin, writing about the origins of desire, asserts, "Men wallow so disgracefully, like beasts, in the filth of vices, for they have no reason which might restrain the blind and dark lusts of the flesh."[85] The "wicked lusts of the flesh" govern a decline, causing men to "degenerate into beasts."[86] Calvin reserves his clearest analysis of the issue of covetousness for this passage, asserting in his exegesis of verse 24 (no man can serve two masters), "The hearts of those who are devoted to riches are alienated from the Lord."[87] The reason for this impossible situation is the utterly damaging consequences of the Fall. Calvin makes the argument here that "it is impossible for any man to obey God, and, at the same time, to obey his own flesh."[88]

These two antithetical masters—the spirit and the flesh—allow Calvin to claim, "Where riches hold the dominion of the heart, God has lost his authority."[89] This language of authority, lordship, and dominion—so evocative of early modern labor relations—finds resolution in Calvin's final proclamation on the passage. He finishes the analysis by linking desire to another form of unfree servitude, slavery: "Whoever gives himself up as a slave to riches must abandon the service of God: for covetousness makes us the slaves of the devil."[90]

Calvin did not neglect the issue that so fascinated Max Weber: the ability of the elect to express religious devotion through the accumulation of wealth. He addressed this critical point through the analysis of the verses in Luke that deal with the question of double masters. Citing first the problem of a person having what he called a "double heart" (and linking this critique to his readings of 1 Chronicles 12:33 and Psalms 12:2), Calvin advances in the commentary the figure of a person who tries simultaneously to serve God and to "devote a great part of [his or her] mind to hunting after honors."[91]

The answer he gives is a fascinating one, because Calvin recognizes that an awareness of sin, like the attempt to transcend it, allows one to escape the trap of having two masters. "It is, no doubt, true," Calvin writes, "that believers themselves are never so perfectly devoted to obedience to God, as not to be withdrawn from it by the sinful desires of the flesh. But as they groan under this wretched bondage, and are dissatisfied with themselves, and give nothing more than an unwilling and reluctant service to the flesh, they are not said to *serve two masters*: for their desires and exertions are approved by the Lord, as if they rendered to him a perfect obedience."[92]

The issue of legitimate wealth surfaces in "On the Christian Life" in a section in which Calvin discusses the ways that avarice generates behaviors that then must be reintegrated into legitimately Christian modes of living:

> Hence, in regard to those who frame their life after their own counsel, we see how restless they are in mind, how many plans they try, to what fatigues they submit, in order that they may gain what avarice or ambition desires, or, on the other hand, escape poverty and meanness. To avoid similar entanglements, the course which Christian men must follow is this: first, they must not long for, or hope for, or think of any kind of prosperity apart from the blessing of God; on it they must cast themselves, and there safely and confidently recline.[93]

It is important to remember, as well, that Calvinist theology retained a space for legitimate wealth. In his 1548 analysis of 2 Corinthians 6:1–10, Calvin notes, "For why should a moderate amount of riches prevent a man from being reckoned a servant of Christ, who, in other respects, is pious, is of upright mind and honorable deportment, and is distinguished by other excellences. As the man that is poor is not on that account to be straightway accounted a good minister, so the man that is rich is not on that account to be rejected."[94]

Calvin continues to argue this point about leaving financial matters in God's hands when he suggests, "However much the carnal mind may seem sufficient for itself when in the pursuit of honour or wealth, it depends on its own industry and zeal, or is aided by the favour of men, it is certain that all this is nothing, and that neither intellect nor labour will be of the least avail, except in so far as the Lord prospers both."[95] Pleasures denied, desires ignored; the wealth generated by the elect has little emotional content beyond that which can be expressed in the form of personal dissatisfaction. From the never-ending search for ways to escape a duality of masters comes a Reformed understanding of covetousness itself.

In his essay "Of Prayer" (found in *Institutes of the Christian Religion*), Calvin presents a novel analysis of greed, defining it as a condition of excess understood in relation to the basic necessities of life: "daily bread." "Those who, not contented with daily bread, indulge an unrestrained insatiable cupidity, or those who are full of their own abundance, and trust in their own riches, only mock God by offering up this prayer [The Lord's Prayer]. For the former ask what they would be unwilling to obtain, nay, what they most of all abominate, namely, daily bread only, and as much as in them lies disguise their avarice from God, whereas true prayer should pour out the whole soul and every inward feeling before him."[96] The inner dialogue with God revealed in prayer would allow the penitent to see the contours of his or her avaricious sins, producing a form of self-knowledge centered on the analysis of sinful desires. Calvin arrived at a similar point in his 1546 exegesis of Corinthians 8:13–17.

Commenting on the spiritual status of the hoarder, Calvin writes, "As in the case of one hoarding the manna, either from excessive greed or from distrust, what was laid up immediately putrified, so we need not doubt that the riches, that are heaped up at the expense of our brethren, are accursed, and will soon perish, and that too, in connection with the ruin of the owner; so that we are not to think that it is the way to increase, if, consulting our own advantage for a long while to come, we defraud our poor brethren of the beneficence that we owe them."[97] This analysis of excess was linked to the critique of greed that Calvin offered in his 1551 understanding of I Peter 5:1–4, in which he describes the ways that "sloth, desire of gain, and lust for power" could be corrected by having a "ready mind," and an "ability to spend himself and his labor disinterestedly and gladly in behalf of the Church." An inability to do this, Calvin asserts, means that one "is not a minister of Christ, but a slave to his own stomach and his purse."[98]

Calvin also examined greed in the larger context of accumulation, a topic he took up in his 1559 exegesis of Habakkuk 2:6. The passage, which is often seen

as a warning to Christians to be wary of being weighed down by their possessions, becomes for Calvin the stepping off point for a description of the moral
hazard implicit in collecting. Calvin argues,

> Every one who has accumulated much, when he comes to old age, is afraid to
> use what he has got, being ever solicitous lest he should lose any thing; and then,
> as he thinks nothing is sufficient, the more he possesses the more grasping he
> becomes, and frugality is the name given to that sordid, and, so to speak, that
> servile restraint within which the rich confine themselves. In short, when any
> one forms a judgment of all the avaricious of this world, and is himself free from
> all avarice, having a free and unblessed mind, he will easily apprehend what the
> Prophet says here,—that all the wealth of this world is nothing else but a heap
> of clay, as when any one puts himself of his own accord under a great heap which
> he had collected together."[99]

In this long passage, Calvin produces a new vision of covetousness, one that
suggests a spiraling desire that reaches a final conclusion only in chaos. This
chaos is reflected most directly in God's punishment. "Then a general truth is
to be drawn from this expression that all the avaricious, the more they heap
together, the more they lade themselves, and, as it were, bury themselves under
a great load. Whence is this? Because riches, acquired by frauds and plunders,
are nothing else than a heavy and cumbrous lump of earth: for God returns
on the heads of those who thus seek to enrich themselves, whatever they have
plundered from others."[100]

If the rich were able to moderate their desires, Calvin suggests, "they might
have lived cheerfully and happily." Instead, those "who inebriate themselves
with riches, find that they carry a useless burden, under which they lie down, as
it were, sunk and buried."[101] Calvin argued a similar point in his 1551 analysis
of James 5:1–6, when he notes, "Those rich men are insane who glory in things
so fading as garments, gold, silver, and such things, since it is nothing else than
to make their glory subject to rust and moths."[102] Calvin continues, attacking
"the vices which he mentions here do not belong to all the rich; for some of
them indulge themselves in luxury, some spend much in show and display, and
some pinch themselves, and live miserably in their own filth."[103] In both passages, Calvin responds to the biblical injunction against avarice by linking accumulated wealth to the decay of objects that have lost their use value. Recalling
the alchemical tradition, Calvin notes the decline from purity associated with
miserliness.

Calvin's personifications of avarice also allow us insight into the larger perambulations of a cultural image. In his 1546 "Argument on the First Epistle
to the Corinthians," Calvin equates avarice with a remarkable set of locations,
professions, and genders. Commenting on the "vices" that "prevailed at Corinth"
and connecting these attributes with the larger context of "mercantile cities,"

Calvin joins avarice to "luxury, pride, vanity, effeminacy, insatiable covetousness, and ambition."[104] The legal profession was particularly under the sway of greed, and Calvin notes that Corinthians displayed "an excessive fondness for litigation, which took its rise from avarice."[105] The embodied qualities of avarice could be turned to a gender critique as well.

Exhibiting a form of sexual panic, Calvin argued in his critique of 1 Corinthians 6:9–11, "Wealth has luxury as its attendant—the mother of unchastity and all kinds of lasciviousness. In addition to this, a nation which was of itself prone to wantonness, was prompted to it by many other corruptions."[106] Indeed, covetousness was the central issue for the Corinthians: "The simple meaning, therefore, is this, that prior to their being regenerated by grace, some of the Corinthians were covetous, others adulterers, others extortioners, others effeminate, others revilers, but now, being made free by Christ, they were such no longer."[107]

The attack continues with Calvin's description of the virtuous and avarice-free magi in his 1561 commentary on Daniel: "The wise men of the Indies, being frugal and austere in their manner of living, were not wholly devoted to gain; for they are known to have lived without any need of either money, or furniture, or anything else. They were content with roots, and had no need of clothing, slept upon the ground, and were thus free from avarice."[108] The magi were then compared to the Chaldeans, who run "hither and thither to obtain money from the simple and credulous." This attack developed into one on the entire culture of the Chaldeans, who

> scattered their prophecies for the sake of gain; and when knowledge is rendered saleable, it is sure to be adulterated with many faults. As when Paul speaks of corruptors of the Gospel, he says,—they trafficked in it, (2 Corinthians 2:7,) because when a profit is made, as we have previously said, even honorable teachers must necessarily degenerate and pervert all sincerity by their lying. For where avarice reigns, there is flattery, servile obsequiousness, and cunning of all kinds, while truth is utterly extinguished. Whence it is not surprising if the Chaldeans were so inclined to deceit, as it became natural to them through the pursuit of gain and the lust for wealth.[109]

The argument that greed undermined legitimate religious leadership resurfaced in Calvin's commentary on Daniel, where he explains, "For where there is no contempt of money, many vices necessarily spring up, since all avaricious and covetous men adulterate God's word and makes, traffic of it. (2 Corinthians 2:17.) Hence all prophets and ministers of God ought to watch against being covetous of gifts."[110] Calvin also developed a connection between avarice and ambition, a topic that also circulated in relation first to effective ministry and pastoral care. "Ambition, therefore, and avarice, and similar vices in a minister, taint the purity of his doctrine, so that Christ has not there the exclusive distinction. Hence, he that would preach Christ alone, must of necessity forget himself."[111]

Calvin's identification of avarice as a component of gendered decline resonated with his arguments about the ways that greed impeded effective statecraft, a topic that Calvin developed most obviously in his exegesis of Daniel. The critique was initiated in Calvin's description of Cyrus II of Persia, who is described as distracted by "his insatiable avarice and ambition."[112] In fact, Calvin comments on the "insatiable" avarice or cupidity of Cyrus in at least three other passages in his analysis of the Book of Daniel. This in turn fosters a larger critique of inadequate monarchical rule—a potentially explosive issue in republican Geneva—in which Calvin notes,

> the heartlessness of kings in these days, who proudly despise God's gifts in all good men who surpass the multitude in usefulness; and at the same time enjoy the society of the ignorant like themselves, while they are slaves to avarice and rapine, and manifest the greatest cruelty and licentiousness. Since, then, we see how very unworthy kings usually are of their empire and their power, we must weep over the state of the world, because it reflects like a glass the wrath of heaven, and kings are thus destitute of counsel.[113]

Avarice signaled deeper problems in the functioning of the state or its leader, and Calvin sees poor leadership as both an individual flaw and a social one. "Whoever aspires to power and self-advancement, without regarding the welfare of others," Calvin writes, "must necessarily be avaricious and rapacious, cruel and perfidious, as well as forgetful of his duties. Since, then, the nobles of the realm envied Daniel, they betrayed their malice, for they had no regard for the public good, but desired to seize upon all things for their own interests."[114]

To label avarice as a sign of morally destitute leadership and to offer it as a critique especially appropriate to monarchs is perhaps nothing new, but its context in republican Geneva remains significant. As Calvin worked through his analysis of Daniel, he returned again and again to a set of stock descriptions of dismayingly damaged leaders. "If a king is avaricious, or cunning, or cruel, or sensual," Calvin establishes, "he desires to have friends and attendants who will not check either his avarice or his craftiness, his cruelty or his lust. Hence they deserve the conduct which they receive, and experience treachery from those whom they ought not to treat with so much honor, if they considered themselves in duty bound to God and to their people."[115]

Calvin then turns to the example of the Romans, adopting a stance that functions as a coded critique of the Catholic Church. The Empire, Calvin asserts, "displayed their avarice, and sold and distributed for the sake of gain, just as much as if all these territories had been immediately reduced into provinces of their empire."[116] Worse, the Romans "never conquered any one without exhausting both the monarch and his dominions to satisfy their insatiable avarice and cupidity," and then "seized everything in the world, and drew all riches, all treasures, and every particle of value into the whirlpool of their unsatisfied covetousness."[117]

The Catholic Erasmus promoted a vision of externalized works as a way to combat greed. Calvin, unsurprisingly, privileged the internalized action of discipline in the service of purity and chastity. Awakened to the presence of God's Law in the wake of an intense conversion experience, Calvin's followers came to understand the body and its desires as fundamentally problematic. Desire—which stemmed from the Fall—was a sign of human depravity. At the same time wealth, if it was earned legitimately, was combined with "honorable comportment," and never generated any emotional or passionate attraction in the believer, was not a reliable sign of greed. Calvin opened the door for a new type of self, one that experienced a fundamentally different relationship with the material world.

We have considered to this point the larger perambulations of avarice and covetousness across differing theological positions in the sixteenth century. What remains is an analysis of the topic in Catholic thought after Calvin's "second Reformation" had absorbed an older Christian suspicion of covetousness into Reformed theology. We get into this topic by examining the great essayist and humanist Michel de Montaigne (1533–92), who was able to maintain the respect of Catholics and Protestants alike during the wars of religion in France.

In the *Essays*, which he began to publish in 1580, Montaigne writes about greed in fourteen of his pieces; the topics have a wide range, but there are some areas of core consistency that allow us to see how the humanist tradition absorbed the larger cultural question of how to define greed and how to discern its logical contours. In his essay "On physiognomy," Montaigne provides a working definition of the vice that recalls an earlier tradition of analysis that defines greed as a bursting of legitimate boundaries that cannot be moderated: "In nothing does Man know how to halt at the point of his need, be it pleasure, wealth or power, he clasps at more than he can hold: his greed is not susceptible to moderation."[118]

In another essay, "On Constancy," Montaigne employs similar language to discuss the ways that emotions—including greed—affect certain types of people. "The Aristotelian sage," Montaigne writes to conclude this essay, "is not exempt from the emotions: he moderates them."[119] The emphasis on moderation in these passages has a special bearing on another theme present in several of Montaigne's texts in which he reflects on how desires and objects interact in the imagination. His understanding of desire was presented in terms of balance, moderation, and finitude. Montaigne writes in one passage from the essay, "One man's profit is another man's loss" and "no profit is ever made except at somebody else's loss: by his [the Athenian Demades] reckoning you would have to condemn earnings of every sort.... And what is worse, if each of us were to sound our inner depths he would find that most of our desires are born and nurtured at other people's expense."[120]

Like other visions of the zero-sum economy, the early modern balance sheet of profit and loss meant that a desire for gain was complicit in depriving another. Greed, as Montaigne indicates here, was an aggressive act, one that helped differentiate the borders of the social and personal. Moderation, Montaigne suggests in his essay "On solitude," provides a counterweight to those fiery emotions of desire: "We must not let our edge be blunted by the pleasure we take in books: it is the same pleasure as destroys the manager of estates, the miser, the voluptuary and the man of ambition."[121]

Montaigne develops a set of arguments about greed, the personal, and the social in his essay "On Solitude." He begins by noting that the differences between what he calls the "solitary life" and the "active" one offers those of bad faith the opportunity to exploit the social for personal gain: "As for that fine adage used as a cloak by greed and ambition, 'That we are not born for ourselves alone but for the common weal,' let us venture to refer to those who have joined in the dance: let them bare their consciences and confess whether rank, office and all the bustling business of the world are not sought on the contrary to gain private profit from the common weal."[122] If profit and gain presented the problem of perhaps depriving others, retention was also implicated in social collapse.

In his fascinating essay "On the Three Kinds of Social Intercourse," Montaigne develops an analysis of the ways that social interaction was lubricated by the desires of humans. Montaigne develops this argument in connection to the creation of his library, an act of possession and collection that bears close resemblance to the larger circulation of the economy. "All the profit which I draw from books," Montaigne writes, "consists in experiencing and applying that proverb ['No need to pity an invalid who has a remedy up his coat-sleeve'] (which is a very true one). In practice I hardly use them more than those who are quite unacquainted with them. I enjoy them as misers do riches: because I know I can always enjoy them whenever I please. My soul is satisfied and contented by this right of possession."[123]

By possessing books, Montaigne is not spurred to possess more of them—the usual emotional trajectory that we are accustomed to seeing on display as a type of unsatisfiable desire; instead the writer feels a sense of balance and completion. The passage, which comes at the end of a long essay in which Montaigne contemplates the distinctions between public and private, provides a helpful introduction to the psychology of the miser, a topic that he developed at greater length in his essay: "The taste of good and evil things depends on the opinion we have of them."

Montaigne acknowledges that plenty—not want—creates the conditions for avarice. "To attain poverty," he argues, "one man cast his golden coins into that self-same sea which others ransack to net and catch riches. Epicurus said that being rich does not alleviate our worries: it changes them. And truly it is not want that produces avarice but plenty."[124] Writing in an autobiographical mode, Montaigne probes the origins of his own relationship to riches, developing a description of the psychological ramification of retention along the way.

The psychology of the miser was demonstrated in what Montaigne called his "second stage" of financial development, a point in time when he had money after a long period of youthful recklessness. He saves a considerable amount, plans for mishap in the future, and sets aside money, but "none of this happened with a painful anxiety. I made a secret of it: I, who dare talk so much about myself, never talked truthfully about my money—like those rich who act poor and those poor who act rich, their consciences dispensed from witnessing truly to what they own."[125] The psychological suffering and intense anxiety that Montaigne experiences when saving were relentless ones.

> The heavier my money the heavier my worries, wondering as I did whether the roads were safe and then about the trustworthiness of the men in change of my baggage; like others that I know, I was only happy about it when I had it before my eyes. When I left my strong-box at home, what thoughts and suspicions I had, sharp thorny ones and, what is worse, ones I could tell nobody about. My mind forever dwelt on it. When you tot it all up, there is more trouble in keeping money than in acquiring it.[126]

When money is removed from circulation by miserliness, this too bears psychological importance to the miser. The accumulated fortune, deprived of exchange value, also loses its use value. Montaigne writes, "I had more to spend, but the spending weighed no less heavily on me, for as Bion said, when it comes to plucking out hairs, it hurts the balding no less than the hairy: once you have grown used to having a pile of a certain size and have set your mind on doing so, you can no longer use it: you do not even want to slice a bit off the top. It is the kind of structure—so it seems to you—that would tumble down if you even touched it. For you to broach it, Necessity must have you by the throat."[127]

One of the central aspects of miserliness that Montaigne diagnosed so acutely in the essay is the way that accumulated wealth exists as a type of limitless desire. Like Paracelsus 150 years before, Montaigne notes the ways that the idea of a border to acceptable behavior—a socially defined limit on activity—allows us to see the mental implications of miserly desire. "The danger," Montaigne writes, "lies in its not being easy to place definite limits on such desires—limits are hard to discover for things which seem good—and so to know when to stop saving. You go on making your pile bigger, increasing it from one sum to another until, like a peasant, you deprive yourself of the enjoyment of your own goods: your enjoyment consists in hoarding and never actually using it. If this is 'using' money, then the richest in cash are the guards on the walls and gates of a goodly city! To my way of thinking, any man with money is a miser."[128]

Recognizing that any accumulation of wealth disposes him to avarice, Montaigne seeks to move beyond this wretched condition and into what he terms the "Third Stage," a point at which he recognizes wealth for what it can do, not just as a pile of useless coins:

> If I do save up now, it is only because I hope to use the money soon—not to purchase lands that I have no use for but to purchase pleasure. *"Non esse cupidum pecunia est, non esse emacem vectigal est."* [Not to want means money: not to spend means income]. I have no fear, really, that I shall lack anything: nor have I any wish for more. *"Divitiarum fructus est in copia, copiam declarat satietas."* [The fruit of riches consists in abundance: abundance is shown by having enough]. I particularly congratulate myself that this amendment of life should have come to me at an age which is naturally inclined to avarice, so ridding me of a vice—the most ridiculous of all human madnesses—which is so common among the old."[129]

The instrumentality of money that Montaigne notes in his essay on taste surfaced again in his essay titled "On Prayer," in which he offers a critique of instrumental religion. Targeting the miser who "prays God for the vain and superfluous preservation of his hoard" alongside the ambitious and the criminal, Montaigne challenges the prayers of evil men, arguing that at "the foot of the mansion which they are about to climb into and blow up, men say their prayers, while their purposes and hopes are full of cruelty, lust and greed."[130]

One of the most important insights that Montaigne developed over the course of the essays was the argument that certain emotions were historical in nature; greed, for instance, was something that was culturally taught. One example of this appears in the legal language of "rights" that Montaigne uses in "The Hour of Parlaying Is Dangerous," where he describes a besieging army: "Before his very eyes they sacked a large section of the town, the rights of greed and vengeance overriding those due to his office and to army discipline."[131] In other essays Montaigne used the example of the New World to indicate that greed and avarice were learned traits associated with European culture and society. While it was certainly tempting to map all sorts of noble qualities onto the first Americans, Montaigne uses indigenous populations as a way to probe what might be called the globalization of European culture. In his rumination on the state of natural man as it was imagined to exist in the New World, Montaigne writes in "On the Cannibals" that there was simply no greed in the garden of the New World:

> I would tell Plato that those people have no trade of any kind, no acquaintance with writing, no knowledge of numbers, no terms for governor or political superior, no practice of subordination or of riches or poverty, no contracts, no inheritances, no divided estates, no occupation but leisure, no concern for kin-

ship—except such as is common to them all—no clothing, no agriculture, not metals, not use of wine or corn. Among them you hear no words for treachery, lying, cheating, avarice, envy, backbiting or forgiveness.[132]

If greed had no place in the Eden of the New World, it was a set of ideas that could be taught through Empire and its civilizing mission. In "On Coaches," Montaigne probes the experience of Empire in the New World, concluding that older forms of conquest, like those found in the classical world, were much different from the experience of colonization in the sixteenth century. Greed— Montaigne uses the word "cupidity" here—was one of the central lessons imparted through the cultural exchanges of the early Atlantic world:

> What a renewal that would have been, what a restoration of the fabric of this world, if the first examples of our behaviour which were set before that new world had summoned those people to be amazed by our virtue and understanding. How easy it would have been to have worked profitably with folk whose souls were so unspoiled and so hungry to learn, having for the most part been given such a beautiful start by Nature. We, on the contrary, took advantage of their ignorance and lack of experience to pervert them more easily towards treachery, debauchery and cupidity, toward every kind of cruelty and inhumanity, by the example and model of our own manners.[133]

Erasmus and Calvin produced theologically informed understandings of greed that resonated in confessionalized ways precisely because they were able to so closely match the religious dramas of the sixteenth century. The humanist Montaigne provides an important counterpoint to these confessionally tinged descriptions of greed. Although rooted in the Catholic tradition, Montaigne oriented his understanding of avarice around selfhood, emotion, and self-mastery. The self, and the emotions it contained, were understood in relation to the material conditions of life. And Montaigne's insistence of the instrumentality of money—one that could be coldly rationalized and understood—offers a useful counterpoint to the lurid emotionality deployed by both Erasmus and Calvin.

The essays written at the end of the sixteenth century by the polymath Michel de Montaigne provide an opportunity to reflect on ways that religion shaped attitudes about economic behavior. We saw in the pre-Reformation writings of Reformers that a charge of avarice could be marshaled in the service of a larger attack on Christian power structures. Even sympathetic Catholics like Erasmus continued to employ religiously inflected understandings of avarice in his post-Reformation writings.

Calvin, of course, filtered his understanding of avarice and greed through his own theology, producing in the process a set of interpretations of key biblical passages that attacked hoarding and accumulation. This theology, naturally, had the potential to discourage savings without encouraging consumerism— exactly the religious foundation that one expects would support a particular worldview conducive to capitalism. Avarice, in Calvin's theology, was subtly transformed from a set of behaviors that could be stopped to one that merely indicated the profound depths of sin that already ensnared people.

Montaigne—writing just after Calvin's death—adopts what might be called a conservatively Catholic approach to the problem. Avarice does not irredeemably corrupt a person; it merely conforms to certain stages of life or adheres to identifiable material practices like Empire. Erasmus's work gives us insight into how the early stages of the Catholic Reformation reinforced certain confessionally significant theological principles in practicing Catholics. Calvin's commentaries, producing new and equally confessionally specific positions on avarice and greed, performed a similar type of cultural work in the mid sixteenth century. And we see, finally, in Montaigne's essays the embeddedness of Catholic positions on avarice expressed in lay writing of the late sixteenth century. Producing a theology of avarice, in other words, was a long-term project.

We have seen how that project unfolded in the previous chapters, and we now turn to a slightly different set of problems, albeit ones hinted at in Calvin and Montaigne: the attempt to understand avarice and greed through a variety of legal structures.

## Notes

1. David M. Luebke et al., *Conversion and the Politics of Religion in Early Modern Germany* (New York: Berghahn Books, 2012).
2. Thomas A. Brady, *German Histories in the Age of Reformations, 1400–1650* (Cambridge: Cambridge University Press, 2009), 289.
3. Susan C. Karant-Nunn, *The Reformation of Feeling: Shaping the Religious Emotions in Early Modern Germany* (Oxford: Oxford University Press, USA, 2010).
4. Max Weber, *The Protestant Ethic and the Spirit of Capitalism*, Routledge Classics (London: Routledge, 2001).
5. See Anthony Gidden's introduction for the main lines of contention; Weber, *Protestant Ethic*, xviii–xxiv.
6. Savonarola, "The Renovation of the Church," in Olin, *Catholic Reformation*, 6.
7. Savonarola, "The Oratory of Divine Love," in Olin, *Catholic Reformation*, 22.
8. John Colet, "Convocation Sermon," in Olin, *Catholic Reformation*, 32.
9. Colet, "Convocation Sermon," 33.
10. Ibid.
11. Ibid., 33–34.
12. Egidio da Viterbo, "Address to the Fifth Lateran Council," in Olin, *Catholic Reformation*, 52.
13. John C. Olin, ed., "Supernae Dispositionis Arbitrio," in Olin, *Catholic Reformation*, 59–60.
14. John C. Olin, ed., "Capuchin Constitutions of 1536," in Olin, *Catholic Reformation*, 162–63.
15. Ibid., 163.
16. Ibid.

17. Ibid.
18. John C. Olin, ed., "Consilium de Emendanda Ecclesia," in Olin, *Catholic Reformation*, 191.
19. Ibid.
20. Ibid., 196.
21. Desiderius Erasmus, "Handbook of the Militant Christian," in *The Essential Erasmus*, trans. John Patrick Dolan (New York: Meridian, 1983), 45–46.
22. Ibid., 46.
23. Ibid., 59.
24. Ibid., 70.
25. Ibid., 78.
26. Ibid., 81.
27. Ibid., 86.
28. Ibid.
29. Ibid.
30. Ibid., 87.
31. Ibid.
32. Ibid., 86.
33. Ibid.
34. Ibid.
35. Ibid.
36. Ibid., 87.
37. Ibid.
38. Ibid.
39. Ibid.
40. Desiderius Erasmus, *The Praise of Folly and Other Writings: A New Translation with Critical Commentary* (New York: Norton, 1989), 10.
41. Ibid., 38–39.
42. Ibid., 49–50.
43. Ibid., 50.
44. Ibid., 67.
45. Ibid., 73.
46. Ibid., 74.
47. John C. Olin, *The Catholic Reformation: Savonarola to Ignatius Loyola* (New York: Fordham Univ Press, 1969), 83.
48. Olin, *Catholic Reformation*, 84.
49. Ibid., 85.
50. Ibid., 88.
51. Desiderius Erasmus, "The Complaint of Peace," in *The Essential Erasmus*, trans. John Patrick Dolan (New York: Meridian, 1983), 182.
52. Desiderius Erasmus, "Concerning the Immense Mercy of God," in *The Essential Erasmus*, trans. John Patrick Dolan (New York: Meridian, 1983), 233.
53. Ibid., 244.
54. Ibid., 268.
55. Desiderius Erasmus, "On Mending the Peace of the Church," in *The Essential Erasmus*, trans. John Patrick Dolan (New York: Meridian, 1983), 332.
56. Ibid., 338.
57. John Calvin, *Commentaries on the Catholic Epistles*, trans. John Owen (Edinburgh: Calvin Translation Society, 1855), 405.

58. John Calvin, *Commentaries on the Four Last Books of Moses: Arranged in the Form of a Harmony*, trans. Charles William Bindham, vol. III (Edinburgh: Calvin Translation Society, 1854), 186–87.

59. Ibid., III:187.

60. Ibid.

61. Ibid.

62. Ibid.

63. John Calvin, *Institutes of the Christian Religion*, trans. Henry Beveridge, vol. III (Edinburgh: Calvin Translation Society, 1845), 269.

64. Calvin, *Commentaries on the Four Last Books of Moses*, III:188.

65. Ibid.

66. Ibid.

67. Ibid.

68. Ibid.

69. Calvin, *Institutes of the Christian Religion*, III:262.

70. Ibid, III:261.

71. Ibid, III:286.

72. Richard Newhauser, ed., *In the Garden of Evil: The Vices and Culture in the Middle Ages*, Papers in Mediaeval Studies 18 (Toronto: Pontifical Institute of Mediaeval Studies, 2005); Richard Newhauser, *Sin: Essays on the Moral Tradition in the Western Middle Ages* (Aldershot, Hants, England: Ashgate/Variorum, 2007); Richard Newhauser, *The Early History of Greed: The Sin of Avarice in Early Medieval Thought and Literature* (New York: Cambridge University Press, 2000).

73. John Calvin, *Commentaries on the Epistles to Timothy, Titus and Philemon*, trans. William Pringle (Edinburgh: Calvin Translation Society, 1856), 158.

74. Ibid.

75. Ibid, 158–59.

76. Ibid, 159.

77. Ibid.

78. Ibid.

79. Ibid.

80. Ibid.

81. Ibid, 160.

82. Ibid.

83. Ibid.

84. John Calvin, *Commentary on a Harmony of the Evangelists, Matthew, Mark, and Luke*, trans. John Pringle, vol. 1 (Edinburgh: Calvin Translation Society, 1845), 336.

85. Ibid.

86. Ibid.

87. Ibid, 1:337.

88. Ibid.

89. Ibid.

90. Ibid.

91. Ibid, 1:338.

92. Ibid.

93. Calvin, *Institutes of the Christian Religion*, III:269.

94. John Calvin, *Commentary on the Epistles of Paul the Apostle to the Corinthians*, trans. John Pringle, vol. II (Edinburgh: Calvin Translation Society, 1849), 250.

95. Calvin, *Institutes of the Christian Religion*, III:269–70.
96. Ibid, III:516.
97. Calvin, *Commentary on the Epistles of Paul*, II:297.
98. Calvin, *Commentaries on the Catholic Epistles*, 142–43.
99. John Calvin, *Commentaries on the Twelve Minor Prophets*, trans. John Owen, vol. IV (Edinburgh: Calvin Translation Society, 1848), 94–95.
100. Ibid., IV:95.
101. Ibid., IV:95–96.
102. Calvin, *Commentaries on the Catholic Epistles*, 343.
103. Ibid., 344.
104. John Calvin, *Commentary on the Epistles of Paul*, 38.
105. Ibid., I:198.
106. Ibid., I:208.
107. Ibid., I:210–11.
108. John Calvin, *Commentaries on the Book of the Prophet Daniel*, trans. Thomas Myers, vol. 1 (Edinburgh: Calvin Translation Society, 1852), 127.
109. Ibid., 1:127–28.
110. Ibid., 1:199.
111. Calvin, *Commentary on the Epistles of Paul*, II:198.
112. Calvin, *Commentaries on Daniel*, 1:344.
113. Ibid., 1:351.
114. Ibid., 1:352.
115. Ibid., 313.
116. Ibid., 2:355.
117. Ibid., 2:356–57.
118. Michel de Montaigne, *The Essays of Michel de Montaigne* (London: Allen Lane, 1991), 1175.
119. Ibid., 49.
120. Ibid., 121.
121. Ibid., 275.
122. Ibid., 266.
123. Ibid., 932.
124. Ibid., 66.
125. Ibid., 68.
126. Ibid.
127. Ibid., 69.
128. Ibid.
129. Ibid., 70.
130. Ibid., 362–63.
131. Ibid., 25.
132. Ibid., 233.
133. Ibid., 1031.

# Bibliography

Brady, Thomas A. *German Histories in the Age of Reformations, 1400–1650*. Cambridge: Cambridge University Press, 2009.

Calvin, John. *Commentary on a Harmony of the Evangelists, Matthew, Mark, and Luke.* Translated by John Pringle. Vol. 1. Edinburgh: Calvin Translation Society, 1845.

———. *Commentary on the Epistles of Paul the Apostle to the Corinthians.* Translated by John Pringle. Vol. I. 2 vols. Edinburgh: Calvin Translation Society, 1848.

———. *Commentary on the Epistles of Paul the Apostle to the Corinthians.* Translated by John Pringle. Vol. II. 2 vols. Edinburgh: Calvin Translation Society, 1849.

———. *Commentaries on the Book of the Prophet Daniel.* Translated by Thomas Myers. Vol. 1. Edinburgh: Calvin Translation Society, 1852.

———. *Commentaries on the Book of the Prophet Daniel.* Translated by Thomas Myers. Vol. 2. Edinburgh: Calvin Translation Society, 1853.

———. *Commentaries on the Catholic Epistles.* Translated by John Owen. Edinburgh: Calvin Translation Society, 1855.

———. *Commentaries on the Epistles to Timothy, Titus and Philemon.* Translated by William Pringle. Edinburgh: Calvin Translation Society, 1856.

———. *Commentaries on the Four Last Books of Moses: Arranged in the Form of a Harmony.* Translated by Charles William Bindham. Vol. III. Edinburgh: Calvin Translation Society, 1854.

———. *Commentaries on the Twelve Minor Prophets.* Translated by John Owen. Vol. IV. Edinburgh: Calvin Translation Society, 1848.

———. *Institutes of the Christian Religion.* Translated by Henry Beveridge. Vol. III. Edinburgh: Calvin Translation Society, 1845.

Colet, John. "Convocation Sermon." In *The Catholic Reformation: Savonarola to Ignatius Loyola; Reform in the Church 1495–1540,* edited by John C. Olin. New York: Harper & Row, 1969.

da Viterbo, Egidio. "Address to the Fifth Lateran Council." In *The Catholic Reformation: Savonarola to Ignatius Loyola; Reform in the Church 1495–1540,* edited and translated by John C. Olin. New York: Harper & Row, 1969.

Erasmus, Desiderius. "The Complaint of Peace." In *The Essential Erasmus,* translated by John Patrick Dolan. New York: Meridian, 1983.

———. "Concerning the Immense Mercy of God." In *The Essential Erasmus,* translated by John Patrick Dolan. New York: Meridian, 1983.

———. "Handbook of the Militant Christian." In *The Essential Erasmus,* translated by John Patrick Dolan. New York: Meridian, 1983.

———. "On Mending the Peace of the Church." In *The Essential Erasmus,* translated by John Patrick Dolan. New York: Meridian, 1983.

———. *The Praise of Folly and Other Writings: A New Translation with Critical Commentary.* New York: Norton, 1989.

Karant-Nunn, Susan C. *The Reformation of Feeling: Shaping the Religious Emotions in Early Modern Germany.* Oxford: Oxford University Press, USA, 2010.

Luebke, David M., Jared Poley, Daniel C. Ryan, and David Warren Sabean. *Conversion and the Politics of Religion in Early Modern Germany.* New York: Berghahn Books, 2012.

Montaigne, Michel de. *The Essays of Michel de Montaigne.* London: Allen Lane, 1991.

Newhauser, Richard. *The Early History of Greed: The Sin of Avarice in Early Medieval Thought and Literature.* New York: Cambridge University, 2000.

———. *Sin: Essays on the Moral Tradition in the Western Middle Ages.* Aldershot, Hants, England: Ashgate/Variorum, 2007.

———, ed. *In the Garden of Evil: The Vices and Culture in the Middle Ages.* Papers in Mediaeval Studies 18. Toronto: Pontifical Institute of Mediaeval Studies, 2005.

Olin, John C., ed. *The Catholic Reformation: Savonarola to Ignatius Loyola.* New York: Fordham Univ Press, 1969.

Olin, John C., ed. "Capuchin Constitutions of 1536." In *The Catholic Reformation: Savonarola to Ignatius Loyola; Reform in the Church 1495–1540.* New York: Fordham Univ Press, 1969.

———. "Consilium de Emendanda Ecclesia." In *The Catholic Reformation: Savonarola to Ignatius Loyola; Reform in the Church 1495–1540.* New York: Fordham Univ Press, 1969.

———. "Supernae Dispositionis Arbitrio." In *The Catholic Reformation: Savonarola to Ignatius Loyola; Reform in the Church 1495–1540.* New York: Fordham Univ Press, 1969.

Savonarola. "The Oratory of Divine Love." In *The Catholic Reformation: Savonarola to Ignatius Loyola; Reform in the Church 1495–1540,* edited and translated by John C. Olin. New York: Fordham Univ Press, 1969.

———. "The Renovation of the Church." In *The Catholic Reformation: Savonarola to Ignatius Loyola; Reform in the Church 1495–1540,* edited and translated by John C. Olin. New York: Fordham Univ Press, 1969.

Weber, Max. *The Protestant Ethic and the Spirit of Capitalism.* London: Routledge, 2001.

# CHAPTER THREE

# Greed and the Law
# in the Seventeenth Century

Michel de Montaigne expressed the opinion that the New World was populated with people who, at least until the Europeans arrived, had no real capacity for greed. The fact that the cross-cultural exchanges of the Atlantic world included an unintended moral education should alert us to the ways that the New World provided a canvas upon which the moral claims of the Old World were recreated. As Europeans sought to make sense of the New World, they also crafted the legal and military tools that were required to solidify and defend their colonies from adversaries. One of the great tasks of seventeenth-century legal scholars and philosophers was to determine how desires could be defined legally in the context of the international extension of colonial empire.

We explore in this chapter the ways that the law in the seventeenth century was a critical space within which ideas about desire, retention, and necessity were given form and institutional cohesion. The evidence indicates that greed was a way for seventeenth-century legal thinkers—and critics—to organize their thinking about law, and we see how legal regimes reflected the societies that created them. We consider four aspects of the problem. An analysis of Hugo Grotius's works on international law and relations will demonstrate the importance of national character and greed to any discussion of imperial rivalries during the period of time when European empires were jockeying for global position.

While Grotius focused on the international, Samuel von Pufendorf used greed to envision a natural law that could govern domestic social interactions, finally coming to imagine an inner and private mental space that was potentially outside the reach of secular legal authorities. We take up the question of how property and right as they were incorporated into the legal structures imagined by John Locke were fundamentally arranged around an attempt to place limits on desire. Finally we engage Francois Fénelon's lengthy critique of French court society during the reign of Louis XIV to examine the ways that critique and criticism of absolutism and mercantilism could be generated through a discussion of greed.

We begin to explore these issues by looking first at a legal text written by the Dutch jurist Hugo Grotius after 1603 titled *De Jurae Praedae*, or *Commentary on the Law of Prize and Booty*.[1] Grotius was responding to a situation characteristic of the globalization of European conflicts: the seizure of a ship belonging to a foreign sovereign and the auctioning of its cargo. The facts of the case were mundane. A Portuguese vessel, the *Santa Catarina*, was captured in the Straight of Singapore by the Dutch captain Jacob van Heemskerck and then auctioned in Amsterdam for a vast sum a year later.[2] Van Heemskerck lacked the authority to attack foreign vessels, and given the political context in which the seizure took place—the Dutch war of independence from the Habsburg empire from the 1570s as well as the formation of the Dutch India Company in 1602—the questions attending to the case were important ones for those trying to make sense of the legal conditions of international trade and warfare alike. Grotius framed the legal issues at hand within the context of desire.

Grotius began by characterizing the attack on the *Santa Catarina* as part of a larger state of war between the Dutch and the Spanish, a state of conflict that allowed acts that would in other times be banned as piracy: "A situation has arisen that is truly novel, and scarcely credible to foreign observers, namely: that those men who have been so long at war with the Spaniards and who have furthermore suffered the most grievous personal injuries, are debating as to whether or not, in a just war and with public authorization, they can rightfully despoil an exceedingly cruel enemy who has already violated the rules of international commerce."[3]

Grotius acknowledges a space for "honorable gain" but then concludes that "the consuming greed for gain, denoted by the Greek term αἰσχροκερδεία (sordid covetousness), is a vile disease of the spirit, characterized by complete disrespect for law and morality."[4] Greed, in other words, is a type of crime governed by the moral codes of humanity as much as by the legal strictures that would seek to eradicate greedy practices. And while greed was certainly a problem, so too was a weak passivity in the face of opportunity: "Yet it is possible to sin in contrary fashion, neglecting opportunities to promote one's own interests, through an anxious and overnice avoidance of things not essentially dishonourable."[5] The proper position to take, Grotius argued, fell in the middle: "It is wrong to inflict injury, but it is also wrong to endure injury."[6]

The task Grotius set for himself with this book was not just to examine the legal and moral questions generated by the creation of the new European empires of the sixteenth and seventeenth centuries but also to determine how older forms of jurisprudence might shed light on these issues. Grotius developed his discussion of these issues around many axes, but three in particular stand out for the purposes of this discussion. Grotius had to envision the ways that acquisitive desire might lead a ruler or a country to war inappropriately; he attempted to figure the point at which honor and greed intersected to configure rules about what might be a legitimate seizure and what could constitute illicit gains; Grotius also sought to attach these questions of honor and illicit acquisition to various national characters.

Grotius opened up the question of gain and its relationship to just or legal warfare by quoting St. Augustine's understanding of the issues. "The greedy urge," Grotius details through St. Augustine, "to inflict harm, cruel vengefulness, an unappeased and unappeasable spirit, savage rebellion, lust for dominion and any similar trait that may appear—these are the things that law finds blameworthy in warfare."[7] In this way, warfare that was carried out merely for the sake of obtaining resources—like the techniques of warfare that sought to punish innocents or to inflict cruelties—was at its heart illegal. While perhaps envisioning the types of catastrophic actions that would characterize fighting during the Thirty Years War a generation later, Grotius's points of reference were the Wars of Religion and the Dutch Revolt, which witnessed not only brutal sectarian fighting but also the political differences between Dutch republicanism and Spanish monarchism.

Grotius was attuned to the idea—predictable in a mercantilist world—that people initiate or join a war with the hope of grabbing resources, an argument that recalls those by Montaigne that we considered in the previous chapter. He dealt with the question of how one might legitimize or justify the seizure of "prize or booty" by noting that "greed for plunder" has historically been a cause for rebellion and revolution.[8] And worse, those instances when a person entered into a war that "did not properly concern him" because he hoped to get rich ("solely for the greed of plunder") was a real problem.[9]

Grotius asserted that warfare should not be undertaken merely to satisfy greed: "Let [people and institutions] remain wholly free from 'deep-seated lust for empire and riches.'"[10] Nonetheless, a central problem for Grotius was not just the seizure of booty but the forced acquisition of something that appeared in excess of what was legitimate. Grotius argues that all the old authorities that dealt with the just war doctrine or who attempted to determine the limits of appropriate seizure do not "condemn ... the seizure of spoils, although many do condemn manifestations of greed in connexion with that practice, that is to say ... 'the acquisition of more than one's due'" that was equated with the exercise of cruelty in war but remained unconnected to the other moral questions centered on the prosecution of organized violence.[11]

Grotius, of course, was a partisan in the larger fights about the legitimacy and justification of Dutch activities—both commercial and martial—at the beginning of the seventeenth century, so we should read his critiques of "Iberian greed and cruelty" that had resulted in the fact that the "Dutch state had been completely drained of resources" with a critical eye.[12] Nonetheless, Grotius's text remains a useful one for the ways that it can indicate how the logic of Empire entered into the larger theoretical debates about virtue and vice. Grotius was writing, after all, in response to the clashes between Dutch and Portuguese sailors in the Pacific, so it should come as no surprise that he disparaged the Portuguese justifications for Empire as part of a larger strategy of upholding the virtue of Dutch extensions into the East Indies.

Grotius broached this subject by offering multiple critiques of the Portuguese imperium, explaining the Lusophone empire could not be justified along the lines of the civilizing mission but was really just a cover story for acquisitive desire. "Long ago," Grotius argues, "Plutarch pointed out that [the civilizing of barbarians] served as [a cloak for greed], or in other words, that shameless lust for another's property was wont to take cover under the excuse of introducing civilization into barbaric regions."[13] Taking an ever more provocative tone, Grotius sought to depict Portuguese actions as ones that stemmed from their long-standing greed, a base condition that was apparent even to more elevated members of the Portuguese nation.

"Writers of ancient times," Grotius argues, "tell us that even long ago the Portuguese people were accustomed to live by robbery and plundering; and persons of the better class among the Portuguese themselves are by no means unaware of the vileness and avarice of the blood that has been intermingled with their race since those bygone times, nor have they failed to note the vast number of Portuguese who are not seriously regarded, among Christians, as Christians."[14] The un-Christian villainy of the Portuguese stood in opposition for Grotius to the virtues of his Dutch compatriots, about whom he writes, "Among all the peoples of these [Germanic] territories there has never been one more free from greed for spoils."[15]

Grotius's slippage into attacks on his national adversaries speaks to the ease with which a critique of another's greed could be extended into a description of national character. Grotius describes "the greedy caprice of the Spaniards."[16] He bluntly writes that the "Portuguese are regarded … not as merchants but as foreign robbers, destructive of human liberty and aflame no less with avarice than with lust for dominion, so that no one associates with them any more than is absolutely unavoidable."[17] The Dutch, naturally, have a more positive set of attributes associated with them. "Dutch sailors," Grotius writes "have cleared themselves satisfactorily of suspicion by disregarding many opportunities for the capture of quite valuable property, and consequently no one can believe that they were motivated merely by greed for spoil in exposing themselves to such great danger; for it is clear that whatever they did, was done because they perceived the impossibility of restraining by any other means the unbounded avidity for gain characteristic of the Portuguese."[18]

Indeed, some Europeans were so incapable of resisting greed that they made predictably foolish decisions. Discussing the loss of ships suffered by the Spanish, Grotius details that this had nothing to do with the skill of French sailors but "of that avarice which had induced the Spaniards to load their ships with merchandise and passengers rather than with arms of any kind."[19] This is not to say, however, that a nation's greed was forever immutable. His critique of the Portuguese centered on how the Iberian kingdom had interfered in the extension of Dutch power into the East Indies in ways that indicated their truly sad moral condition. The Portuguese no longer were to be characterized as possessing an "insane greed for gain," but instead exhibited "envy pure and simple."[20]

The theoretical principle that Grotius used in *Mare Liberum* (Freedom of the Seas, 1609) to articulate his claim of open access on the foundation of a moral universe was oriented around greed and its avoidance: "If in a thing so vast as the sea a man were to reserve to himself from general use nothing more than mere sovereignty, still he would be considered a seeker after unreasonable power. If a man were to enjoin other people from fishing, he would not escape the reproach of monstrous greed. But the man who even prevents navigation, a thing which means no loss to himself, what are we to say of him?"[21] Grotius's conception of right of access—and his identification of barriers to access as a type of greed (or worse)—suggests that an organizing principle of international law in the seventeenth century should not be possession but transit. Inhibiting motion through space is the great crime that prevents the connective tissue of early modern imperialism to form.

Grotius asserts that taking something—even an intangible like the right to traverse the sea—is the greatest injustice: "In fact, injustice simply consists of taking what belongs to someone else, and it does not matter whether it stems from greed, or lust, or anger, or an improvident benevolence; or from the desire to excel, which is the source of the greatest injustices."[22] One answer to this perceived injustice was to be found in the just exercise of organized violence: "The theologians and the philosophers have leveled many severe criticisms at such causes as ambition, avarice, and dissension; yet the same authorities, despite their censorious attitude towards un-just wars, do not by any means deny that certain wars are just."[23]

Thus we see that the foundational texts of a fledgling version of international relations and international law were organized around a language of greed. Indeed, we see in the seventeenth century—and Grotius's *Commentary on the Law of Prize and Booty* and *Freedom of the Seas* are good examples of the process—the ways that greed was integrated in new ways into law and into new forms of legal thinking.

The legal thought that coalesced around greed in the seventeenth century was then later refined and extended in the eighteenth century in terms of a new logic of economics that looked backward to the baroque order for its religious sensibilities and forward toward a set of market relations that would help shape the sensibilities of liberal economics. Following Grotius's example, however, we see other thinkers of the seventeenth century work out more carefully how greed helped organize legal thinking. Grotius's protégé, Samuel von Pufendorf, linked a set of moral claims that circled around the crime of avarice and the need for a new set of laws that would allow nations to come to terms peacefully with one another.

Samuel von Pufendorf's 1660 text on the just war doctrine and the rules of war titled *Two Books of the Elements of Universal Jurisprudence* established a connection between avarice and unjust war that he would embellish over the next thirty-five years. In *Universal Jurisprudence*, Pufendorf asserted that one major—but illegitimate, in his view—cause of war was the greedy "prospect of making gain" on the part of a rogue state. Just as a state was required to police the actions of greedy individuals ("as if, in truth, there were less injustice, cruelty, and avarice in what is found to have been done often by those whose crimes have gone unpunished among men, because they had no one over them, and so they have not been vehemently castigated, since the rest of men do not shrink from perpetrating the same crimes"), so too must there be an international set of agreements that could rein in those states who went to war merely in the hope that there would be financial or territorial reward.[24]

As Pufendorf details, "If some special law ought to be set up on the basis of the common usage of nations, the very first heading in it will treat of the legitimate waging of wars for mere ambition, or with the prospect of making gain, than which nothing is more frequent among most nations."[25] Like Grotius before him, Pufendorf exhibits a critical attack on a type of "national greed" that was reflected in the actions of a particular state and in its approach to other sovereign entities.

The foundation of his critique of the international ramifications of greed—most upsetting, war—cannot be seen if we limit our view to the national and international levels. The individual as it was understood in the context of Lutheran theology and Berlin court society was still the primary vector for the moral and religious crimes of greed. Individuals and their greed produced a very special relationship between the individual and the legal apparatus and, in fact, helped provide a new class of crimes that should not be punished because people were simply too weak to resist the temptations that they represented or that were perhaps unreachable by the long arm of the law.

Pufendorf essentially claims that some emotions were so strong as to make people not fully responsible for their actions, at least in a secular sense. As Pufendorf argues in his 1673 text *The Whole Duty of Man*, greed could be understood in the context of duty and desire. "The *Desire of outward Possessions, Riches, and Wealth*," Pufendorf writes in this text "does also prevail greatly in the Minds of Men; and no wonder, since Men have not only need thereof for their own Support and Preservation in the World, but also often lie under an indispensible Duty to provide them for others."[26]

The all-important connection between wealth and charity remains a cornerstone of the principled position that Pufendorf advocates, but it is useful to remember that this notion of duty is divorced from any clear religious principle. Pufendorf explains, "Because our Wants are not infinite, but lie in a very narrow Compass, and since Nature is not wanting in a plentiful Provision for the Necessities of her Sons; and lastly, since all that we can heap together must, at our Death, fall to others; we must moderate our Desire and our Pursuit of those Things, and govern our selves in the Use of them according to the just Occasions of Nature, and the modest Demands of Temperance and Sobriety."[27]

As we will see in the subsequent chapter, the idea of balance or moderation in desire was a pillar of German thought about economics and trade, and it is important to see Pufendorf's appeal to moderation in that light. Pufendorf also counseled against "profligacy," which stood in contrast to retention and hoarding: "We must do no dishonest or base Thing for the procuring them; we must not increase them by sordid Avarice, nor squander them away by profuse Prodigality, nor in any ways make them subservient to vicious and dishonest Purposes."[28]

Finally, Pufendorf also notes that wealth could be fleeting, and its loss could precipitate a deeper crisis of selfhood. "Since Riches are of a very perishable Nature," Pufendorf writes, "and may be taken from us by many Accidents and Casualties, we must, with respect to 'em, put our Mind in so even a Temper, as not to lose it self if it should happen to lose them."[29] The fear that one's mind might be unsettled if one lost a possession was a normal one, but we see here in Pufendorf's writings on desire and necessity the beginning of an idea about privacy and the individual that takes on a special significance if we place him in a broader intellectual context.

Pufendorf expects people to attempt to police their own desires and behaviors; he imagines people to be capable of respecting God's laws. Human laws must be of a different nature. Pufendorf writes later in the text, "It is absolutely necessary, That *all those Disorders of the Mind should be exempted from Punishment, that are the Effects of the common Corruption of Mankind*; such as Ambition, Avarice, Rudeness, Ingratitude, Hypocrisy, Envy, Pride, Anger, private Grudges, and the like."[30] Human law and punishment can only reach so far. Those actions that stemmed from the pitifully "corrupt" nature of humankind should not fall under the legal sway of the sovereign; they are instead of a legal category much nearer to insanity. Indeed, Pufendorf explained in paragraph XI of Chapter 13 of his *Whole Duty of Man* that some crimes were so internalized (and never resulted in action) that they could not really fall under the terms of human justice. Greed, it would seem, could be excused of certain transgressions:

BUT if, together with the End of Punishments, we consider the Condition of Human Nature, we shall see, That *all Sins are not of that Quality, that they must necessarily fall under the Sentence of a Court of Justice. The Acts of the Mind within it self,* which are merely internal; such as, Thinking upon a Sin with Delight, coveting, desiring, resolving to do an ill Thing, but without effect; though they should be afterward made know by a Man's own Confession, yet are all exempted from the Stroke of human Punishments.[31]

We see again how a notion of the privacy of one's thoughts—even if those thoughts are morally problematic—cannot be the subject of secular legal reach. Thinking about people thinking about greed, Pufendorf begins to articulate a claim to the existence of the freedom of thought.

The distinction that Pufendorf drew between divine and natural laws in *The Whole Duty of Man* reappeared in his 1687 treatise *Of the Nature and Qualification of Religion in Reference to Civil Society.* Pufendorf first argued that Christian precepts "had not the least relation to the Establishment of a Sovereign State," clearly indicating a division of powers between the secular and the divine.[32] Indeed, the state could work at cross-purposes to the divine order: "A State cannot be without a Supream Head, who having Power to bestow Honours and Dignities, this generally proves the occasion of ambitious Designs. A State cannot be maintained without considerable Revenues, which entices Men to Avarice. But, if we look upon our Saviour, we shall find that his main Endeavour is to keep his Disciples from ambitious Designs and Covetousness."[33]

The logic of two legal systems—one secular, one divine—had its appeals, but it could not account for a larger set of concerns revolving around the behaviors of people in the secular realm. How might people be encouraged to behave if the only real threat was a divine one?

Pufendorf wrestled with this issue in his 1695 text *The Divine Feudal Law,* writing that there were multitudes of people who could not police their own extravagant desires: "How many are there who might live at Ease, a quiet, pleasant, Life, if they knew how to set Bounds to Avarice and Ambition, and could forbear to strive, that they might get more, and rise higher, than fair and favourable Opportunity, the certain Indication of the Divine good Pleasure in the Case, invites them to do?"[34] Pufendorf clearly considered avarice a problem affecting individuals, but he promoted an easier answer in the form of society and he envisioned a type of social contract that would work its magic by creating a third way between the sovereign (who might actually encourage greed in some, as we saw before) and the divine (which could only punish in the hereafter).

Civil society provided a bridge between these two poles, at the same time reining in the threat of unjust territorial expansion, returning him at the end of his life to some of the questions of international jurisprudence that animated his earlier work. Wondering what "numberless Multitude of Evils does the Wickedness of some Men bring upon others?" Pufendorf articulated an answer

to his own question: "All which might be prevented, if Men would rather perform the common Duties which they owe to one another, than obey enormous
Lusts. What else is it that destroys whole Nations by Wars, in which one Word
a mighty Inundation of Woes is included, but an ungovern'd Desire of Rule,
and of extending Empire without Bounds?"[35]

Pufendorf's attempt—with only limited success—to work out a secular legal
framework through which to govern desires indicates how complex the problems had become by the end of the seventeenth century. Sovereigns, bound by
the demanding pace of court society, the need for a bureaucratized military,
and (often) important territorial and commercial ambitions, could no longer
merely police desires by joining forces with Church officials. Ecclesiastical officials might have wished for more worldly authority, but the commercial revolution of the late seventeenth century provided a whole new set of worldly
temptations against which religious officials were increasingly powerless. Only
a social definition and critique of greed could help produce a legal framework
that could satisfy everyone, and this definition had to be worked out in terms of
legal codes capable of justly governing property rights, use, and need.

John Locke, noting the presence of "evil Concupiscence" in people, sought
just this sort of legal framework, and one way to read his 1689 *Two Treatises
of Government* is to note the ways that avarice acts as a kind of backbone upon
which the claims of a larger legal structure could be built.[36] Locke scholar Peter
Laslett observes that Locke's work hinges on the question and definition of
property oriented around its appropriate—and not wasteful—use, writing in
his introduction to Locke's *Two Treatises of Government*, "Property so acquired
was not unlimited, for it was confined originally to what a man and his family
could consume or use, and must not be wasted."[37] Laslett's insight into Locke's
position on property and waste is a useful entry point into how property rights,
ownership, and waste were understood in the Anglophone world after the Glorious Revolution of 1688–89.

Laslett suggests that Locke's "whole argument is intended to show that individual property did not arise from the common consent of all mankind, though
in the end the actual distribution of it is held to be due to money, which is
a matter of consent, perhaps even worldwide consent."[38] We must, in other
words, come to terms with Locke's theory of money if we want to understand
how acquisition figured into his view of economic exchange. As Laslett argues
in his introduction, "Half-conscious traditionalism or plain hypocrisy must be
held to account for Locke's description of unlimited acquisitiveness as '*amor
sceleratus habendi*, evil Concupiscence.'"[39]

In Locke's *First Treatise*, Section 42 revolves around these questions of need
and charity. Locke is firm in his commitment to a type of social justice, explaining, "A Right to the Surplusage of his Goods" could not "justly be denied" to
one in need.[40] Miserly retention, in other words, remained just as much a crime

in Locke's time as it had been in Paracelsus's. Charity, in fact, provided the legal mechanisms needed for social cohesion. Locke shows in the section that "*Charity* gives every Man a Title to so much out of another's Plenty, as will keep him from extream want, where he has not means to subsist otherwise."[41] Charity is important to Locke because its absence can deprive the poor of sovereignty; charity creates the conditions for human freedom.

In his *Second Treatise*, Locke returns to similar themes. He writes in his section on property that property comes from labor and the argument revolves around the way labor adds value by allowing a person to distinguish the natural and common from the belabored and uncommon. But property has to be exchanged in order for society to function, and he explains in Section 46 that property can over time be diminished, which leads Locke in the following section to describe the invention of money. The origin of money is found in the desire to hoard: "And thus came in the use of Money, some lasting things that Men might keep without spoiling, and that by mutual consent Men would take in exchange for the truly useful, but perishable Supports of Life."[42] Section 50 provides the key passage:

> But since Gold and silver, being little useful to the Life of man in proportion to Food, Rayment, and carriage, has its value only from the consent of Men, whereof Labour yet makes, in great part, the measure, it is plain, that Men have agreed to disproportionate and unequal Possession of the Earth, they having by a tacit and voluntary consent found out a way, how a man may fairly possess more land than he himself can use the product of, by receiving in exchange for the overplus, Gold and Silver, which may be hoarded up without injury to any one, these metals not spoiling or decaying in the hands of the possessor. This partage of things, in an inequality of private possessions, men have made practicable out of the bounds of Societie, and without compact, only by putting a value on gold and silver and tacitly agreeing in the use of Money.[43]

We see in Section 50 the ways that a money economy, at least in Locke's estimation, functions best when excess property is exchanged rather than retained. The miser, and we will see echoes of this argument in later chapters, mistakes money for property and therefore refuses to participate in sociable exchange. Perhaps one way of connecting Locke's two treatises would be to see evidence here of the argument that just as the poor have the right to another's "Surplusage" in the form of charity, all of society has a claim to the miser's hoarded wealth.

There is further evidence for this reading when we consider Section 184 of the *Second Treatise*, in which Locke writes that money's value is created through various effects of the imagination. Locke writes,

> For as to Money, and such Riches and Treasure taken away, these are none of Natures Goods, they have but a Phantastical imaginary value: Nature has put

no such upon them: They are of no more account by her standard, than the Wampompeke of the Americans to an European Prince, or the Silver Money of Europe would have been formerly to an American…. Which will be easily granted, if one do but take away the imaginary value of Money, the disproportion being more, than between five and five hundred.[44]

Money's value is generated culturally and contextually; to his mind it does not "translate" across cultural borders. We will see in later chapters how this effect of money and money's value reappeared as a central problem in the philosophy of money at the end of the nineteenth century.

Locke made his most direct commentary on the issue of greed and avarice in Section 111 of his *Second Treatise*. The passage at hand is a complex one, so it is best to quote the entire section before moving on to the analysis. Locke writes in Section 111,

But though the Golden Age (before vain Ambition, and *amor sceleratus habendi*, evil Concupiscence, had corrupted Mens minds into a Mistake of true Power and Honour) had more Virtue, and consequently better Governours, as well as less vicious Subjects; and there was then no stretching Prerogative on the one side to oppress the People; nor consequently on the other any Dispute about Priviledge, to lessen or restrain the Power of the Magistrate; and so no contest betwixt Rulers and People about Governours or Government: Yet, when Ambition and Luxury, in future Ages would retain and increase the Power, without doing the Business, for which it was given, and aided by Flattery, taught Princes to have distinct and separate Interests from their People, Men found it necessary to examine more carefully the Original and Rights of Government; and to find out ways to restrain the Exorbitances, and prevent the Abuses of that Power which they having intrusted in another's hands only for their own good, they found was made use of to hurt them.[45]

One way to read this passage is to focus on the temporal qualities that drew Locke's attention at the outset. He notes the existence of a former "Golden Age" that existed before greed helped ruin humanity, corrupting "Mens minds." The lasting implications of that fall include a division between ruler and ruled. Greed, like ambition and luxury, had helped shape a political environment that was fundamentally unstable. He does not use the term "revolution" in the passage, but Locke's warning that people might "examine more carefully" the ways their government was founded and functioned should perhaps be read as a warning to those in power.

That an accusation of greed might be a useful way to critique legal structures and political power is in some ways unsurprising, yet Locke's integration of greed, law, and sovereignty in his *Two Treatises* is a useful indication of how revolution—in Locke's case the Glorious Revolution of 1688—could be legitimized. If we turn our attention to similar critiques of the French monarchy from the same period, we can see another dimension of the problem. Francois Fénelon's 1699 *The Adventures of Telemachus, the Son of Ulysses* issues a similar set of critiques of the French monarchy. The book takes as its source material the education of Ulysses's son, Telemachus, by his teacher "Mentor" (shown near the conclusion to be Minerva). The book, which proved to be extremely popular, was understood to be an extended critique of Louis XIV's court and rule and led ultimately to Archbishop Fénelon's dismissal from Versailles.

Fénelon's references to court society were only thinly veiled. One passage describes the greedy duplicity of the courtier Metophis, who dupes the king, allowing Fénelon to initiate a larger critique of court society: "'They [the people] pretend to love the king, when in fact they have no attachment but to the riches which he gives: far from loving him, they, in order to obtain his favors, first flatter and then betray him.'"[46] Another ruler, Pygmalion, is a noted *avarus*, who "tormented by an insatiable thirst after riches, becomes everyday more and more miserable and odious to his subjects. To be wealthy at Tyre is criminal: avarice rendering him distrustful, suspicious, cruel, he persecutes the rich, and fears the poor.[47] Indeed, King Pygmalion is in all respects completely lacking in virtue.

He represents the absolute failure of sensible kingship, and he reduces his court and his subjects to poverty in his relentless pursuit of more wealth. Fénelon writes that Pygmalion "only sought to make himself happy: he thought to make himself so by the possession of riches and absolute power; he possesses everything that he could desire, and yet has made himself miserable by them."[48] Fénelon characterizes Pygmalion further as a king whose rule is continually undermined by his passions for money. Fénelon intimates that if Pygmalion could begin to control his own passions and embrace a simpler and more virtuous life, his rule would be more secure and more effective:

> If he were a shepherd ... he would not have more great riches, which are as useless to him as sand, since he dares not touch them; yet he would enjoy freely the fruits of the earth, and would suffer no real need. This man seems to do everything he wants, and yet this is far from being the case; he does as his ferocious passions decree, and is continually preyed upon either by avarice, fear, or suspicion. He seems to command all other men, and yet has not the command of himself, for he has as many masters and executioners as he has violent desires."[49]

Critiquing the rule of Louis XIV by analogy, and offering a blunt assessment of the psychological dynamics at work in court society, Fénelon offers in *Telemachus* an indication of the ways that political rule might be conditioned by a type of avarice that then renders the entire political apparatus suspect.

The court of Pygmalion is bad enough, but Fénelon painted in a picture of alternative societies and differing legal structures. Telemachus is told in the novel to "do ... as is done here [Tyre]; give a ready and kind reception to all strangers; let them find in your havens security, convenience, and entire liberty; never suffer yourself to be blinded by avarice or pride. The true secret to gain a great deal, is never to grasp at too much, and to know how to lose suitably."[50] Telemachus's teacher, Mentor, describes another vision of an ideal society in a different passage, articulating a type of cameralist vision of Crete:

> The more people there are in a country, the greater plenty they enjoy, provided they are industrious. They never have occasion to be jealous of one another: the earth, that kind mother, multiplies her gifts according to the number of her children who merit her fruits by their labor. The ambition and avarice of men are the only sources of their misfortunes: men want to have everything, and render themselves unhappy by the desiring the superfluous: if they would live in a simple manner, and be content with satisfying the real needs, we should see plenty, joy, peace, and union reign everywhere.[51]

Fénelon argues that the children of this king are able to avoid the usual litany of awful behaviors: "They do not make courage consist solely in despising death amidst the dangers of war, but also in disdaining excessive wealth, and shameful pleasures. Here they punish three vices, which remain unpunished in other countries: ingratitude, dissimulation, and avarice."[52] Fénelon's utopian visions reveal something important about the economic vision of the late seventeenth century. We see how rule and economic development could be coordinated in ways that generated a healthy and prosperous society.

Economic development—and the maintenance of healthy commerce—were of course central problems facing European rulers at the end of the seventeenth century. But we also see in Fénelon's work a warning that mercantilist policies could in fact be self-limiting and self-defeating. Fénelon explains in another passage in the text,

> There are several mines of gold and silver in this beautiful country; but the inhabitants, simple in their manners and happy in that simplicity, do not deign to count them as any part of their wealth; they account nothing such that does not serve to supply the real needs of men. When we first began to trade with them, we found gold and silver employed for the same purposes as iron—as, for instance, to make plowshares. Since they have no foreign commerce, they had no occasion for money. They are all either shepherds or laborers.[53]

We see here that Fénelon seeks to challenge the emphasis on foreign commerce that was such a part of mercantilist thought. Economic extraction—especially when it came at the expense of social cohesion and happiness—was a dangerous pursuit.

The social ramifications of *un*-mercantilist economics were central to Fénelon's critique. Superfluity leads to unhappiness. Describing one region, Fénelon writes of its inhabitants, "They must be jealous of one another; mean;

spiteful, and envious; and continually harassed by avarice, fear, and ambition; incapable of true, genuine pleasure, since they are enslaved by so many false necessities, on the supply of which they make their happiness depend."[54]

Fénelon shows in another passage that rulers are responsible for the social and economic character of their countries: "About these kings too were seen flitting, like owls in the night, cruel jealousies, vain alarms, and distrusts, which give the people their revenge for the hard-heartedness of their kings, insatiable avarice, false glory, which is always accompanied by tyranny, and unmanly sloth, which doubles every evil that befalls us and can yield no solid pleasure."[55] The "people's revenge" for monarchical avarice is a concept perhaps more in tune with the France of 1789 than it was with the France of Fénelon's time, but it nonetheless indicates the dramatic changes of the seventeenth century.

In 1628 William Harvey, dedicating his *De Motu Cordis* to King Charles I, explained that the "heart of animals is the foundation of their life, the sovereign of everything within them, the sun of their microcosm, that upon which all growth depends, from which all power proceeds. The King, in like manner, is the foundation of his kingdom, the sun of the world around him, the heart of the republic, the fountain whence all power, all grace doth flow."[56] Typical of absolutist discourse, the king's body and the realm were joined, and just as typical of Renaissance thought, the natural and metaphysical worlds were homologized. As the circulation of the heavens, so too the circulation of blood; together they indicated harmonies between inner and outer, big and small, human and divine. But as Fénelon's critique of Louis XIV demonstrates, it was also understood that the absolutist fish rotted from its head—and if the monarch exhibited moral failures then the entire legal structure was potentially imperiled.

We have seen in this chapter the ways that greed helped organize legal thinking in the seventeenth century. The initial concerns of Grotius with national character and the legal framework within which imperial rivalries were conducted demonstrated the ways in which avarice and greed were midwives attending the birth of international relations. Pufendorf's attempt to create a natural law that would be suitable to govern social relations was equally organized around the categories of desire, greed, and necessity. His unwillingness to police the "thought crimes" of greed—those mental pleasures of contemplation that never reached the point of action—provided a private zone unreachable by the codes of justice. Greed, while terrible, helped to construct the notion of the private and the very idea of freedom of thought.

Coming to the question of property, right, and revolution we see with Locke how greed, property, and charity revolved around new ways of thinking about ownership and money. Finally, Fénelon provides insight into the ways that political critique—organized through a language of greed—also turned on a mercantilist axis. By understanding how economic extraction was framed in terms of the moral codes of greed, we are able to see anew the birth of a new economic order beginning in the eighteenth century.

## Notes

1. Hugo Grotius, *Commentary on the Law of Prize and Booty*, trans. Martine Julia van Ittersum (Indianapolis: Liberty Fund, 2006), 9.
2. Ibid. See the introduction by Martine Julia van Ittersum for greater detail on the seizure.
3. Ibid., 9.
4. Ibid., 11.
5. Ibid., 12.
6. Ibid.
7. Ibid., 66.
8. Ibid., 80.
9. Ibid., 85.
10. Ibid., 186.
11. Ibid., 88.
12. Ibid., 252.
13. Ibid., 309.
14. Ibid., 384.
15. Ibid.
16. Ibid., 397.
17. Ibid., 259.
18. Ibid., 455.
19. Ibid., 481.
20. Ibid., 258.
21. Hugo Grotius, *The Freedom of the Seas: Or, The Right Which Belongs to the Dutch to Take Part in the East Indian Trade* (Oxford: Oxford University Press, 1916), 38.
22. Hugo Grotius, *The Rights of War and Peace*, vol. 3 (Indianapolis: Liberty Fund, 2005), 1758.
23. Grotius, *Commentary on the Law*, 52–53.
24. Samuel Pufendorf, *Two Books of the Elements of Universal Jurisprudence*, trans. William Abbott Oldfather (Indianapolis: Liberty Fund, 2009), 227.
25. Ibid.
26. Samuel Pufendorf, *The Whole Duty of Man*, trans. Andrew Tooke (Indianapolis: Liberty Fund, 2003), 76.
27. Ibid.
28. Ibid.
29. Ibid.
30. Ibid., 229.
31. Samuel Pufendorf, *The Whole Duty of Man according to the Law of Nature*, ed. Jean Barbeyrac, trans. Andrew Tooke (London: R. Gosling, 1735), 262.
32. Samuel Pufendorf, *Of the Nature and Qualification of Religion in Reference to Civil Society*, trans. Jodocus Crull (Indianapolis: Liberty Fund, 2002), 54.
33. Ibid.

34. Samuel Pufendorf, *The Divine Feudal Law: Or, Covenants with Mankind, Represented*, trans. Theophilus Dorrington (Indianapolis: Liberty Fund, 2002), 11.
35. Ibid.
36. John Locke, *Two Treatises of Government*, ed. Peter Laslett (Cambridge: Cambridge University Press, 1988), 342.
37. Ibid., 101.
38. Ibid., 101–102.
39. Ibid., 106.
40. Ibid., 170.
41. Ibid.
42. Ibid., 300–1.
43. Ibid., 301–302.
44. Ibid., 391–92.
45. Ibid., 342–43.
46. François de Salignac de La Mothe-Fénelon, *Telemachus, Son of Ulysses*, Cambridge Texts in the History of Political Thought (Cambridge: Cambridge University Press, 1994), 25.
47. Ibid., 32.
48. Ibid., 34.
49. Ibid.
50. Ibid., 36.
51. Ibid., 59.
52. Ibid., 60.
53. Ibid., 109.
54. Ibid., 110.
55. Ibid., 250.
56. William Harvey, Robert Willis, and Sydenham Society, *The Works of William Harvey, M.D.* (London: Sydenham Society, 1847), 3.

# Bibliography

Fénelon, François de Salignac de La Mothe. *Telemachus, Son of Ulysses*. Cambridge Texts in the History of Political Thought. Cambridge: Cambridge University Press, 1994.

Grotius, Hugo. *Commentary on the Law of Prize and Booty*. Translated by Martine Julia van Ittersum. Indianapolis: Liberty Fund, 2006.

———. *The Freedom of the Seas: Or, The Right Which Belongs to the Dutch to Take Part in the East Indian Trade*. Oxford: Oxford University Press, 1916.

———. *The Rights of War and Peace*. Vol. 3. 3 vols. Indianapolis: Liberty Fund, 2005.

Harvey, William, Robert Willis, and Sydenham Society. *The Works of William Harvey, M.D.* London: Sydenham Society, 1847.

Locke, John. *Two Treatises of Government*. Edited by Peter Laslett. Cambridge: Cambridge University Press, 1988.

Pufendorf, Samuel. *The Divine Feudal Law: Or, Covenants with Mankind, Represented*. Translated by Theophilus Dorrington. Indianapolis: Liberty Fund, 2002.

———. *Of the Nature and Qualification of Religion in Reference to Civil Society*. Translated by Jodocus Crull. Indianapolis: Liberty Fund, 2002.

————. *Two Books of the Elements of Universal Jurisprudence.* Translated by William Abbott Oldfather. Indianapolis: Liberty Fund, 2009.

————. *The Whole Duty of Man.* Translated by Andrew Tooke. Indianapolis: Liberty Fund, 2003.

————. *The Whole Duty of Man according to the Law of Nature.* Edited by Jean Barbeyrac. Translated by Andrew Tooke. London: R. Gosling, 1735.

# CHAPTER FOUR

# Greed, Consumerism, and the State

Published at the very end of the seventeenth century, François Fénelon's *Telemachus* (1699) includes a fascinating description of the catastrophic invention of money:

> I [Erycthon] am much afraid, my children, that I have made you a fatal present, by inventing money. I foresee that it will be an incitement to avarice, ambition, and vanity; that it will give rise to an infinity of pernicious arts, directly tending to soften and corrupt manners, that it will make you despise agriculture, which is the support of human life, and the source of all its true riches: but the gods are my witnesses that my intention was good and upright, in introducing among you this invention, which is useful in itself.[1]

We see encapsulated in this passage many of the themes that animated eighteenth-century understandings of greed: concern about the money economy, the softness that consumerism might engender in a population, and the identification of a set of "main sins" (avarice, ambition, and selfishness) that might corrupt an entire population. We consider these issues in this chapter, looking at how thinkers in the eighteenth century responded to the collapse of the baroque order, the growing power of consumer capitalism, and the debates about the proper role of the state and its financial resources.

This chapter is mainly concerned with events in the eighteenth century, a period of time that saw the rise of enlightenment discourse about the state, economics, and the self as well as new systems of economic exchange. We begin by considering the ways that cameralism—a system of economic thought associated with the German-speaking lands—connected an old language of moral collapse surrounding greed with a new set of problems that revolved around the development of consumer society. We consider as well some of the ways that frugality and prodigality—rather than avarice and greed—were employed in gradually more positive ways over the course of the eighteenth century.

We also take up the question, through an analysis of Christian Wolff, of how the new languages of economics, trade, and law indicated a reconfiguration of global interaction in the eighteenth century oriented mainly around circulation. Anything that impeded the flow—such as miserly accumulation—could then be presented as a problem to be solved. We also investigate how states attacked the problem of expenditure, looking for instance at Frederick the Great's Prussia in order to understand better how problems like the husbanding of resources, the promotion of exchange, and the moral implications of consumer exchange were handled in the mid eighteenth century. The chapter concludes by considering the growth of Smithian economic terms, looking especially at the ways that Adam Smith took up the question of avarice and greed in his works.

We begin to consider these problems by looking at the work of Christian Thomasius (1655–1728), a wide-ranging thinker who spent his most productive years at the University of Halle (arriving in the area in 1690). Thomasius developed, beginning in the 1690s, a series of arguments about the role of desire and its relationship to an ethical life. Thomasius is known both as an "inventor" of the German Enlightenment and as a central figure of Halle Pietism, a rigorous form of German Protestantism that "encouraged personal renewal and new birth ... social activism and postmillennialism."[2]

Thomasius's legal training (he was a professor of law until his death in 1728), his philosophical positions, and his religious sensibilities make him a useful figure to uncover the intellectual contexts not only of Halle Pietism but also of the reworking of economic theory at the end of the seventeenth century as the baroque order began to collapse and a market logic expanded its sway. We begin by examining one of Thomasius's texts in order to probe the connections that existed between a Pietist worldview and how the nature of financial desire was understood at the end of the seventeenth century. Thomasius in fact wrote two books that deal with this topic. *Einleitung zur Sittenlehre* (Introduction to Moral Theory) was published in 1692.[3] The other is called *Ausübung der Sittenlehre* (Application of Moral Theory) and was published four years later, in 1696.[4]

Both texts, however, were written in the context of Thomasius's involvement with August Hermann Franke, the theologian responsible for institutionalizing Pietism in the city of Halle and the creation of the University of Halle in 1694. In these texts, Thomasius wrestles with the problem of desire, especially as it was connected to a set of subsidiary forms of sin that had a long tradition in Christian thought, and he isolated in this text three *Hauptlaster* (main sins): *Geld-Geiz*, *Wollust*, and *Ehrgeiz*—greed, lust, and ambition. Greed, as Thomasius explained it, is a pretty simple concept; he identified it as the "desire for gold or for gold's value."[5]

Thomasius's understanding of the connections between religion and economy at the end of the seventeenth century allows us to better see the connections between Pietism and the emergence of a new understanding of consumption. Understanding the ways that consumerism was viewed by German Pietists is important because Pietism had a significant global impact, Pietists held significant sway over the court in Berlin, and they offered a challenge to both Lutheran and Catholic theological positions on greed and acquisition. One Pietist tract from 1721, for instance, argued, "God is capitalist."[6] These texts by Thomasius add an important dimension to our understanding of what Deborah Valenze has called the "acquisitive self" that was produced over the seventeenth and eighteenth centuries and, in particular, give insight into some of the ways that Pietism perhaps put a type of brake on the production of an acquisitive self by reminding people of the moral dangers of acquisition.[7]

The Pietist critique of greed was produced in part on the basis of I Timothy 6:10, typically rendered in German as *der Geitz, der eine Wurtzel alles Uebels ist*. August Hermann Francke noted the passage in at least two sermons, and the verse, as we have seen, figured in Luther's theology as well. Whereas Luther was concerned about the types of mental conflict that could arise when an honorable person tried to avoid avarice, Pietists had a slightly different vision of the economy of the soul than did orthodox Lutherans.

While both Lutherans and Pietists envisioned greed as a thought crime that took place in the imagination of a person and that created the impetus for social division, Pietists understood greed both as an antisocial emotion, an individual crime that held the potential to harm the entire Christian community, and as a form of imbalance that had spiritual manifestations. As Thomasius notes in the text, "A miser has no desire to unite with other people," indicating the degree to which Thomasius understood greed as something that created a barrier to social interaction and feelings of community.[8]

*Application of Moral Theory* is useful for its descriptions—both positive and negative—of the Pietist search for a balanced state of calm, what Thomasius calls the "reasonable desires" of "peaceful people."[9] One way of performing this didactic task was through a method of comparison and contrast. The ideal type is contrasted with the characteristics of those falling under the sway of lust, ambition, and greed. Where the reasonable and balanced person is governed by the humor of air, the material of phlegm, and the virtue of justice, the attributes pertaining to what Thomasius called the "passions" tells us much about the ways that greed and its allied dangers were understood at the end of the seventeenth century. Greed, Thomasius tells his readers, was linked to poverty (not, interestingly enough, to wealth), its alchemical source was salt, it was governed by Earth, and it produced the feeling of melancholia in its victims.

Unlike lust, which was localized in the lower belly, or ambition, which Thomasius associated with the brain, greed was connected to the heart. This is interesting because in other contexts greed is looked at in embodied ways, but it is usually associated with the stomach (the greedy guts, for example), and the heart is the site of more elevated feelings like love. Fortune was greed's virtuous opposite (justice, temperance, and prudence were joined to the other categories), and it was particularly apparent in what Thomasius called "very old" men—rather than in youth (who were prone to lust) or adults (whose passion was ambition). If greed had a particular outlook, it was "theoretical philosophy" (not student or practical philosophy); if it had an academic specialty, greed was joined to theology, while lust was connected to medicine and ambition to law. Who might be greedy? Peasants, merchants, and soldiers (although to be fair, soldiers were listed under all three categories: greed, lust, and ambition).[10]

Thomasius followed this metaphysical description of the passions with a list of categories that charted the central distinctions between calm and reasonable desire and desire that had spun out of control. Where reason produced a quality of "discrete openness," greed was demonstrated through "vicious lies and false presentation [*Simulirung*]." Instead of "freely given munificence," greed produced "pitiable miserliness and stinginess." The reasonable person's ability to experience "equanimous friendship" was not the same as the "crazy, self-important moochers," who fell under the sign of greed.

Thomasius contrasted "patient heartiness" with greed's "gleeful cruelty"; reason's "matter-of-fact moderation or chastity" was quite unlike the "wretchedly servile hatred of the female sex" (*Schindhuendisch. Haß des wiebl. Geschlechts*). And down the list it goes. Reason, Thomasius tells us, demonstrates thrift, efficiency, and generosity; it cultivates "joyful service" and produces "moderate memories." Greed, on the other hand, might encourage industriousness and "hard steady work," but it also was responsible for producing "stifling vindictiveness" and the "envious joy of other's misfortunes." Moreover, he noted that greedy people have incredible memories as opposed to the merely "moderate memory" of the reasonable.[11]

Thrift, which would be associated later in the eighteenth and nineteenth centuries with miserliness, is actually a function of reason. Industriousness and steady work, which again has a different value or charge in the nineteenth century, appears in *Application of Moral Theory* quite differently, as a sign of greed. Ultimately, Thomasius claims in the text, greed is a desire different not in degree from other desires but in kind. Thomasius, following Matthew 6:21/Luke 12:34, writes that the "essential difference of greed from reasonable desire, lust, ambition, or from all other human loves is exposed: Where our treasure is, so too is our heart."[12] Instead of a "modern" vision or critique of acquisitiveness, we get a taste of what acquisition might have meant in a mercantilist and early modern context.

One example of this is the way that Thomasius explores greed through references to the alchemical tradition—a tradition that not only infused the natural world with signs of vice and virtue but also was concerned centrally with the creation of new forms of wealth that could burst the static barriers of economic finitude. Thomasius writes, for instance, "Just as when the greedy one sees a Thaler, he thinks of hundreds or thousands of them; he also would imagine a hundred trillion through a new multiplication. If he could have all the gold in the world, he would through the use of the Philosopher's Stone make as much gold as Midas."[13] This connection between gold, gold's value, and the possession of new commodities helped produce the *Geiziger*, the greedy one. Thomasius asserts in one passage, "Property is the soul and the life of greed."[14]

By noting how the physical and the metaphysical—property and soul—were joined in peculiarly tight ways in the avaricious, Thomasius identified what I think might be the best way to understand the Pietist anxiety about financial desire. Thomasius argues in one section of the text, "The greedy person finds in his greed an endless unease."[15] He remarks on this idea in another passage, in which he describes the terrible desires people have to possess certain luxury goods, in this case a set of perfumed gloves, that once possessed lead people to a continual sense of lack, like "children with their dolls who lay in bed for two days and on the third tear off its head" because the object of desire has shifted away from the object of possession.[16] Indeed, Thomasius remarks that "it isn't the specific pleasure of possession but the pleasure of the constant accumulation of new things" that drives the greedy to such heights of spiritual turmoil.[17]

Time and again, Thomasius identifies *Unruhe* (turmoil) as both the symptom and sign of greed. The emphasis on a normative vision of equilibrium and peace rather than turmoil and imbalance perhaps gives us insight into the connections between the theological positions of Pietism and the economic logic of the early modern period, a system of thinking that also depended heavily on metaphors of balance in the absence of a logic of infinite economic growth more connected to thinkers in the eighteenth century. Instead, we might see in Thomasius's predilection for peace, balance, and calm a religioeconomic corollary to his Halle colleague Georg Ernst Stahl's phlogiston theory of medicine, which also established humoral balance and flow as the critical mechanism undergirding human health.[18]

What does all of this tell us about the status or nature of consumer society, especially its moral dimension, at the end of the seventeenth century? We can identify two important things: we see the flowering of a type of consumer revolution indicated by the list of objects that excite desire; and a recognition of desire as something that by definition cannot be satisfied. First, Thomasius recognized in consumer desire the unsatisfiable desire to possess things, things that when held suddenly lose their allure, in other words, a kind of acquisitive self that interacted with others through the marketplace and attempted to satisfy desire through possession. Second, he did not produce a psychological or a medical critique of this desire but a religious and moral one. The greedy person who could not tame his or her desire or cultivate it in productive ways was in some ways a sinner, a person always tempted, never satisfied, and, therefore, never at peace. It is not the case that desires are wrong, but desires untempered by moral discipline create the seedbeds for a type of sinning self that acts with reckless self-regard and is tormented by its own desires.

Thomasius generated one type of reaction to the new economic realities of the early eighteenth century, a reality formed in part by the explosive powers of global commerce and the consumer revolution.[19] Bernard Mandeville's *Fable of the Bees* (1714), based on a poem Mandeville wrote in 1705, provides evidence of a larger shift in understanding economic and social transitions centered on the turn of the eighteenth century and focuses our attention on the fear of hoarding and what miserly retention might mean for the responsible husbanding of resources and the careful management of "prodigality." Written just after Thomasius's works on morals and education, Mandeville's text takes on many of the larger issues associated with a new way of thinking about economics.

If we focus our attention on the section of the book with the subtitle "The Root of Evil, Avarice, That damn'd ill-natur'd baneful Vice, Was Slave to Prodigality," we see that Mandeville saw avarice as occupying a historically new position in the hierarchy of sins. "Avarice," he writes, "is no longer the Reverse of Profuseness, than while it signifies that sordid love of Money, and narrowness of Soul that hinders Misers from parting with what they have, and makes them covet it only to hoard up. But there is a sort of Avarice which consists in a greedy desire of Riches, in order to spend them, and this often meets with Prodigality in the same Persons, as is evident in most Courtiers and great Officers, both Civil and Military."[20]

Not only did Mandeville recognize that avarice was adopting a new guise in the early eighteenth century, but he also isolated a critical difference between older forms of retention—which he identifies in the passage as avarice—and a new form of acquisition or accumulation (the "greedy desire of Riches"), which could serve as the foundation for prodigality and, therefore, economic change. Avarice, overall, might still be a problem for Mandeville, but it does retain something of a positive attribute in the new historical context in which he wrote. Importantly, however, Mandeville might have intuited a new economic environment, but he still lived in a world of financial finitude, to which he attributed the moral critique of miserliness. Mandeville argues, "For the more the Money is hoarded up by some, the scarcer it must grow among the rest, and therefore when Men rail very much at Misers there is generally Self-Interest at Bottom."[21] In a world of limited resources, hoarding remained very much a problem.

Mandeville repeated this charge in another passage of the book, writing, "When Men find that the trouble they are put to in getting Money is either more or less, according as those they would have it from are more or less tenacious, it is very natural for them to be angry at Covetousness in general; for it obliges them either to go without what they have occasion for, or else to take greater Pains for it than they are willing."[22] Despite the worrisome qualities of avarice, and the comfort that one could take in being "angry at Covetousness," Mandeville articulated a range of positive elements for avarice. Never rising to the blunt claim that "greed is good," Mandeville nonetheless began to portray pecuniary desire in positive ways.

The most significant of the ways that avarice could shade into more elevated tones was through its connection to prodigality. Having money and spending it—the foundation in some ways of a functioning consumer economy—was connected to avarice in Mandeville's thought. "Avarice," Mandeville wrote, "notwithstanding it is the occasion of so many Evils, is yet very necessary to the Society, to glean and gather what has been dropt and scatter'd by the contrary Vice. Was it not for Avarice, Spendthrifts would soon want Materials; and if none would lay up and get faster than they spend, very few could spend faster than they get. That it is a Slave to Prodigality, as I have call'd it, is evident from so many Misers as we daily see toil and labour, pinch and starve themselves to enrich a lavish Heir."[23]

Indeed, avarice provided a foundation to prodigality that was nothing less than a "Blessing" to the entire community: "When I speak thus honourably of this Vice, and treat it with so much Tenderness and good Manners as I do, I have the same thing at Heart that made me give so many Ill Names to the Reverse of it, viz. the Interest of the Publick; for as the Avaricious does no good to himself, and is injurious to all the World besides, except his Heir, so the Prodigal is a Blessing to the whole Society, and injures no body but himself."[24]

Mandeville was not the only writer who noticed how money was adopting new powers in the early eighteenth century. Jonathan Swift's *Gulliver's Travels* (1726) advanced a similar avarice/profusion connection. In a passage that recalls Fénelon's *Telemachus*, Gulliver describes the origins of money to the Yahoos:

> Whereupon I was at much pains to describe to him the use of *money*, the materials it was made of, and the value of the metals; that when a Yahoo had got a great store of this precious substance, he was able to purchase whatever he had a mind to, the finest clothing, the noblest houses, great tracts of land, the most costly meats and drinks, and have his choice of the most beautiful females. Therefore since *money* alone was able to perform all these feats, our Yahoos thought they could never have enough of it to spend or to save, as they found themselves inclined from their natural bent either to profusion or avarice. That the rich man enjoyed the fruit of the poor man's labour, and the latter were a thousand to one in proportion to the former. That the bulk of our people was forced to live miserably, by laboring every day for small wages to make a few live plentifully.[25]

Retaining wealth, in other words, was the great problem of the early eighteenth century. Spending—even in the morally vexed situations that Thomasius examines—could be recoded as virtue. We see in these passages fresh evidence for the ways that the consumer revolution powerfully reworked the moral universe of eighteenth century Europeans.

Mandeville's attempt to cast avarice in a new light, promoting its link to profligacy as a positive mode of economic behavior, held important implications for the community as a whole. Avarice no longer presented an unassailably dangerous moral condition. Indeed, it could now be seen as offering flavor notes in the composition of a national brew: "I would compare the Body Politick (I confess the Simile is very low) to a Bowl of Punch. Avarice should be the Souring and Prodigality the Sweetning of it. The Water I would call the Ignorance, Folly and Credulity of the floating insipid Multitude; while Wisdom, Honour, Fortitude and the rest of the sublime Qualities of Men, which separated by Art from the Dregs of Nature the fire of Glory has exalted and refin'd into a Spiritual Essence, should be an Equivalent to Brandy."[26]

As if this taster's guide were not enough, Mandeville also informed his readers that the proper balance of avarice and prodigality had significance when it came to the larger question of national health. "I look upon Avarice and Prodigality in the Society as I do upon two contrary Poisons in Physick, of which it is certain that the noxious Qualities being by mutual Mischief corrected in both, they may assist each other, and often make a good Medicine between them."[27] Together we see that Mandeville, an early proponent of capitalism, revalued avarice in important ways. Not only was it one way to promote economic growth, but its connection to prodigality allowed a reworking of the moral universe as well.

Growth—economic and otherwise—was a topic of extreme interest in the early eighteenth century, and we turn now to a brief analysis of how growth in the economic plane was understood by appeals to the biological. The metaphors of growth derived from a fantasy of limitless vitalism, and the subsequent political transformations that that model promoted were central to a reimagining of the nature of nature. For these reasons, it is useful to consider the metaphorical and conceptual universe that terms like "growth," "nature," and "balance" inhabited in the first half of the eighteenth century. In order to probe these issues and to see how greed, avarice, retention, and miserliness were thought to affect the functioning of the global economy, we turn to an analysis of the German academic and polymath Christian Wolff. Wolff described in the 1710s certain fantasies of explosive, limitless, infinite agricultural growth relayed by the French agronomist Pierre Le Lorrain (the Abbé de Vallemont), who imagined that by soaking seeds in a combination of bog water and saltpeter,

> all those Ears which in a thousand and more Years grow successively out of one grain, do exist in that very grain perfectly formed, be they never so little. According to this opinion, there lies concealed in that single Grain, which this Year is

thrown into the Earth, the perfect Stalk with the Ear and all its grains. Moreover there is all the Ears in it, that grow out of these Grains the ensuing Year; also all the Ears that grow out of the Grains of the second Year, in the third Year; no less the Ears that sprout forth in the fourth Year out of the Grains of the third, and so further *in infinitum.*[28]

Sadly the expected explosion of fecundity did not come to pass. Wolff was forced to dismiss Vallemont's claims, and instead he initiated a series of experiments to determine the various yields that could be obtained through conscientious rational cultivation and husbandry.

We see here Wolff as a practitioner of the Enlightenment but more importantly one who openly fantasized about limitless growth and the happiness and welfare that would result. We need, briefly, to consider the application of vitalist principles in three areas—botany, political theory, and international law— to see how those areas of scientific endeavor intersected with the problem of desire. This will allow us to examine how growth and generation, rule and organization, connection and sympathy, communication and equilibrium appeared in different areas of knowledge in the early eighteenth century.

The fantasies of growth and the notions of value that they expressed arose at the same time that "vitalism" was a dominant theory animating the life sciences. Vitalism, which purported to seek out the harmonies, sympathies, and mystical forces that united nature into a growing, living thing, is seemingly at odds with a capitalist economic order that promoted a competitive and chaotic society of individual actors. Nonetheless, vitalism's emphasis on organic growth is connected to capitalist visions of infinitely expanding economic wealth in important ways.

We take up these ideas by examining three of Wolff's texts. The first we have already considered: his botanical/agricultural text "A Discovery of the True Cause of the Wonderful Multiplication of Corn; with Some General Remarks on the Nature of Trees and Plants" by Dr. Wolfius (Christian Wolff; written 1718; printed 1734). The second is Wolff's controversial political philosophy text "The Real Happiness of a People under a Philosophical King" (written 1721; printed 1750), and the third is his study of international law, *Jus Gentium Methodo Scientifica Petractatum* (Law of Nations Treated according to a Scientific Method; 1749).[29]

Christian Wolff (1679–1754) helped invent the academic disciplines in Germany of economic theory, cameralism, and political economy. He also worked on theories of life and self and on ontology. He was a correspondent of Leibniz and was patronized by Frederick the Great. Wolff taught at Halle until he started spouting off about the virtues of Confucianism in 1721, which angered not only the Pietists but also Frederick William I, who in 1723 gave Wolff twenty-four hours to leave Prussia or be killed. Wolff fled to Marburg and initiated a successful career there, becoming a popular professor. When Frederick II came to the throne in 1740, Wolff was invited back to the University of Halle. He accepted the position and remained in Halle until the end of his life.

Wolff lived and worked when both economic and biological theories were being reworked by academics and philosophers across Europe. Peter Reill argues that in terms of the natural sciences, "the basic failure of mechanism was its inability to account for the existence of living matter. Mechanists had posited a radical separations between mind and matter that only God's intervention could heal, either as the universal occasion for all phenomena or as the creator of a preestablished harmony between mind and matter."[30] Vitalism provided a solution to this problem: "Enlightenment vitalists sought to bridge or dissolve this dichotomy by positing the existence in living matter of active or self-activating forces, which had a teleological character. Living matter was seen as containing an immanent principle of self-movement or self-organization whose sources lay in active powers, which resided in matter itself."[31]

Moreover, "Enlightenment vitalists envisioned it [nature] as a teeming interaction of active forces vitalizing matter, revolving around each other in a developmental dance." and "In the world of living nature, each constituent part of an organized body was both cause and effect of the other parts, all symbiotically linked through the universal power of sympathy."[32]

Economic science of the later eighteenth century was also informed by a connection between vitalist thinking and the problem of commerce. Barbara Packham writes,

> [Adam] Smith's exposition of his economic system in *Wealth of Nations* is enlivened by intermittent references to bodies, both male and female, alive and dead. Such bodies pepper what might otherwise be an overly dry and abstract discussion with resonant and often startling analogies: the effects of luxury and poverty on fertility, for instance, are discussed in an implicit comparison of reproduction with economic productivity, and references to channels, organs, and vessels draw on a circulation metaphor founded ultimately on Harvey's discovery of the circulation of the blood in 1628 and the seventeenth-century discourse of the body politic.[33]

Packham goes on to argue, "It is a very specific kind of body, then, that Smith depicts in his image of the economy: a body powered by internal forces and vital energies which steer it unconsciously and independently to well-being, ease, and health."[34] If we are to believe Packham, by the time of the Scottish Enlightenment and Adam Smith's *Wealth of Nations*, vitalism had infected political economy. We turn now to the integration of vitalist codes into the German variants of political economy, especially cameralism in the first half of the eighteenth century.

We take up these issues by looking more closely at Wolff's agricultural text from 1718. While he dismissed as ridiculous Vallemont's assertion about soaking a seed in bog water, saltpeter, or some other mixture of water with old bones, he did offer a coded vitalism when he discussed the ways that generation operated in the cultivation of oats. He indicated for instance that there was a type of biological intuition that took place, and this urge to life was an important strategy in the attempt to recover from trauma: "Parting the Cluster of Oats, the Ears whereof were partly blighted, I saw plainly, that each of this great Number of Halms grew on the Eye of the other, at the Bottom where its Root began, and that its Root had no Communication with the Root of another Halm."[35]

Life sought out new pathways that allowed the organism to regulate and maintain its growth. When blight occurred, it was related to the problem of flow and circulation. The "deform'd figures" and "monstrous bodies" of blighted plants were described in the language of corruption that was caused "because fluid Matter spoil when their Current is stopt, the radical Moisture which circulates in all Plants, being hinder'd in its Circulation by an ill shap'd Figure, must corrupt."[36] Blending a Harveyite description of circulation with a vitalist conception of the inner spirit of life—figured in this case as "radical" moisture—Wolff proposed a vision of botanical blight in which an outer form frustrated the inner spirit's free movement. Such theories were not unique to botany and agriculture, of course, but were also freely applied to other forms of medical and physical knowledge.

The point of this discussion of botany, generation, and cultivation is to identify how these categories were at their base informed by economic thinking. Wolff writes midway through the text,

> I know very well, that those, who have a great many Fields to till, and who direct their Thoughts only upon getting of Money, will hardly like my Invention. For they don't care much for a Science, which teacheth them the Faculties of Nature, because the getting of Money is not immediately annexed to it, and they cannot see as yet, how to make any other Use of my Invention, than to make the Ground very loose, and to put the Grains of Seed separately into it, which Labour I would not advice 'em myself to go through. I should do them a more agreeable Piece of Service, if I could propose a Way to get a thousand-fold Crop by the usual Labour that's bestowed upon the Field; and then they would not desire to know the Secret, how Nature can afford it, but be willing to submit their Reason to the Direction of their Senses.[37]

The rational pursuit of the inner truth of nature—the ability to increase crop yields by better understanding the interior logic of botanical generation and regeneration—would pay clear financial dividends to those willing to pursue a scientifically derived application of natural law. In this text from 1718 (published 1734) Wolff provides a vitalist-informed rationale for the rational cultivation of plants. The application of science to the problem of agriculture had the potential to increase wealth and happiness throughout society.

A similar motive of promoting the common wealth and its relationship to statecraft informed Wolff's work on Confucianism from the 1720s. He published this as "The Real Happiness of a People under a Philosophical King" in 1750 (German and French versions of the text had appeared sporadically in the 1730s and 1740s). The text is significant not only for its "globalized" approach to political theory but also for its vitalist theory of social organization, political leadership, and communal welfare. Outside of the framers of the American Constitution, few political theorists in the eighteenth century were as concerned with happiness as the German cameralists.

Indeed, Wolff posed at the outset of his pamphlet the argument that "a Community will then be happy, when either Philosophers rule, or the Rulers are Philosophers."[38] Society, he thought, is formed by people "with joint powers to promote a common Good," and "Happiness consists in one uninterrupted Progress towards greater Degrees of Perfection."[39] The government, then, is given the task of promoting happiness, something that Wolff suggests is best accomplished when the rulers have some type of philosophical bent, so that the head of the social order may direct the social body in fruitful and harmonious ways to the benefit of the entire society.

Where might such a philosopher-ruler be found? In a German and vitalist vision of Han China, naturally. Wolff argued, "Confucius, who employed much Labour in explaining it, and who is thought to have succeeded best therein, contends, that from the natural Connexion of Things, their Order, their Vicissitudes and Powers of acting, the most excellent Instructions may be derived for regulating both the personal and domestic Life, and chiefly the publick Government of Towns, Provinces, and of a whole Empire."[40] Wolff's depiction of Chinese bureaucracy and its Confucian underpinnings not only demonstrates the importance of administration that was based on the promotion of the commonwealth and the happiness of the population—classic cameralist notions—but also was larded with vitalist language that depicted the self-regulating and connected social body. Vitalism provided a language to understand not only the botanical and biological but also the administrative and political.

While "connection" and "regulation" indicated the application of vitalist principles to the functioning of the social and political bodies, other language, based on the "similitudes" between kinship and the social organism also employed vitalist notions. Again discussing the Chinese, Wolff argued, "[The Chinese emperors] had, and not unhappily, reduced the Direction or Conduct of a Family or House to Self-Direction, arguing by Virtue of a determinate Similitude from Self-Direction, or the Conduct of one's own Person or Body to the Management of a Family; so at length they came to reduce the Notion of a *Commonwealth* to that of a House of Family, and under the Person of the Head of the Family represented to themselves a Ruler, or Governor, thus arguing again by Virtue of a determinate Similitude from a Family to a civil Society."[41] Wolff funneled Confucianism through the filter of vitalism and expressed the result as a blend of biological, familial, and political relations that had further resonance for Wolff because, as he put it in a different section of the text, "that manifold Connection and Dependence of every Thing in Nature upon each other" made it possible to view the connections that linked large and small, important and insignificant, into a mutually constitutive social organism.[42]

The vitalist homologies that joined the biological and social realms had a larger importance to the functioning of society. Isabel Hull, writing in part about Christian Wolff, argues, "Civil society for the cameralists was always society in its organized entirety, not just as a collection of economic relations."[43] This idea is reflected in Wolff's 1721 text *Vernuenfftige Gedanken von den gesellschaftlichen Leben der Menschen...* (Reasonable Thoughts on the Social Life of People...), in which he employs vitalist codes like "striving," "unification," and "perfection" to suggest that the rules of social interaction were written in the language of nature:

> Because individual houses could not by themselves create all the comforts of life [*alle Bequemlichkeiten des Lebens*] of which they were capable, nor could they alone secure life and limb, and consequently could not attain the highest good for which they are bound to strive, so it was necessary that as many should come together and with united energy promote their best, so that they would be able to create all the comforts of life and, in conformity with natural obligation, advance unhindered from one perfection to the next and protect themselves adequately against all injury. When this occurs, they form a society [*Gesellschaft*], and the untrammeled progress in encouraging the common best, which they may achieve with their united energy, is the welfare of this society. This society is called the common entity [*das gemeine Wesen*].[44]

Vitalist language crept into other sections of this text as well: descriptions of satisfied urges and harmonious interactions provided Wolff with a way to describe the proper functioning of civil society. He writes, "Generally there is always more to be gained when one is disposed to something by an internal urge [*Trieb*], than when one is merely held to it against oneself by external coercion"[45] and "Perfections consists in the harmonizing [*Zusammenstimmung*] of the diverse."[46]

If vitalism governed not just the biological but also the social and political, it also functioned as a way to understand and to regulate larger regional and global processes as well. Wolff's *Jus Gentium Methodo Scientifica Pertractatum* (written 1749) provides a way to understand how vitalism was applied to the question of international law. One aspect of the text indicates the ways that commerce was connected to the larger functioning of a global civil society that reflected on the international level the vitalist regulation of the body, the household, the state, and the society. Wolff defined commerce as "the right to buy and to sell again anything whatsoever, movable and moving, as well as the necessaries, as things useful and for pleasure."[47]

Commerce is useful, he argues, again raising the idea of pleasure, because it can provide things for the "necessity, advantage, and pleasure of life."[48] The phrase is repeated again and again. When discussing the "advantages" of foreign trade, Wolff suggests, "External commerce has this advantage, that the things which are lacking in one nation, but needed for the necessity, advantage, or pleasure of life, can be purchased from another nation, and since things are bought and sold for money, if more things are sold to other nations than are purchased from them, the nation grows in wealth, nay more it can attain to the greatest wealth."[49]

Wolff envisioned the global economy humming along as a harmonious and self-directed organism that not only existed for the "pleasure" of different nations but also promoted "friendship" based upon natural law. Wolff writes, "Every nation ought to love and cherish every other nation as itself, even though it be an enemy. For every man ought to love and cherish every other man as himself. Therefore, since the law of nations is originally nothing else than the law of nature applied to nations, every nation too ought to love and care for every other nation as for itself."[50] Wolff went on to argue, "Nations ought to cultivate friendship with each other and every one ought to do its best not to make others hostile to itself. For nations ought to love one another as themselves," and he concluded,

> Nations are bound by nature to engage in commerce with each other, so far as is in their power.[51] For whatever a nation can contribute that another may have an abundance of the things which are required for the necessity, advantage and pleasure of life, that it ought to contribute, and the right belongs to every nation to procure for itself at a fair price the things which it needs from other nations and of which they themselves have no need. Therefore, since commerce consists in the right to buy and sell in turn everything, movable and immovable, as well necessaries as things useful and for pleasure, and consequently is the means of obtaining those things which are required for the necessity, advantage and pleasure of life, but which nations do not have in their own territory, nations are bound by nature to engage in commerce with each other, so far as is in their power.[52]

This global civil society, bound together by commerce, friendship, and pleasure, existed in a state of equilibrium, but one that could be undermined and subverted. While the concept of balance or equilibrium is mechanical in nature, for Wolff equilibrium needed to be maintained and regulated, which indicates a straying from vitalist theory. Wolff writes, "Equilibrium among nations is defined as such a condition of several nations so related to each other in power that the combined power of the others is equal to the power of the strongest or to the joint power of certain ones. In our native vernacular it is called *das Gleichgewichte der Voelcker.*"⁵³ War represented a state of exception, a moment of unnatural disequilibrium that impeded not only trade but also liberty, and Wolff suggested that a series of mutual defensive pacts were necessary to maintain a "balance of power."

Such a vision of the external controls necessary to maintain balance were of course not yet entirely like Adam Smith's "integrated, autonomous, self-regulating system, whose unconscious pursuit of its best interest should be allowed to operate without external interference," but it does represent an attempt on the brink of the Seven Years War to imagine a global commercial system in which the mercantile relations of core and periphery were to be made porous.⁵⁴

We see in these texts the integration of vitalism and the biological not just into the directly agricultural and economic texts of Wolff's work but also into his social, political, and legal ones as well. While the autonomous economy of Smith and the Scottish Enlightenment is not recognizable here, there are important elements that suggest that German cameralists, cut off as they were from the material bounty of a colonial system, sought new ways to understand and to "embody" the fiscal, social, and political structures of the early eighteenth century. While the economy was not yet an "invisible hand" animated by the desires of the social, it did have urges, drives, a demand for balance, and a set of harmonies to which it aspired.

As the Confucian household provided the homology for good government in Han China, the social body, guided by the wise ruler, offered a similarly harmonious vision of civil society. Like the blighted plants whose outer form impeded the free flow of "vital moisture" that concerned Wolff in the 1710s or the healthy society whose social relations were harmoniously bound and structured by the family, the image of global commerce indicated by Wolff around 1750 not only marked the inclusion of vitalism in legal discourse but also gave a hint of the ways that intellectuals would begin to envision and understand the economy through the language of biology later in the eighteenth century.

Wolff enjoyed the patronage of Frederick the Great, who also had much to say on the topic of greed and avarice, especially as it related to the larger issue of statecraft. Writing to Voltaire in September 1737, Frederick the Great declared, "Gaiety makes us gods; austerity devils. This austerity is a kind of greed that deprives men of happiness they may enjoy."⁵⁵ We see here a hint of the ways that Frederick—ruler of Prussia from 1740 to 1786—imagined the connections between greed and statecraft. The evidence, drawn from Frederick's collected papers, allows us to see how the "first servant of the state" reconciled the demands for state thrift while avoiding the charge of miserliness and greed. Frederick indicates that trying to balance "generosity and greed" was a great task of the state in the mid eighteenth century.

We are accustomed to looking at new ways of understanding the role of the state as a factor in economic growth in the eighteenth century that was reflected earlier in cameralism and a shift from the collapsing baroque order of the late seventeenth century to a model of sustained growth and capital development. In this context greed is usually thought to take on a set of connotations that culminate by the end of the eighteenth century in a logic of self-interested economic actors.[56] But one of the main questions we must consider is how greed, austerity, and miserliness as state policy were understood earlier in the eighteenth century. How, in other words, did political leaders reconcile some of the moral and religious critiques of financial tightness with the larger demands of state fiscal policy?

One of the issues at hand in the eighteenth century seems to be a splitting apart of greed, with its connotations of obsessive acquisition and consumption, from miserliness and austerity, which focus attention on an equally obsessive form of retention. Consumption and retention are not, of course, the same thing, and one of the tasks of political leaders in the eighteenth century was to determine how to recognize those differences.

To trace out how "enlightened absolutists" like Frederick dealt with the moral and economic implications of the new economic forms of the eighteenth century, we consider three sources of information. One body of material on this topic can be culled from Frederick's letters, especially those like the one quoted above that were written to Voltaire. Another important text is Frederick's reworking of Machiavelli's *The Prince*, the so-called *Anti-Machiavel*, drafted in 1739. The other is his third "Epistle," titled "Ueber Ehrgeitz und Habsucht/ Sur la gloire et l'intérêt," written on 15 April 1740, just six weeks before he ascended the throne. One of the most interesting aspects of this particular problem is the question of timing. There were a cluster of texts that revolve around the issue of greed that were all written in the late 1730s through the spring of 1740. In other words, greed, austerity, and statecraft were recurring problems for Frederick the Great as he awaited the throne.

Frederick took up the issue of austerity, miserliness, and statecraft in a letter sent to Voltaire at the end of July 1739 (dated 27 July) in which he reflected on the power of the king to transform the economic character of a region, in this case the newly acquired territory of Lithuania. He notes with particular disdain the extravagant character of his grandfather Frederick III/I's funeral ("Frederick I died…, and he was buried with his false grandeur, consisting of vain pomp and the ostentatious display of frivolous ceremonies") and then pays his father—known for his frugality—a rare compliment: "Since that time [Frederick William's ascension to the throne], the King has spared no expense in allowing his salutary views to succeed. He first promulgated wise regulations, he rebuilt all that the plague made sorrowful, he brought thousands of families from all parts of Europe. The land was cleared, the country was repopulated, trade flourished once again and abundance reigns more than ever in this fertile country."

What is important here, especially in light of Frederick II's theoretical positioning on this issue in his following text, the *Anti-Machiavel*, is the way he notes his father's willingness to spare no expense. Indeed, Frederick William was characterized by his son as one "who not only directed, who designed the plans, and fulfilled them alone, but who has himself presided over their execution; He spared neither care nor pains, nor immense treasures, or promises or rewards to ensure the happiness and lives of half a million thinking beings."

The sad condition of Lithuania before Frederick William's arrival was caused first by plague, but the real problem, as Frederick argues in the letter, was the "sordid avarice of Ministers" who had, with their ludicrously austere practices, left the countryside bereft of inhabitants and the economy in shambles. The evidence suggests that as Frederick was gearing up to assume the throne the question of austerity, profligacy, and economic management of the kingdom was an important set of interlocking problems that he wrestled with, and he not only used Voltaire as a sounding board but also contrasted his ideas with the examples provided to him by his father and grandfather.

Frederick worked out these ideas in a more organized way in the fall of 1739 and the winter of 1740. His work the *Anti-Machiavel* more or less consists of Frederick the Great's reactions and systematic responses to Machiavelli's *The Prince* (1515). The chapter most germane to our concerns centers on Frederick's rewriting of Chapter 16 of *The Prince*, "On Liberality and Parsimony." Machiavelli's argument in that chapter is that parsimony and austerity are good qualities in a leader, ones that indicated the careful stewardship of resources. Even if one is called a miser, that would be preferable to being poor and powerless.

Machiavelli argues, "A prince ought to care little—if he wishes not to have to rob his subjects, to be able to defend himself, not to become poor and contemptible, and not to be forced to become rapacious—about incurring the name of miser."[57] Luxury and profligacy—or "liberality" in spending—indicated not just a weak ruler, but one that would be unable to afford the basic necessities of the state, which would then lead the ruler to issue increasingly unpopular demands for new taxes. The ruler who spent, Machiavelli argued, was a fool. And it was better to be a miser than a fool.

Frederick the Great, writing 225 years after Machiavelli's text was presented to Lorenzo de Medici, not only lived in a much different economic environment but also fundamentally disagreed with Machiavelli's precepts. And more interesting, the language he uses to discuss the economic health of a state was radically different from the range of metaphors open to Machiavelli. Frederick II opened his critique of Machiavelli's position on state spending by first suggesting that one must be mindful of the size of the polity in question. Small states, or those with a limited population and tax base, might do well to heed Machiavelli's advice, but large states like Prussia operated in a completely different environment. Frederick put it like this:

> The luxury which comes from abundance and makes riches circulate through all the veins of a state makes a great kingdom flourish. It maintains industry and multiplies the needs of the rich and opulent, thus tying them to the poor and indigent. Luxury is to a great empire what the diastolic and systolic movements of the heart are to the human body. It is the spring which sends the blood through the great arteries to our extremities and makes it circulate through the small veins back to the heart for redistribution.[58]

This is no proto-Keynesianism; luxury and state spending were not imagined to be tools that could be employed to return a sick body to health, but the passage does indicate the extent to which the biorhythms of the vitalist body could be used to understand economic flows.

Frederick's descriptions of the surging and pulsing powers of luxury to power the economic body of Prussia present an example of how luxury could be valued differently in the changed moral landscape of desire being crafted in the mid eighteenth century. If luxury was not a problem for a large state like Prussia, a larger moral critique of avarice could be unleashed, thus deflecting an argument like Machiavelli's that suggested that miserliness was preferable to other more foolish behaviors. Frederick the Great—again retreating to bodily metaphors for analytical purchase—suggests in one section of his text, "Avarice is a voracious hunger that is never satiated, a cancer that corrupts everything around it. A miser desires riches, he envies those who possess them, and he takes all he can. Greedy men fall to the lure of profit, and avaricious judges are corruptible. The vice is such that it can eclipse the greatest virtues."[59]

What is interesting here is not Frederick's avoidance of religious reasoning when unchaining his attack on greed and miserliness. What is more significant is that this critique comes in the wake of his father's reign. Frederick's father, Frederick William I, was a notorious spendthrift who produced a court society that Ben Marschke has usefully described as "infamously miserly."[60] In this passage, it is clear that state expenditures generate positive outcomes—spending helps to grow money, and this spending is not done to generate just one person's fortune—that spending improves the entire society. One way to read this passage, in other words, might be to see in it a veiled critique of his father, who as a younger man had worked so hard to restore Lithuania to something like a functioning economy but who, over time, came to exhibit a suite of odd behaviors that could perhaps be chalked up to the "cancer" of avarice "that corrupts everything around it."

There may be evidence for this reading when we consider aspects of Frederick's writing just prior to his taking the throne. Frederick drafted and revised the *Anti-Machiavel* in the fall of 1739 and winter of 1740, just months before coming to the throne. He revisited aspects of these themes in one of his "Epistles" to Voltaire, this one sent on 15 April 1740 (he became king six weeks later, on 31 May) and titled "Ueber Ehrgeitz und Habsucht/Sur la gloire et l'intérêt." The piece is a long one, and there is more there than we can deal with at this point, but we should consider how Frederick used the poem as a way to look at larger themes pertinent to this chapter: statecraft, legitimate rule, and economics.

In the piece, Frederick offers a set of recurring critiques of the "despicable miser Harpagon"—the titular character in Moliere's 1668 play *L'Avare* (The Miser). Frederick the Great offered his critique of the moral collapse indicated by the "vile villainy" expressed by the miser. When we note the larger context of avaricious fathers (or fathers-in-law) that populated the literary imagination of Europeans in the seventeenth and eighteenth centuries, we also see the ways that thrifty fathers not only appeared in Frederick's own life but could also be linked to the larger idea of political rule and paternalism. The "starving" Harpagon, as Frederick describes in one passage, is "surrounded by abundance" yet only "scrapes together his gold dust and silver bullion." Frederick goes on to claim in another passage that the "miser is himself the most troubling enemy.... He has violated the most sacred rights of the people."

Harpagon fulfilled a role in the eighteenth century similar to the one filled by the character Scrooge today—a recognizable literary character found safely in the past who could be unleashed as a negative example of a character type. Unable to speak openly about the situation with his father, Frederick employed the figure of Harpagon—the miserly father—as a way of discussing the self-subverting qualities of avaricious rule. That Frederick organized this critique not through an older language of individual sin but through a language of right and law indicates how the connections between state, society, and economy were undergoing revision in the mid eighteenth century.

We have seen here a few instances of the ways that Frederick the Great wrestled with the question of luxury and austerity, miserliness and profligacy. We see evidence for the apparent role that Frederick imagined being played by the state in ensuring the health of the economy. He saw a strong role for the paternalistic state; it is this confluence of policies seemingly built upon the promotion of commerce in the cameralist mode and his developing understanding of state finance that tells us much about how to connect state and economy in the mid eighteenth century. There were a number of theories of economic development at the time. That Frederick chose to organize his writings around a critique of lazy and avaricious ministers who undermined their own efforts at development through a misapplied fixation on savings is certainly significant.

Overall, and coincident with Frederick's seeming preoccupation with the problem of development and greed as he was gearing up to take the throne, was that mid-eighteenth-century rulers like Frederick were seeking ways to further uncouple greed from consumption. His willingness to see miserly retention at the level of the state as something that limited economic development while still seeing greed as something morally troubling at the individual level gives us insight into the range of possible configurations at work before the twin revolutions of the late eighteenth century.

Frederick the Great sought to undermine the validity of greed at the level of the state, preferring instead to promote a different vision of fiscal responsibility. Nonetheless, greed remained a troublesome area for writers in the mid eighteenth century who sought to understand some of the ways that individuals and communities were connected. As we saw in Paracelsus's writings, financial inequality was imagined to be a consequence of avarice. A similar concern animated a variety of writers who related the interior emotional life of individuals to the exterior health of the political order. Some, like Henry Fielding in *Tom Jones, A Foundling* (1749), traced one's physical health back to the mental equilibrium imperiled by avarice. "Now there is no one Circumstance in which the Distempers of the Mind bear a more exact Analogy to those which are called Bodily, than that Aptness which both have to a Relapse. This is plain in the violent Diseases of Ambition and Avarice."[61]

Jean Jacques Rousseau, who dated his own tendency toward avarice to his anxiety over his mother's financial situation, connected the avoidance of avarice to a functioning social contract.[62] Importantly, however, Rousseau located avarice and greed in the lower orders, not in the wealthy. As he writes in *Social Contract* (1762), "No citizen should be sufficiently opulent to be able to purchase another, and none so poor as to be forced to sell himself. This supposes on the side of the great, moderation in wealth and position, and, on the side of the lower classes, moderation in avarice and greed."[63] In both circumstances, the "passions and the interests" that helped eighteenth-century thinkers situate greed in the new moral context remained a tool for inducing the necessary thought experiments that could in turn change the ways that people acted.[64]

Fielding asked his readers to probe their own passions and to synchronize their emotional lives with those they read about.[65] "To deny the Existence," Fielding writes, "of a Passion of which we often see manifest Instances, seems to be very strange and absurd; and can indeed proceed only from that Self-Admonition which we have mentioned above: but how unfair is this! Doth the Man who recognizes in his own Heart no Traces of avarice or Ambition, conclude, therefore, that there are no such Passions in Human Nature?"[66] Neither Fielding nor Rousseau placed greed in a central location of their larger works; neither used avarice to promote some larger didactic agenda. Yet each of them—albeit in different ways and in different genres—recognized the transformed moral context in which economic behaviors unfolded in the mid eighteenth century.

Adam Smith—arguably the most significant economic thinker of the eighteenth century—sought to understand individual financial desires, and he was particularly concerned with miserliness and accumulation. Like other thinkers from the mid and late eighteenth century, Smith offered a blunt assessment of avarice as an economic problem. He writes in *The Theory of Moral Sentiments* (1759) that the desperate search for status generated all sorts of problematic economic behaviors: "Nay, it is chiefly from this regard to the sentiments of mankind, that we pursue riches and avoid poverty. For to what purpose is all the toil and bustle of this world? what is the end of avarice and ambition, of the pursuit of wealth, of power, and preeminence? Is it to supply the necessities of nature? The wages of the meanest labourer can supply them."[67] In another passage, Smith notes that status "is the end of half the labours of human life; and is the cause of all the tumult and bustle, all the rapine and injustice, which avarice and ambition have introduced into this world."[68]

Smith chalked up the cause of "both the misery and disorders of human life" to the asymmetries of the social order. "The great source of both the misery and disorders of human life seems to arise from overrating the difference between one permanent situation and another. Avarice overrates the difference between poverty and riches: ambition, that between a private and a public station: vainglory, that between obscurity and extensive reputation."[69] We see, in other words, how a religious language of sin (avarice, ambition, and vainglory) was translated into a logic of individualism that generated a range of behaviors that sought to promote one at the expense of others. Capitalism was the economic dimension of this logic, and Smith notes how behaviors like avarice and ambition came with a set of negative connotations. Smith never rehabilitated avarice in his writings—he never came to the position that greed was good— but he did promote other, less morally charged, terms in its place.

In *Theory of Moral Sentiments*, Smith noted the way that avarice created desires that were directed in particular ways and generated particular emotional responses. "The objects of avarice and ambition," Smith writes, "differ only in their greatness. A miser is as furious about a halfpenny as a man of ambition about the conquest of a kingdom."[70] Smith then helped promote another way of talking about avarice that avoided some of the negative associations that he had identified earlier in the text. Instead of avarice or greed, Smith increasingly employed terms like "frugality" and "parsimony" to talk about certain economic behaviors. The "virtue of frugality," for instance, "lies in a middle between avarice and profusion, of which the one consists in an excess, the other in a defect, of the proper attention to the objects of self-interest."[71] This analysis leads Smith to craft a definition of the border between miserliness and frugality. Describing the "most severe economy and the most exact assiduity," Smith articulates a "tenor of conduct" that avoids avarice in favor of parsimony:

His parsimony to-day must not arise from a desire of the particular threepence which he will save by it, nor his attendance in his shop from a passion for the particular tenpence which he will acquire by it: both the one and the other ought to proceed solely from a regard to the general rule, which prescribes, with the most unrelenting severity, this plan of conduct to all persons in his way of life. In this consists the difference between the character of a miser and that of a person of exact economy and assiduity. The one is anxious about small matters for their own sake; the other attends to them only in consequence of the scheme of life which he has laid down to himself.[72]

Smith continued this new approach to discussing economic behavior and accumulation in other passages as well. When discussing how fortunes might grow over time, Smith argues that growth was engendered by "real knowledge and skill in our trade or profession, assiduity and industry in the exercise of it, frugality, and even some degree of parsimony, in all our expenses."[73] Elsewhere, he imagined the situation in which "the man who lives within his income is naturally contented with his situation, which, by continual, though small accumulations, is growing better and better every day. He is enabled gradually to relax, both in the rigour of his parsimony and in the severity of his application; and he feels with double satisfaction this gradual increase of ease and enjoyment, from having felt before the hardship which attended the want of them."[74]

Parsimony and self-denying frugality provide a way to talk about certain economic behaviors in ways that avoid the chaos and injustice of avarice. Smith's great contribution to the language of economic morality, in other words, was not to permit ambition and greed to characterize economic or social motivations but to provide a definition of parsimony and frugality that emphasized its care and "assiduity" and future orientation in ways perhaps characteristic of Calvinist approaches to money.

In his great *Wealth of Nations* (1776), Smith returned again to a description of the social and political instabilities that certain economic behaviors—those most clearly avaricious on the part of elites—generated. When discussing the hydraulics of the grain market, Smith noted how avarice could create self-defeating outcomes in producers. "Though from excess of avarice," Smith writes, "the inland corn merchant should sometimes raise the price of his corn somewhat higher than the scarcity of the season requires.... The corn merchant himself is likely to suffer the most by this excess of avarice; not only from the indignation which it generally excites against him, but [also through a change in market conditions]."[75]

The social instabilities created by miserly behavior on the part of growers also undermined their larger goals of economic consolidation: "In years of scarcity the inferior ranks of people impute their distress to the avarice of the corn merchant, who becomes the object of their hatred and indignation. Instead of making profit upon such occasions, therefore, he is often in danger of being utterly ruined, and of having his magazines plundered and destroyed by their violence."[76]

As we saw in our discussion of Luther, the passions triggered by capitalist market exchanges could fray the social fabric. "Men may live together in society with some tolerable degree of security," Smith writes,

> though there is no civil magistrate to protect them from the injustice of those passions. But avarice and ambition in the rich, in the poor the hatred of labour and the love of present ease and enjoyment, are the passions which prompt to invade property, passions much more steady in their operation, and much more universal in their influence. Wherever there is great property, there is great inequality. For one very rich man, there must be at least five hundred poor, and the affluence of the few supposes the indigence of the many. The affluence of the rich excites the indignation of the poor, who are often both driven by want, and prompted by envy, to invade his possessions.[77]

The miserly behavior of the rich—and the social and economic inequalities that derived from it—put in place the conditions for radical change.

Adam Smith, of course, understood the virtues of economic and political freedom, but he was also wary of the consequences of that freedom and sought to encourage what might today be called socially responsible economic behavior. But what mechanisms, other than invisible appendages, might be used to craft this new economics? Utilitarianism provided one answer at the end of the eighteenth century. Jeremy Bentham, writing in his *Introduction to the Principles of Morals and Legislation* (1780, 1789), notes that wealth provides a certain degree of pleasure and that the pains associated with wealth are primarily negative ones: "The only pains opposed to them are pains of privation."[78]

Seeking to produce a "calculus of pleasure and pain" that could guide proper behavior, Bentham sought mainly to understand what he called the "motives" of behavior. Greed was an important emotion in this sense. Language, he suggests, may "denote a certain fictitious entity, a passion, an affectation of the mind, an ideal being which upon the happening of any such incident is considered as operating upon the mind, and prompting it to take that course, toward which it is impelled by the influence of such incident. Motives of this class are Avarice, Indolence, Benevolence, and so forth."[79]

Although Bentham saw wealth as a potential source of both pleasure and pain, he—like Smith—sought to forge a tighter definition of the border between legitimate parsimony and illegitimate greed. "To the pleasures of wealth corresponds the sort of motive which, in a neutral sense, may be termed pecuniary interest: in a bad sense, it is termed, in some cases, avarice, covetousness, rapacity, or lucre: in other cases, niggardliness: in a good sense, but only in particular cases, economy and frugality; and in some cases the word industry may be applied to it: in a sense nearly indifferent, but rather bad than otherwise, it is styled, though only in particular cases, parsimony."[80] He continued this argument by demanding that if readers wished to "do a real service to mankind, show them the cases in which sexual desire *merits* the name of lust; displeasure, that of cruelty; and pecuniary interest, that of avarice."[81]

One way of reading Bentham's demand for a clearer line between the avaricious and the merely parsimonious or frugal is to say that in the wake of the eighteenth-century reconfiguration of economics and exchange the moral language of earlier periods no longer made complete sense. Whereas in the past critics could point out the social decay that adhered to retention and accumulation, after Smith's work that language had fallen apart. There was no longer a clearly situated expression of miserly behavior. As we will see in future chapters, this definitional chaos allowed avarice and greed to be reworked and integrated into new systems of economics, religion, and medicine in the nineteenth century.

## Notes

1. François de Salignac de La Mothe-Fénelon, *Telemachus, Son of Ulysses*, Cambridge Texts in the History of Political Thought (Cambridge: Cambridge University Press, 1994), 259.
2. Peter Hanns Reill, *The German Enlightenment and The Rise of Historicism* (Berkeley: University of California Press, 1975); The quote comes from Douglas H. Shantz, *An Introduction to German Pietism: Protestant Renewal at the Dawn of Modern Europe*, Young Center Books in Anabaptist & Pietist Studies (Baltimore: Johns Hopkins University Press, 2013), 7.
3. Christian Thomasius, *Einleitung zur Sittenlehre* (Hildesheim: G. Olms, 1968).
4. Christian Thomasius, *Ausübung der Sittenlehre* (Hildesheim: G. Olms, 1968).
5. Ibid., 261.
6. J.A. Wiegleb, *GOTT ist Capitalist* (Halle, Germany, 1721). My thanks to Wolfgang Breul and Benjamin Marschke for organizing the "Pietismus und Ökonomie ca. 1650–1750" conference in Mainz in 2012 and for calling my attention to Wiegleb's striking claim.
7. Deborah M. Valenze, *The Social Life of Money in the English Past* (New York: Cambridge University Press, 2006), 145–78.
8. Thomasius, *Ausübung der Sittenlehre*, 271.
9. Ibid., 170.
10. Ibid., 170–71.
11. Ibid., 172–73.
12. Ibid., 272.
13. Ibid., 266.
14. Ibid., 278–79.
15. Ibid., 266.
16. Ibid., 268.
17. Ibid.
18. Barbara Duden, *The Woman beneath the Skin: A Doctor's Patients in Eighteenth-Century Germany* (Cambridge, MA: Harvard University Press, 1998).

19. Maxine Berg, *Luxury and Pleasure in Eighteenth-Century Britain* (Oxford: Oxford University Press, 2005).

20. Bernard Mandeville, *The Fable of the Bees, Or, Private Vices, Publick Benefits* (Indianapolis: Liberty Classics, 1988), 102.

21. Ibid., 100–101.

22. Ibid., 101.

23. Ibid.

24. Ibid., 103.

25. Jonathan Swift et al., *Gulliver's Travels* (London: Penguin Books, 1985), 298.

26. Mandeville, *Fable of the Bees*, 105.

27. Ibid., 106.

28. Christian Wolff, *A Discovery of the True Cause of the Wonderful Multiplication of Corn with Some General Remarks upon the Nature of Trees and Plants. By Dr. Wolfius, …* (London: Clarendon Press, 1734), 6.

29. Ibid.; Christian Wolff, *The Real Happiness of a People under a Philosophical King Demonstrated* (London: Clarendon, 1750); Christian Wolff, *Jus Gentium Methodo Scientifica Pertractatum*, trans. Joseph H. Drake, Classics of International Law 13 (London: Clarendon Press; H. Milford, 1934).

30. Peter Hanns Reill, *Vitalizing Nature in the Enlightenment* (Berkeley: University of California Press, 2005), 7.

31. Ibid.

32. Ibid.

33. Catherine Packham, "The Physiology of Political Economy: Vitalism and Adam Smith's Wealth of Nations," *Journal of the History of Ideas* 63, no. 3 (2002): 467.

34. Ibid., 469.

35. Wolff, *Discovery of the True Cause*, 18.

36. Ibid., 30.

37. Ibid., 36–37.

38. Wolff, *Real Happiness of a People*, 2.

39. Ibid., 3.

40. Ibid, 12–13.

41. Ibid., 22–23.

42. Ibid., 50.

43. Isabel V. Hull, *Sexuality, State, and Civil Society in Germany, 1700–1815* (Ithaca, NY: Cornell University Press, 1996), 161.

44. Qtd. in Hull, *Sexuality, State, and Civil Society*, 161.

45. Ibid., 168.

46. Ibid., 171.

47. Wolff, *Jus Gentium Methodo Scientifica Pertractatum*, 38.

48. Ibid., 39.

49. Ibid.

50. Ibid., 87.

51. Ibid., 90.

52. Ibid., 97–98.

53. Ibid., 330.

54. Packham, "Physiology of Political Economy," 476.

55. Letter to Voltaire, 27 (20) September 1737. "Œuvres de Frédéric Le Grand—Werke Friedrichs Des Großen," accessed 10 July, 2013, http://friedrich.uni-trier.de/de/oeu

vres/toc/text/: "La gaîté nous rend des dieux; l'austérité, des diables. Cette austérité est une espèce d'avarice qui prive les hommes d'un bonheur dont ils pourraient jouir."

56. Albert O. Hirschman, *The Passions and the Interests: Political Arguments for Capitalism before Its Triumph* (Princeton, NJ: Princeton University Press, 1977); Emma Rothschild, *Economic Sentiments: Adam Smith, Condorcet, and the Enlightenment* (Cambridge, MA: Harvard University Press, 2001).

57. Niccolo Machiavelli, *The Prince: With Related Documents*, The Bedford Series in History and Culture (Boston: Bedford/St. Martin's, 2005), 89.

58. Frederick II, *The Refutation of Machiavelli's Prince: Or, Anti-Machiavel*, trans. Paul Sonnino (Athens: Ohio University Press, 1981), 103.

59. Ibid., 104.

60. Benjamin Marschke, "Princes' Power, Aristocratic Norms, and Personal Eccentricities: Le Caractère Bizarre of Frederick William I of Prussia (1713–1740)," in *The Holy Roman Empire, Reconsidered*, ed. Jason Philip Coy, Benjamin Marschke, and David Warren Sabean, Spektrum: Publications of the German Studies Association 1 (New York: Berghahn Books, 2010), 50.

61. Henry Fielding, *The History of Tom Jones, a Foundling*, ed. Fredson Bowers (Hanover: Wesleyan University Press, 1975), 198.

62. Jean-Jacques Rousseau, *The Confessions of Jean-Jacques Rousseau*, trans. John Michael Cohen (London: Penguin Classics, 1953), 198.

63. Jean-Jacques Rousseau, *The Social Contract*, Hafner Library of Classics, no. 1 (New York: Hafner, 1947), 47.

64. Hirschman, *Passions and the Interests*.

65. Lynn Hunt, *Inventing Human Rights: A History* (New York: Norton, 2008).

66. Fielding, *Tom Jones*, 271.

67. Adam Smith, *The Theory of Moral Sentiments*, New ed (London: H.G. Bohn, 1853), 70.

68. Ibid., 80.

69. Ibid., 210.

70. Ibid., 247.

71. Ibid., 400.

72. Ibid., 246.

73. Ibid., 311.

74. Ibid., 314.

75. Adam Smith, *The Wealth of Nations* (New York: Modern Library, 2000), 562.

76. Ibid., 564–66.

77. Ibid., 766.

78. Jeremy Bentham, *The Principles of Morals and Legislation* (Oxford: Clarendon, 1879), 39 fn 1.

79. Ibid., 98–99.

80. Ibid., 107.

81. Ibid., 119.

# Bibliography

Bentham, Jeremy. *The Principles of Morals and Legislation*. Oxford: Clarendon, 1879.

Berg, Maxine. *Luxury and Pleasure in Eighteenth-Century Britain*. Oxford: Oxford University Press, 2005.

Duden, Barbara. *The Woman beneath the Skin: A Doctor's Patients in Eighteenth-Century Germany.* Cambridge, MA: Harvard University Press, 1998.

Fénelon, François de Salignac de La Mothe-. *Telemachus, Son of Ulysses.* Cambridge Texts in the History of Political Thought. Cambridge: Cambridge University Press, 1994.

Fielding, Henry. *The History of Tom Jones, a Foundling.* Edited by Fredson Bowers. Hanover: Wesleyan University Press, 1975.

Frederick II. *The Refutation of Machiavelli's Prince: Or, Anti-Machiavel.* Translated by Paul Sonnino. Athens: Ohio University Press, 1981.

Hirschman, Albert O. *The Passions and the Interests: Political Arguments for Capitalism before Its Triumph.* Princeton, NJ: Princeton University Press, 1977.

Hull, Isabel V. *Sexuality, State, and Civil Society in Germany, 1700–1815.* Ithaca, NY: Cornell University Press, 1996.

Hunt, Lynn. *Inventing Human Rights: A History.* New York: Norton, 2008.

Machiavelli, Niccolò. *The Prince: With Related Documents.* Boston: Bedford/St. Martin's, 2005.

Mandeville, Bernard. *The Fable of the Bees, Or, Private Vices, Publick Benefits.* Indianapolis: Liberty Classics, 1988.

Marschke, Benjamin. "Princes' Power, Aristocratic Norms, and Personal Eccentricities: Le Caractère Bizarre of Frederick William I of Prussia (1713–1740)." In *The Holy Roman Empire, Reconsidered,* edited by Jason Philip Coy, Benjamin Marschke, and David Warren Sabean. Spektrum: Publications of the German Studies Association 1. New York: Berghahn Books, 2010.

"Œuvres de Frédéric Le Grand—Werke Friedrichs Des Großen." Accessed 10 July, 2013. http://friedrich.uni-trier.de/de/oeuvres/toc/text/.

Packham, Catherine. "The Physiology of Political Economy: Vitalism and Adam Smith's Wealth of Nations." *Journal of the History of Ideas* 63, no. 3 (2002): 465–81.

Reill, Peter Hanns. *The German Enlightenment and the Rise of Historicism.* Berkeley: University of California Press, 1975.

———. *Vitalizing Nature in the Enlightenment.* Berkeley: University of California Press, 2005.

Rothschild, Emma. *Economic Sentiments: Adam Smith, Condorcet, and the Enlightenment.* Cambridge: Harvard University Press, 2001.

Rousseau, Jean-Jacques. *The Confessions of Jean-Jacques Rousseau.* Translated by John Michael Cohen. London: Penguin Classics, 1953.

———. *The Social Contract.* Hafner Library of Classics, no. 1. New York: Hafner, 1947.

Shantz, Douglas H. *An Introduction to German Pietism: Protestant Renewal at the Dawn of Modern Europe.* Young Center Books in Anabaptist & Pietist Studies. Baltimore: Johns Hopkins University Press, 2013.

Smith, Adam. *The Theory of Moral Sentiments.* New ed. London: H.G. Bohn, 1853.

———. *The Wealth of Nations.* New York: Modern Library, 2000.

Swift, Jonathan, Peter Dixon, John Chalker, and Michael Foot. *Gulliver's Travels.* London: Penguin Books, 1985.

Thomasius, Christian. *Ausübung der Sittenlehre.* Hildesheim: G. Olms, 1968.

———. *Einleitung zur Sittenlehre.* Hildesheim: G. Olms, 1968.

Valenze, Deborah M. *The Social Life of Money in the English Past.* New York: Cambridge University Press, 2006.

Wiegleb, J.A. *GOTT ist Capitalist.* Halle, Germany, 1721.

Wolff, Christian. *A Discovery of the True Cause of the Wonderful Multiplication of Corn with Some General Remarks upon the Nature of Trees and Plants*. London: Clarendon Press, 1734.

———. *Jus Gentium Methodo Scientifica Pertractatum*. Translated by Joseph H. Drake. Classics of International Law 13. London: Clarendon; H. Milford, 1934.

———. *The Real Happiness of a People under a Philosophical King Demonstrated*. London: Clarendon, 1750.

# CHAPTER FIVE

# Greed and the Oscillations between Liberalism and Socialism

If we compare three English-language Bibles dating from the end of the eighteenth century to the beginning of the nineteenth, we find further evidence of important cultural shifts in the meaning of greed and avarice correlated to the development of industrial economies in Western Europe. Confining ourselves to just I Timothy 6:10, we find the following translation in the John Worsley Bible of 1770: "For the love of money is the root of all evils, which some coveting after have been led astray from the faith, and pierced themselves through with many sorrows." Worsley's Bible reproduced—with variations for spelling and occasional authorial embellishments and annotations—the language that has dominated Western critiques of greed for two thousand years. Indeed, the passage has been remarkably unchanged in English since Wycliffe's Bible of the 1380s ("Sothly the roote of alle yuels is coueityse, the which 'sum men coueitynge,' or desyringe, erreden fro the feith, and bisettiden hem with many sorwis").

Over time "coveting" was replaced with "love of money." Indeed, Noah Webster's 1833 Bible reproduced yet again this familiar phrase: "For the love of money is the root of all evil: which while some have coveted, they have erred from the faith, and pierced themselves through with many sorrows."

And then an important change was introduced in the 1858 Leicester Ambrose Sawyer Bible. The passage at hand reads: "For the love of money is a root of all evils, which some having desired have been misled from the faith, and pierced themselves through with many sorrows." Greed, instead of being *the* root of all evil, has been demoted to merely one of many: *a* root of all evils. Evil—whether singular or plural—no longer had a universal origin. The question of what might constitute the source of evil was complicated further in the 1904 Twentieth Century New Testament, which produced the following: "Love of money is a source of all kinds of evil; and in their eagerness to be rich some have wandered away from the Faith, and have been pierced to the heart by many a regret."

Compared to the long line of Bibles that employed the definite article to talk about the source of evil, it is remarkable that it was only in the mid nineteenth and early twentieth centuries that the passage was presented differently, using the indefinite article. The Wycliffe (both early and late, ca. 1380s–90s), Tyndale (1530–34), Coverdale (1535), Great (1540), Thomas Matthew (1549), Bishop's (1568), Rheims Douai (1582–1610), Geneva (1587), King James (1611), Daniel Mace (1729), Richard Challoner (1750–52), John Wesley (1755), and New English (1970) Bibles all use the phrase "the root." Of the ones I consulted, only the Leicester Ambrose Sawyer (1858), the Twentieth Century New Testament (1904), and the Good News Bible (1976) departed from this tradition, using "a source" of evils (or a similar construction). Unlike our concern in Chapter One with understanding the ways that *cupiditas* and *avaritia* were imported into vernacular texts, we see here aspects of a different problem: changes in the proposed relationship between *cupiditas* and evil.

We see in this evidence a weakening of greed over time. From *the* source of evil, to *a* source of evil, to a source of "kinds" of evil, covetousness can be seen losing its connotations of sinfulness over the course of the nineteenth century. We seek in this chapter to understand what this semantic shift indicates about how greed intersected with a larger set of concerns more typically associated with nineteenth-century intellectual history. Hidden inside that small shift from "the" to "a" is a story about how greed came to be located in the wider world of liberalism and socialism. We consider, in other words, how a description of greed was inherent to and implicated in the ways people made sense of the new world of industrial capitalism as it emerged in the early nineteenth century.

We start our analysis of these issues with a look at the preface to the first edition of Thomas Malthus's *An Essay on the Principle of Population*, published in 1798, which begins by acknowledging the debt of the author to the radical William Godwin, Mary Wollstonecraft's husband and Mary Shelley's father. "THE following Essay," Malthus notes in the preface, "owes its origin to a conversation with a friend, on the subject of Mr Godwin's essay on 'Avarice and Profusion' in his Enquirer."[1] Greed, in other words, helped launch a suite of fields dominating early nineteenth-century European intellectual life: utilitarianism, liberalism, the social science of population analysis, and socialism. Indeed, Godwin saw in his essay comparing the merits of avarice and profusion the "germs of a code of political science, … intimately connected with the extensive diffusion of liberty and happiness."[2]

William Godwin's "Of Avarice and Profusion," published in *The Enquirer* in 1797, is organized around the effort to distinguish the proper modes of acquisition and expenditure, and Godwin describes a goal of social equality promoted through exchange. Acknowledging, like Adam Smith before him, that the root of value was located in labor, Godwin also notes the virtues of a robust economy. "Industry has been thought a pleasing spectacle," he writes.[3] The virtuous signs of capitalist exchange were everywhere: "What more delightful than to see our provinces covered with corn, and our ports crowded with vessels? What more admirable than the products of human ingenuity? Magnificent buildings, plentiful markets, immense cities?"[4]

The source of this human ingenuity, and all the delights that flowed from it, was greed: "How many paths have been struck out for the acquisition of money? How various are the channels of our trade? How costly and curious the different classes of our manufactures? Is not this much better, than that the great mass of society should wear out a miserable existence in idleness and want?"[5] Here we see a clear description of the profit motive and an articulation of the social benefits produced by allowing people to seek riches through application of their own industry and labor. Put simply, capitalist self-interest produces not only rich individuals but also a panoply of social goods.

Godwin identified in the essay three modes of economic behavior: indebtedness, avariciousness, and profligacy. Both the debtor and the profligate spender were unable to govern their behaviors, and they were subjected to all sorts of psychological torments as a result. The debtor, for instance, continually worries about finances, his ability to experience happiness warped by the black hole of anxiety that indebtedness causes. A "continual accumulation of debt," Godwin writes, "is eminently pernicious." He argues further:

> It does not contribute to his own happiness. It drives him to the perpetual practice of subterfuges. It obliges him to treat men, not according to their wants or their merits, but according to their importunity. It fixes on him an ever gnawing anxiety that poisons all his pleasures. He is altogether a stranger to that genuine lightness of heart, which characterises the man at ease, and the man of virtue. Care has placed her brand conspicuous on his brow. He is subject to occasional paroxysms of anguish which no luxuries or splendour can compensate. He accuses the system of nature of poisonous infection, but the evil is in his own system of conduct.[6]

The gravitational pull exerted by debt makes it impossible for the debtor to act within normal social bounds. All his relationships are characterized by gross inauthenticity; all his pleasures hollowed out by the obsessive worrying generated by indebtedness.

The debtor represents a failed relationship with money; riches present an equally false path to happiness, for the idle rich merely spend their money on useless passions and regrettable trifles. Luxury, after all, "unnerves and debases."[7] It is only the *avarus*, Godwin argues, who navigates between indebtedness and profligacy to find a golden mean of disciplined approach to financial matters. As Godwin described it in a different essay: "Avarice is not so thoroughly displayed in the preservation, as in the accumulation, of wealth."[8] The *avarus*, Godwin suggests, "recognises, in his proceedings at least, if not as an article of his creed, that great principle of austere and immutable justice, that the claims of the rich man are no more extensive than those of the poor, to the sumptuousness and pamperings of human existence. He *watches* over his expenditure with unintermitted scrupulosity; and, though enabled to indulge himself in luxuries, he has the courage to practise an entire self-denial."[9]

Asceticism, in other words, is the key. One should delay pleasure and constantly survey and conserve resources. Accumulation is of central importance, yet the act of accumulation is understood in a slightly different way than miserliness had been understood in the past. Rather than accumulating merely to generate a pile of money, Godwin's *avarus* generates a reservoir of money that retains a potential use value.

It is a characteristically modern idea to consider one's savings not as a type of avarice defined by sin but instead as a psychological approach to money that considers saving and ascetic self-denial to be a conservative safety net. Spending just to spend, like saving merely to enjoy the pleasure of accumulation, is wrong: "The miser considers himself as a man, entitled to expend upon himself only what the wants of man require. He sees, and truly sees, the folly of profusion."[10] The proper approach to money is through rationality and cold realism: "Money, though in itself destitute of any real value, is an engine enabling us to vest the actual commodities of life in such persons and objects, as our understandings may point out to us. This engine, which might be applied to most admirable purposes, the miser constantly refuses to employ."[11]

This refusal to switch on the engine of money and thus to open the gates of expenditure makes the miser into a new type of figure. Recognizably conservative and ascetic, Godwin's miser approaches the limit of nonrational behavior but then could be seen to apply a logic that comes from a realistic worldview. Indeed, the miser's realism is a part of his or her character, coloring his or her actions in recognizable ways. Godwin argues that the miser attains a finely calibrated ability to determine value that is not conditioned necessarily by the constraints of morality: "He strips the world of its gaudy plumage, and views it in its genuine colours. He estimates splendid equipages and costly attire, exactly, or nearly, at their true value. He feels with acute sensibility the folly of wasting the wealth of a province upon a meal."[12] Miserliness, in other words, is more than just the opposite of profligacy; it is also an approach to object relations that is predicated on the ability to measure value accurately and coldly, uncolored by emotion or raw desire.

Godwin's analysis of avarice and of miserly behavior leads him to consider the social ramifications of this form of selfhood. Contrasting the miser to the person who contributes generously to charity, Godwin comes down on the side of the miser: "It may however almost be doubted whether the conduct of the miser, who wholly abstains from the use of riches, be not more advantageous to mankind, than the conduct of the man who, with honourable intentions, is continually misapplying his wealth to what he calls public benefits and charitable uses."[13] Generating a large reservoir of wealth, in other words, might do more for society than charitable contributions. If we consider the implications of this argument—that spending, even on charity, is bad and saving is good— we see a reversal of Frederick II's position on state expenditures that he worked out in the *Anti-Machiavel*.

Seeing a dramatic shift in the valuation of avarice when we consider the movement from the mid eighteenth century to the late eighteenth century should not come as a surprise. Godwin's emphasis on individual behavior, on asceticism, on planning for the future and coldly assessing value in the present provides an astute description of the psychology necessary for liberal capitalism. More than the production of an acquisitive self, or a trading self, or a future-oriented self, we see in Godwin's descriptions of miserliness a valuation of certain economic modes that may be projected—as Malthus himself demanded—into liberalism.

A year after the appearance of William Godwin's essay "Avarice and Profusion," the first edition of Thomas Malthus's *An Essay on the Principle of Population* was published.[14] As we noted earlier, Malthus's *Essay* was inspired by a discussion of Godwin's work. The *Essay*, revised several times over the next two decades, attempted to provide an answer to the question: why are people poor? Malthus's answer to that question helped produce a new vision of resource allocation and of social obligation. For those unfamiliar with this text, Malthus argues that population growth has become unsustainable in the context of the then-available stocks, and he suggests that demographic decline (in the form of both increased mortality and reduced fecundity) would allow sufficient resources.

Poverty, in other words, stems from an unsustainably large population. Naturally, there was a moral logic to these claims, and Malthus identified "promiscuous intercourse" as one element contributing to the problem of poverty.[15] Advocating strategies of limiting births and suggesting a cultural shift that would judge spinsterism less harshly, Malthus is quite clear in his assessment of the fact that human sexuality was a culprit in the crime of poverty.

Thinking of ways to improve the condition of the poor, Malthus notes the sexual exuberance of the working class, linking the social and sexual practices of certain types of people to their economic station. Because poverty is first generated and then perpetuated by inappropriately excessive sexuality, any critique of the rich for paying insufficiently high wages is wrong. "When the wages of labour," Malthus asserts, "are hardly sufficient to maintain two children, a man marries and has five or six. He of course finds himself miserably distressed. He accuses the insufficiency of the price of labour to maintain a family. He accuses his parish for their tardy and sparing fulfillment of their obligation to assist him. He accuses the avarice of the rich, who suffer him to want what they can so well spare. He accuses the partial and unjust institutions of society, which have awarded him an inadequate share of the produce of the earth."[16]

The poor, in other words, find themselves in that unhappy position because they have too many children, not because the value of their labor is artificially suppressed by their employers. To be fair, Malthus was genuinely concerned with the problem of poverty and sought ways to alleviate it. His promotion of what could be called a kind of liberal "morality"—viewing poverty as the result of individual actions (most significantly sexuality and an inability to practice frugality) and not as the outcome of the systemic flaws of a liberal economic order—should be seen as a valuable indication of the ways that old moral problems like avarice were recast in the early nineteenth century. Unlike Paracelsus, for instance, who envisioned inequality as a social crime of the rich, Malthus indicates the ways that the "crime" of avarice could no longer be faulted for inequality.

Despite this shift in the valuation of avarice in liberal political economy, Malthus does take the time to imagine what it might be like to be poor. In an appendix to the book included in the 1806 edition, Malthus engages in a thought experiment about the experience of poverty, its origins, and its social effects. Adopting the voice—if not the persona—of a poor person Malthus begins by acknowledging that "I cannot indeed conceive anything more irritating to the human feelings than to experience that degree of distress which, in spite of all our poor laws and benevolence, is not unfrequently felt in this country."[17]

Poor relief and charity have a limited effect, Malthus recognizes. Again assuming the voice of the poor, Malthus continues the argument: "and yet to believe that these sufferings were not brought upon me either by my own faults, or by the operation of those general laws which, like the tempest, the blight, or the pestilence, are continually falling hard on particular individuals, while others entirely escape, but were occasioned solely by the avarice and injustice of the higher classes of society."[18] In other words, the poor are wrong to blame their condition on the greed of the rich. They should instead, as personally painful as it may be, locate the origins of their troubles either in their own "faults" or in the nature of modern economic relations as a whole, which appears as depersonalized and abstract in its force as some unpredictable natural disaster. It is not a question of the rich exhibiting avaricious behaviors. By the time Malthus wrote in 1806, such a statement was presumably one that raised few eyebrows. And yet it is important to note that Malthus was quite clear that the critique of greed issued by the poor was an unfair one.

A perfect storm of behaviors, then, accounts for the existence of poverty. The poor, it seems, are victims of their own choices and irrational desires; the rich bear no responsibility for the poor. Even charity and poor relief have only a limited effectiveness. Modern capitalist economies and a relentless downward pressure on wages in the labor market conspired to establish a poverty that was difficult to escape. Even colonies—the one thing aside from the management of fertility that could relieve the escalating population pressure afflicting the poor—was of only limited value as a relief valve. "It must be acknowledged," Malthus writes,

> that the class of people on whom the distress arising from a too rapidly increasing population would principally fall could not possibly begin a new colony in a distant country. From the nature of their situation, they must necessarily be deficient in those resources which alone could ensure success: and unless they could find leaders among the higher classes, urged by the spirit of avarice or enterprize; or of religious or political discontent; or were furnished with means and support by government; whatever degree of misery they might suffer in their own country from the scarcity of subsistence, they would be absolutely unable to take possession of any of those uncultivated regions, of which there is yet such an extent on the earth.[19]

Finally we see the value of avarice. If the "leaders of the higher classes" are to show the impoverished a way forward, it is via the "spirit of avarice." Indeed, greed is good for the liberal thinker. While Godwin interpreted miserliness as a form of economic behavior that possessed a number of good elements, Malthus was much more approving of the "spirit of avarice" that he saw producing a range of virtuous outcomes. Godwin still had some qualms about recoding avarice as a virtue; Malthus was convinced of it. Avarice—expressed as self-interest—was a way to escape the trap of limited resources.

The question remains, however, how liberal thinkers that followed Malthus worked over some of the implications of the way he revalued greed. Jean-Baptiste Say, probably most famous for Say's law, the idea that supply generates demand, gives one of the clearest examples of the ways that liberal economists of the early nineteenth century built upon this potential reworking of sin that we see expressed in Malthus's thoughts on poverty. Say's most significant book, the 1803 *A Treatise on Political Economy*, takes up the question of avarice and its relation to economic behavior in multiple places. The book, in which Say advocates an open market, lets us examine the ways that continental liberals conceptualized avarice.

Unlike Malthus, Say continued to have reservations about avarice and greed and only in a few instances saw clearly positive consequences to the behavior. Indeed, Say often uses avarice, greed, or an adjectival variant of the word to indicate his suspicion of the emotion. For example, in the section of the book dedicated to an analysis of "unproductive capital," Say recapitulated the hoary images of the "unproductive" nature of "Asiatic luxury," noting especially the economic consequences of hoarding that was meant to subvert "the greedy eyes of power," thus rendering a significant sector of the economy "invisible, without being inactive."[20] Orientalist conceptions of the greedy state aside, Say also connected what he saw as economically unrational practices like slavery with avarice. Even the "soft impulse of sexual attraction is subject to the avaricious calculations of the master," indicating exactly how invasive avarice is with its ability to undermine the logical economic functioning of slave and colonial society.[21]

Avarice had other effects as well, and Say identified state lotteries as another example of how greed had a destructive potential both for states and for individuals. "When a government," Say writes, "derives a profit from the licensing of lotteries and gambling-houses, what does it else but offer a premium to a vice most fatal to domestic happiness, and destructive of national prosperity? How disgraceful is it, to see a government thus acting as: the pander of irregular desires, and imitating the fraudulent conduct it punishes in others, by holding out to want and avarice the bait of hollow and deceitful chance!"[22] Predictably, avarice was not distributed equally across a population; women were especially prone to the vice: "The weaker sex is, from the very circumstance of inferiority in strength of mind, exposed to greater excess both of avarice and prodigality."[23]

We see, then, that avarice was connected to a range of improperly functioning systems. It was linked to what was often described as "Asiatic despotism." It perpetuated some of the worst aspects of Atlantic slavery, allowed governments to prey on the inappropriate desires of unsophisticated citizens, and revolved around the feminine. But perhaps the worst aspect of avarice in Say's view was the effect that it had on the functioning of the free market. Indeed, he saw greed as a constant threat to the mechanics of free trade. Say bluntly argues that avarice works to undermine what he calls the "first principles" of political economy: open markets. Both political rulers and the greed of the merchant class were to blame, but the end result was a system that did not live up to its theoretical possibilities. On the question of trade balances, Say writes,

> To speak the truth, it is because the first principles of political economy are as yet but little known; because ingenious systems and reasonings have been built upon hollow foundations, and taken advantage of, on the one hand, by interested rulers, who employ prohibition as a weapon of offence or an instrument of revenue; and, on the other, by the personal avarice of merchants and manufacturers, who have a private interest in exclusive measures, and take but little pains to inquire, whether their profits arise from actual production, or from a simultaneous loss thrown upon other classes of the community.[24]

Avarice gets in the way of trade, undermining its smooth functioning.

Say continued in this vein, taking up the problem of trade monopolies and "privileged trading companies," which he saw as having a similarly detrimental effect on the operation of the economy. "The privileged traders," Say argues, "being thus exempted from all competition by the exertion of the public authority, can raise their prices above the level that could be maintained under the apellation of a free trade."[25] Prices, he says, may be fixed, which helps producers but also represents an "injustice" affecting consumers. The entire situation, Say believes, represented a form of collusion between the government and the producer that was engineered to satisfy greed:

> This unnatural ratio of price is sometimes fixed by the government itself, which thus assigns a limit to the partiality it exercises towards the producers, and the injustice it practises upon the consumers: otherwise, the avarice of the privileged company would be bounded only by the dread of losing more by the reduction of the gross amount of its sales, in consequence of increased prices, than it would gain by their unnatural elevation. At all events, the consumer pays for the commodity more than its worth; and government generally contrives to share in the profits of the monopoly.[26]

Writing about the decline of the Dutch control over the spice trade, Say details that monopolies related to overseas trade were equally problematic, and the colonial system was built in part in order to satisfy the avaricious grasp of the monopolist nation.[27] Another threat to the open market could be located in the form of counterfeiting, which again Say connected to the inappropriate hold of avarice on the minds of some people. "The only danger," Say writes, "is that of counterfeits, which there is the strongest stimulus for avarice to fabricate, in proportion as the difference between the intrinsic, and the current value, grows wider."[28]

Even the labor market was not immune to the problem of avarice, and Say takes on employers whose avarice leads them to undervalue labor: "One sometimes meets with masters, who, in their anxiety to justify their avaricious practices by argument, assert roundly, that the labourer would perform less work, if better paid, and that he must be stimulated by the impulse of want."[29] Describing his country in 1812, Say was blunt in his assessment of the ways that the government had undermined economic success because public expenditures had subverted the functioning of the private sector of the economy. There is, Say argues, "a system of administration uniformly avaricious and hostile to private interest, [which] had rendered all enterprises of industry difficult, hazardous and ruinous in the extreme."[30]

If, as Say suspected, greed could explain why the free market did not function correctly, his explanation for how to correct that scenario was a savvy one. If greed subverted the free market, perhaps only the free market could in turn subvert greed. One way that this scenario could develop was through the segmentation of the market and the development of a robust division of labor. A division of labor is useful, Say argues, because it allows efficiencies and savings that develop despite the profit motive and the avarice of producers. The "division of labour enables the regular dealer to execute the business for them [regular traders] much cheaper than they can do it themselves."[31] By employing an expert, Say writes, regular traders come out better in the end:

> Let them reckon up the trouble it costs them, the loss of time, the money thrown away in extra charges, which is always proportionally more in small than in large operations, and see if all these together do not amount to more than the two or three per cent. that might be saved on every paltry item of consumption; even supposing them not to be deprived of what little advantage they might expect, by the avarice of the cultivator or manufacturer they would have to deal directly with, who will of course impose, if he can, upon their inexperience.[32]

Additionally, Say recognized the power of market logic to break apart the old static view of the world. Even if the market were freed, it still existed in a field of constraints. The desire—and the value of—different commodities fluctuate, and profit motivates behaviors in direct ways. Say writes,

> Such profits must operate as a powerful stimulus to the cultivation of that particular kind of products, there must needs be some violent means, or some extraordinary cause, a political or natural convulsion, or the avarice or ignorance of authority, to perpetuate this scarcity on the one hand, and consequent glut on the other. No sooner is the cause of this political disease removed, than the means of production feel a natural impulse towards the vacant channels, the replenishment of which restores activity to all the others. One kind of production would seldom outstrip every other, and its products be disproportionately cheapened, were production left entirely free.[33]

We see in this passage the ways that market forces and the desire to generate profits could in fact tear apart political and economic systems that engineered false conditions of constraint. This logic led Say to argue in a different part of his *Treatise* that market conditions of scarcity or supply encourage new solutions, and thus greed has some part in its own destruction: "Ingenuity is set at work to find a substitute for the scarce article of food, and not a particle is wasted. Thus, the avarice of one part of mankind operates as a salutary check upon the improvidence of the rest; and, when the stock withheld at length appears in the market, its quantity tends to lower the price in favour of the consumer."[34]

The preceding discussion of the ways that avarice and market forces interacted in Say's book has not yet addressed the larger issue of how he envisioned economic behavior, and specifically what role the profit motive could play. Say addressed this issue in one passage in which he asserted that in the future, greed would not be understood in quite the same way, and in fact economic behavior could be decoupled from morality in critical ways. Say approached this topic through a discussion of interest:

> The progressive advance of industry has taught us to view the loan of capital in a different light. In ordinary cases, it is no longer a resource in the hour of emer-

gency, but an agent, an instrument, which may be turned to the great benefit, as well of society, as of the individual. Henceforward, it will be reckoned no more avaricious or immoral to take interest, than to receive rent for land, or wages for labour; it is an equitable compensation adjusted by mutual convenience; and the contract, fixing the terms between borrower and lender, is of precisely the same nature, as any other contract whatsoever.[35]

If economic behavior could be recast as a zone in which discussions of morality were inappropriate, then all sorts of rational approaches to behavior could be developed, and it is in this realm that Say perhaps was most closely aligned with Godwin and Malthus.

Like Godwin, Say investigated the distinctions between profligacy and greed. Looking at the realm of consumption and its effects, for instance, Say asserted, "In respect to consumption, prodigality and avarice are the two faults to be avoided: both of them neutralize the benefits that wealth is calculated to confer on its possessor; prodigality by exhausting, avarice by not using, the means of enjoyment."[36] Launching an analysis of the divergent operation of these two modes of economic behavior, Say advocates a middle path, one he labels "economy" and describes as being "equally distant from avarice and profusion," which consists of a "sober," "rational," "just," and "generous" approach to the question of spending.[37] Avarice, as Say defined it, was the practice of hoarding, "not for the purpose of consuming or re-producing, but for the mere sake of hoarding; it is a kind of instinct, or mechanical impulse, much to the discredit of those in whom it is detected."[38]

Economy, on the other hand, "is the offspring of prudence and sound reason and does not sacrifice necessaries to superfluities."[39] And it is important to note that for Say, economy did not preclude luxury or consumption. As he put it, "The most sumptuous entertainment may be conducted with economy, without diminishing, but rather adding to its splendour, which the slightest appearance of avarice would tarnish and deface."[40] A new type of person is created, "economical man," who, Say argues, "balances his means against his present or future wants, and those of his family and friends, not forgetting the calls of humanity."[41] The connection that Say makes between economical man and the larger society is important, because again that connection is lacking in the person of the miser, who "regards neither family nor friends; scarcely attends to his own personal wants, and is an utter stranger to those of mankind at large" and demonstrates "a vile propensity to sacrifice every thing to the sordid consideration of self."[42]

Avarice was not just a key element in liberal economic discourse at the turn of the nineteenth century. An analysis of just a handful of the canonical novels from the time reveals a type of obsession with the problem that indicates a wider cultural importance to greed and avarice than one might assume to be the case. A central problem found in early nineteenth-century novels was the changing nature of the marriage market. No longer centered only on the economic logic of the early modern household and also not yet fully integrated into the putatively "modern" logic of the sentimental love match, bourgeois marriage in the first half of the nineteenth century sought to reconcile emotion and financial stability. Novels from the period were a forum to work through those tensions. Greed, marriage, inheritance, and matchmaking were intertwined in hundreds of fictional settings.

In Jane Austen's *Sense and Sensibility* (1811), for instance, the plot centers in many ways on characters who must choose between a marriage of love and one based on financial security. As Mr. Willoughby—a rake who seduces one young woman, falls in love with another, and nearly marries a third—put it: "Well may it be doubted; for, had I really loved, could I have sacrificed my feelings to vanity, to avarice?—or, what is more, could I have sacrificed hers?—But I have done it. To avoid a comparative poverty, which her affection and her society would have deprived of all its horrors, I have, by raising myself to affluence, lost every thing that could make it a blessing."[43]

Austen's *Pride and Prejudice* (1813) recapitulates aspects of this dilemma. One passage of the novel probes the question of avarice as a motivation for marriage directly: "Pray, my dear aunt, what is the difference in matrimonial affairs, between the mercenary and the prudent motive? Where does discretion end, and avarice begin? Last Christmas you were afraid of his marrying me, because it would be imprudent; and now, because he is trying to get a girl with only ten thousand pounds, you want to find out that he is mercenary."[44]

Honoré de Balzac's *Eugénie Grandet* (1833) dwells on a set of similar themes. Eugénie's father, the miser Monsieur Grandet, enacts a series of intricate financial plots that will not only enrich his heir and daughter but also impoverish and embarrass his nephew, because as one passage in the book shows, "Money without honor is a disease."[45] When Eugénie and her cousin fall in love, the question of money, affection, and greed become intertwined. After Eugénie's cousin, Charles, leaves France to pursue his fortune (because he cannot bring himself to marry when he himself has no financial security), the results are horrifying. Charles's activities in the Caribbean deform him: "From unremitting contact with selfish interests, his heart grew cold; his feeling for others contracted and withered away.... Charles became hard and ruthless in his pursuit of gain. He sold Chinamen, negroes, swallows' nests, children, theatrical performers."[46]

The desire to secure financial success so that one could enter the marriage market warped the European man of business by his connection to the forces of exchange (especially when they were located in colonial spaces). Balzac's description of Charles in *Eugénie Grandet* is quite similar to a character appearing in a 1847 novel: Mr. Rochester in Charlotte Brontë's *Jane Eyre*. Rochester's father (like Eugénie's) was an "avaricious, grasping man," who could not bear to split his inheritance, thus requiring Rochester to seek a "wealthy marriage." Rochester's father seeks to leverage his business contacts to facilitate a union: "He sought me a partner betimes. Mr. Mason, a West India planter and merchant, was his old acquaintance. He was certain his possessions were real and vast: he made inquiries. Mr. Mason, he found, had a son and daughter; and he learned from him that he could and would give the latter a fortune of thirty thousand pounds: that sufficed."[47]

Ebenezer Scrooge, a "a squeezing, wrenching, grasping, scraping, clutching, covetous old sinner," developed those characteristics in part because of the unhappy circumstance of his own engagement, which was called off by his fiancée when he began to dedicate himself single-mindedly to his business.[48] Charles Dickens's *A Christmas Carol*, published in 1843, describes Scrooge soon after he has jilted his fiancée, Belle: "For again Scrooge saw himself. He was older now, a man in the prime of life. His face had not the harsh and rigid lines of later years, but it had begun to wear the signs of care and avarice. There was an eager, greedy, restless motion in the eye, which showed the passion that had taken root, and where the shadow of the growing tree would fall."[49]

The scene in which Scrooge's greed and his inability to carry through his marriage plans indicates the decisive quality of the moment. Belle declares that Scrooge has replaced her with a "golden idol" and then exclaims, "All your hopes have merged into the hope of being beyond the chance of its [the world] sordid reproach. I have seen your nobler aspirations fall off one by one, until the master passion, Gain, engrosses you."[50] Scrooge, she says, "you ... weigh everything by Gain"[51] To be clear, however, this form of greed seems to have been more or less explicitly attached to men. Emily Brontë's Heathcliff in *Wuthering Heights* (published in 1847) is described: "He'd be quite capable of marrying your fortune and expectations: avarice is growing with him a besetting sin."[52]

One of the characters in Balzac's *Eugénie Grandet*, while discussing the ideas of Jeremy Bentham, claims, "Money is a commodity and whatever represents money becomes a commodity as well."[53] This is a striking claim, especially when we note that it surfaces in relationship to the founder of utilitarianism. We considered Bentham's ideas about the utility of pleasure and pain as they were worked out in his text *Introduction to the Principles of Morals and Legislation* (1780) in the previous chapter; we now turn to the question of how thinkers in the mid nineteenth century applied utilitarian principles to the problem of greed.

In his essay "Utilitarianism," drafted between 1854 and 1856 and published in 1861 in *Frazer's Magazine*, John Stuart Mill broaches the topic of the "love of money" by noting that there "is nothing originally more desirable about money than about any heap of glittering pebbles. Its worth is solely that of the things which it will buy; the desires for other things than itself, which it is a means of gratifying."[54] And then, matching earlier arguments about the seductive qualities of money to absorb one's desires because of its transformative powers, Mill argues, "The desire to possess it [money] is often stronger than the desire to use it, and goes on increasing when all the desires which point to ends beyond it, to be compassed by it, are falling off. It may be then said truly; that money is desired not for the sake of an end, but as part of the end."[55] Money, in short, becomes an ingredient necessary to the creation of a person's overall happiness. As Mill asserts,

> From being a means to happiness, it has come to be itself a principal ingredient of the individual's conception of happiness.... The person is made, or thinks he would be made, happy by its mere possession; and is made unhappy by failure to obtain it. The desire of it is not a different thing from the desire of happiness, any more than the love of music or the desire of health. They are included in happiness. They are some of the elements of which the desire of happiness is made up. Happiness is not an abstract idea, but a concrete whole.[56]

Incorporating money and an analysis of greed into Benthamite utilitarian principles, Mill noted the increasingly important role that money played—as a fungible source of pleasure itself—in the psychological outlook of modern people. As Mill became increasingly dissatisfied with utilitarianism as a way of understanding the forces shaping human behavior, he reconsidered the ways that greed and financial desire were valued. The topic, for instance, appeared in his essay "The Subjection of Women" (published in 1869 and probably written in 1861) connected to the brutality of the transatlantic slave trade. In "The Chapters on Socialism" (published in 1879 and probably written in 1870), Mill notes how "the bad quality of the goods is more than an equivalent for their cheapness; while at the same time the much greater fortunes now made by some dealers excite the cupidity of all, and the greed of rapid gain substitutes itself for the modest desire to make a living by their business."[57]

Mill found an answer to the crisis generated by the profit motive and the greed that sustained it by looking to communism, suggesting, "It will be said that at present the greed of personal gain by its very excess counteracts its own end by the stimulus it gives to reckless and often dishonest risks. This it does, and under Communism that source of evil would generally be absent."[58] Mill's turn toward socialism, and his inclusion of the problem of greed in his analysis of its appeal, indicates one of the prime intellectual events of the late nineteenth century, and its centrality to later developments requires an analysis of how Karl Marx understood financial desire, profit motives, and the functioning of the industrial capitalist economy in the latter part of the nineteenth century.

Karl Marx recognized that capitalism depends on avarice for its emotional underpinning. "At the historical dawn of the capitalist mode of production," Marx writes in volume one of *Capital*, "and every capitalist upstart has to go through this historical stage individually—avarice [*Geiz*], and the drive for self-enrichment, are the passions which are entirely predominant."[59] There are scattered references to greed and avarice across Marx's writings, but we need to consider three texts in order to trace the ways that the problem was worked out across Marx's career: *The German Ideology* (written in 1846), the *Grundrisse* (written in 1858), and *Capital* (1867). In the *German Ideology*, which Marx authored with Friedrich Engels in 1846, there is an extended evaluation of Max Stirner's *Der Einzige und sein Eigentum* (The Ego and Its Own, 1845). The passage, titled "St. Max—the New Testament: 'Ego,'" seeks to explore the connections between "egoism" and economic behavior.

Avarice, as we have noted in other chapters, is fundamentally connected with a type of self. Marx built upon this connection in the passage, noting how Stirner labeled "the avaricious one" as a "selfless egoist." The section of the book with the most extended analysis of avarice, however, appears under the subtitle "On Communism and Morality" and is centered on an analysis of the ways that Stirner collapsed avaricious behavior, egoism, and self-denial, which prompted Marx and Engels to suggest that this was a complete misreading of the economic logic of the "representative avaricious bourgeois," who, they assert, "have no need to deny the 'promptings of conscience', 'the sense of honour', etc., or to restrict themselves to the one passion of avarice alone. On the contrary, their avarice engenders a series of other passions—political, etc.—the satisfaction of which the bourgeois on no account sacrifice."[60]

Marx and Engels extended this critique in the section titled "Consciousness," in which avariciousness is presented as a defining characteristic of bourgeois selfhood, a way of thinking about desire and its satisfaction that helps produce alienation. Avarice is not really about self-denial. Marx and Engels suggest that avarice is greed for money and, as such, is the motivation for a range of subsidiary behaviors and forms of consciousness.

In the *Grundrisse* (1858) Marx gave a blunter assessment of greed, focusing on the power of money to channel emotional life and arguing near the end of the "Chapter on Money," "Money is therefore not only an object, but is *the* object of greed [*Bereicherungssucht*].... Money is therefore not only the object but also the fountainhead of greed."[61] Unsurprisingly, Marx was quite clear on the position that greed was a product of certain historical forces. As he writes, "Greed itself is the product of a definite social development, not *natural*, as opposed to *historical*. Hence the wailing of the ancients about money as the source of all evil."[62] In the "Chapter on Money," Marx advanced the position—like many before him—that greed and avarice worked in different ways. He noted the psychological implications on behavior of "hedonism" (consumption) and miserliness (*Geiz*) and noted the corrosive effects of each on historical conditions. "Monetary greed," as he put it, "necessarily brings with it the decline and fall of the ancient communities."[63]

In its place—and as a direct result of the power of greed to transform the world—was the development of "modern industrial society," which Marx argued, "opens with general greed for money on the part of individuals as well as of states."[64] As a form of desire that had come to be peculiarly attached to one form of wealth—a form of wealth that was itself completely mutable—Marx envisioned greed as a type of desire that had enormous power to remake the world in its own image. "Greed, as the urge of all, in so far as everyone wants to make money, is only created by general wealth. Only in this way can the general mania for money become the wellspring of general, self-reproducing wealth."[65] As this evidence demonstrates, Marx was tuned in to the problem of greed early in his writings, and he was particularly aware of the ways that greed had exerted a transformational power over larger economic structures. These were themes that he developed further as he applied his critical insight not just to the problem of money but to the development of capital as well.

In *Capital* (1867), Marx elaborated on many of the issues that had animated his interest in money in his earlier career. Hoarding was a topic of central importance for Marx because hoarding represented a point around which discussions of wealth, capital, and exchange pivoted. We begin this discussion by noting that Marx, by the time he wrote *Capital*, no longer saw (if indeed he ever did) a complete identification between the avaricious person and the capitalist. "His aim," Marx wrote of the person who possessed quantities of wealth, "is rather the unceasing movement of profit-making. This boundless drive for enrichment, this passionate chase after value, is common to the capitalist and the miser [*Schatzbildner*]; but while the miser is merely a capitalist gone mad, the capitalist is a rational miser. The ceaseless augmentation of value, which the miser seeks to attain by saving his money from circulation, is achieved by the more acute capitalist by means of throwing his money again and again into circulation."[66]

The tight linkage between the actions of an individual and the movements of the economy as a whole were central to the problem of hoarding: "But what appears in the miser [*Schatzbildner*] as the mania of an individual is in the capitalist the effect of a social mechanism in which he is merely a cog."[67] As he had already argued in the *Grundrisse*, Marx saw the mutative qualities of wealth—and the desire to possess money—to be especially suited to the conditions of industrial capitalism. "With the possibility of keeping hold of the commodity as exchange-value, or exchange-value as a commodity," Marx wrote, "the lust for gold [*Goldgier*] awakens. With the extension of commodity circulation there is an increase in the power of money, that absolutely social form of wealth which is always ready to be used."[68] Naturally enough, these conditions produced a certain type of person, the money-obsessed bourgeois: "Work, thrift and greed [*Sparsamkeit und Geiz*] are therefore his three cardinal virtues, and to sell much and buy little is the sum of his political economy."[69]

Marx recognized the psychological dimension of greed, and he was attuned to its powerful ability to transform behaviors and mindsets in ways that we now see as being a part of the modern economic order. Much of the discussion of greed and its relationship to modern economic relations revolved around a discussion of pleasure and its satisfaction or renunciation. Accumulation of money produced a type of pleasure response that operated in uniquely modern ways. As Marx writes, "While the capitalist of the classical type brands individual consumption as a sin against his function, as 'abstinence' from accumulating, the modernized capitalist is capable of viewing accumulation as 'renunciation' of pleasure."[70]

Nonetheless, the whipsawing action of desire and pleasure—especially when the question of luxury and its enjoyment entered the arena—produced an especially diabolical set of behaviors. Acknowledging that the "capitalist gets rich, not, like the miser [*Schatzbildner*], in proportion to his personal labour and restricted consumption, but at the same rate as he squeezes out labour-power from others, and compels the worker to renounce all the enjoyments of life," Marx identifies the capitalist first with the "dashing feudal lord" and then writes that the modern conditions of capital exchange are ordered by the restraints of "sordid avarice [*schmutzigster Geiz*] and anxious calculation lurking in the background."[71] The ultimate result is a schizophrenic one: "There develops in the breast of the capitalist a Faustian conflict between the passion for accumulation and the desire for enjoyment."[72]

Other socialist thinkers identified greed much more systematically as a sign or consequence of modern capitalist relations, and in their critiques of acquisitive behavior they joined an attack on capitalist forms with a critique of modernity more generally. William Morris, the socialist, craftsman, and artist, is an example of left-wing critics who valued premodern social relations and saw in modern capitalist economic relations a type of demoralizing self-interestedness. Feudalism, in fact, produced a much healthier set of social relations. As one Morris scholar argues, "If feudalism was hierarchical, it at least created a society with clearly defined roles and responsibilities, not an individualist jungle in which only the ruthless greedy could survive. For greed is the natural enemy of the fulfillment Ruskin celebrates. Medieval culture, as he describes, died with the advent of mercantilism at the end of the fifteenth century—when the pursuit of material gain superseded the love of God and the beauty of his handiwork."[73]

In "The Lesser Arts," an essay dating from 1877, Morris takes up the question of the place of art in modern society and culture. His diagnosis of the problem was not hopeful: "The only way in which we can get a supply of intelligent popular art: a few artists of the kind so-called now, what can they do working in the teeth of difficulties thrown in their way by what is called Commerce, but which should be called greed of money?"[74] In this formulation, the integration of artistry into the money economy was a process of debasement. Indeed, any buying and selling—or "greed for money," as he put it—resulted in catastrophe for workers and consumers alike.

He continued this argument in another passage in the essay, claiming first, "A greed of unfair gain, wanting to be paid for what we have not earned, cumbers our path with this tangle of bad work, of sham work."[75] The root causes of this bad faith—greed—brought about all sorts of other difficulties as well. The passage continues: "So the heaped-up money which this greed has brought us (for greed will have its way, like all other strong passions), this money, I say, gathered into heaps little and big, with all the false distinction which so unhappily it yet commands amongst us, has raised up against the arts a barrier to the love of luxury and show, which is of all obvious hindrances the worst to overpass: the highest and most cultivated classes are not free from the vulgarity of it, the lower are not free from its pretence."[76]

Morris continued this theme in his 1884 essay "Useful Work versus Useless Toil," in which he linked a declining modern architecture to the catastrophic impulses of capitalist greed: "Beginning by making their factories, buildings, and sheds decent and convenient like their homes, they would infallibly go on to make them not merely negatively good, inoffensive merely, but even beautiful, so that the glorious art of architecture, now for some time slain by commercial greed, would be born again and flourish."[77] The following year, 1885, Morris's essay on utopian socialist Robert Owen contained similar language: Owen was the "lifter of the torch of Socialism amidst the dark days of the confusion consequent on the reckless greed of the early period of the great factory industries."[78]

While Morris would include in his utopian *News from Nowhere* (1890) the stock liberal critique of workers, he placed these critiques of the greed of workers in the mouths of "reactionists": "'The insatiable greed of the lower classes much be repressed.'"[79] Morris recognized the fluid nature of a charge of greed: it could work as well for socialists attacking capital as it could for "reactionists" critiquing the poor. In both cases, however, modern economic relations were to blame for liberating the passions that he believed had perhaps been held in check in earlier economic systems like feudalism.

There is evidence for this claim in a long sentence that Morris included in his 1887 essay "A Dream of John Ball." The passage opens with an expression of the freedom that Morris believed could be found in the deeply hierarchical society of medieval England: "I say if the men be still men, what will happen except that there should be all plenty in the land, and not one poor man therein, unless of his own free will he choose to lack and be poor, as a man in religion or such like; for there would then be such abundance of all good things, that, as greedy as the lords might be, there would be enough to satisfy their greed and yet leave good living for all who laboured with their hands."[80] Morris continues, contemplating the social, intellectual, and economic effects of the medieval division of labor:

> So that these should labour far less than now and they would have time to learn knowledge, so that there should be not learned or unlearned, for all should be learned; and they would have time also to learn how to order the matters of the parish and the hundred, and of the parliament of the realm so that the king should take no more than his own; and to order the rule of the realm, so that all men, rich and unrich, should have part therein; and so by undoing of evil laws and making of good ones, that fashion would come to an end whereof thou speakest, that rich men make laws for their own behoof; for they should no longer be able to do thus when all had part in making the laws; whereby it would soon come about that there would be no men rich and tyrannous, but all should have enough and to spare of the increase of the earth and the work of their own hands.[81]

Morris may be fairly attacked as a utopian who misread the virtues of the medieval past, overemphasizing the qualities of social cohesion and moral economy, but his understanding of modern economic relations was not a hollow one; for as much as he may have misunderstood about the tenor of medieval life, he also got much right about his own society.

Morris offered his critique of modern capitalism (preferring, perhaps naively, the old medieval guild system), and he too saw in the mass production of ugly and needless goods a monstrous outgrowth of modern capitalism that gave free rein to people's consumerist desires while never promoting a correlative celebration of workers' skill. Marx's analysis of greed, avarice, and hoarding produces a significant recognition of the way critics in the nineteenth century packaged their discussions of motivations, historical conditions, and economic transformations. We see in Marx how the liberal tendency to promote individuals and their desires as the prime engine of economic change would, by the end of the nineteenth century, appear in some way as a type of pathology. Indeed, the psychology of greed—and its incorporation into medical analysis at the end of the nineteenth and the beginning of the twentieth century—reflected a major reconstitution of the problem that allowed its incorporation into newly emerging scientific, economic, and religious fields of the period.

## Notes

1. Thomas Malthus, *An Essay on the Principle of Population* (Oxford: Oxford University Press, 1993), 3.
2. William Godwin, *The Enquirer: Reflections on Education, Manners and Literature, in a Series of Essays* (London: G.G. and J. Robinson, 1797), 164–65.
3. Ibid., 153.
4. Ibid.

5. Ibid.
6. Ibid., 151–52.
7. Ibid., 162.
8. Ibid., 195.
9. Ibid., 159–60.
10. Ibid., 162.
11. Ibid., 163.
12. Ibid., 161.
13. Ibid., 163–64.
14. T.R. Malthus, *An Essay on the Principle of Population, Or, A View of Its Past and Present Effects on Human Happiness: With an Inquiry into Our Prospects Respecting the Future Removal or Mitigation of the Evils Which It Occasions*, Cambridge Texts in the History of Political Thought (Cambridge: Cambridge University Press, 1992).
15. Ibid., 225.
16. Ibid., 227.
17. Ibid., 346.
18. Ibid., 346.
19. Ibid., 85.
20. Jean Baptiste Say, *A Treatise on Political Economy: Or, The Production, Distribution, and Consumption of Wealth*, trans. Clement Cornell Biddle (Philadelphia: Grigg & Elliot, 1832), 62.
21. Ibid., 152.
22. Ibid., 422.
23. Ibid., 354.
24. Ibid., 104–5.
25. Ibid., 129.
26. Ibid.
27. Ibid., 159.
28. Ibid., 210.
29. Ibid., 295.
30. Ibid., 305.
31. Ibid., 35.
32. Ibid., 35–36.
33. Ibid., 79–80.
34. Ibid., 138.
35. Ibid., 300.
36. Ibid., 364.
37. Ibid., 365.
38. Ibid.
39. Ibid.
40. Ibid.
41. Ibid.
42. Ibid.
43. Jane Austen, *Sense and Sensibility* (London: Dent, 1922), 258.
44. Jane Austen, *Pride and Prejudice* (Harmondsworth: Penguin Books, 1972), 188–89.
45. Honoré de Balzac, *Eugénie Grandet* (Oxford: Oxford University Press, 2009), 101.
46. Ibid., 173.
47. Charlotte Brontë, *Jane Eyre* (Baltimore: Penguin Books, 1966), 332.

48. Charles Dickens, *A Christmas Carol: And Other Christmas Stories* (New York: Signet Classic, 1984), 31.
49. Ibid., 71–72.
50. Ibid., 72.
51. Ibid., 73.
52. Emily Brontë, *Wuthering Heights* (Middlesex: Penguin Books, 1965), 142.
53. Balzac, *Eugénie Grandet*, 99.
54. John Stuart Mill, *On Liberty and Other Essays* (Oxford: Oxford University Press, 1998), 170.
55. Ibid.
56. Ibid., 170–71.
57. John Stuart Mill, *Principles of Political Economy: And, Chapters on Socialism*, The World's Classics (Oxford: Oxford University Press, 1994), 406.
58. Ibid., 418.
59. Karl Marx, *Capital: A Critique of Political Economy* (London: Penguin Books in association with New Left Review, 1981), 741.
60. Karl Marx and Friedrich Engels, "The German Ideology by Marx and Engels: Saint Max," accessed 26 June 2014, http://www.marxists.org/archive/marx/works/1845/german-ideology/ch03a.htm.
61. Karl Marx, *Grundrisse* (London: Penguin, 1993), 222.
62. Ibid.
63. Ibid., 223.
64. Ibid., 225.
65. Ibid., 224.
66. Marx, *Capital*, 254–55.
67. Ibid., 739.
68. Ibid., 229.
69. Ibid., 231.
70. Ibid., 740–41.
71. Ibid., 741.
72. Ibid..
73. William Morris, *News from Nowhere and Other Writings* (London: Penguin Classics, 1994), xxv.
74. Ibid., 242.
75. Ibid., 250–51.
76. Ibid., 251.
77. Ibid., 302.
78. Ibid., 319.
79. Ibid., 139.
80. Ibid., 33.
81. Ibid., 33–34.

# Bibliography

Austen, Jane. *Pride and Prejudice*. Harmondsworth: Penguin Books, 1972.
———. *Sense and Sensibility*. London: Dent, 1922.
Balzac, Honoré de. *Eugénie Grandet*. Oxford: Oxford University Press, 2009.

Brontë, Charlotte. *Jane Eyre*. Baltimore: Penguin Books, 1966.

Brontë, Emily. *Wuthering Heights*. Middlesex, UK: Penguin Books, 1965.

Dickens, Charles. *A Christmas Carol: And Other Christmas Stories*. New York: Signet Classic, 1984.

Godwin, William. *The Enquirer: Reflections on Education, Manners and Literature, in a Series of Essays*. London: G.G. and J. Robinson, 1797.

Malthus, Thomas. *An Essay on the Principle of Population*. Oxford: Oxford University Press, 1993.

Malthus, T.R. *An Essay on the Principle of Population, Or, A View of Its Past and Present Effects on Human Happiness: With an Inquiry into Our Prospects Respecting the Future Removal or Mitigation of the Evils Which It Occasions*. Cambridge Texts in the History of Political Thought. Cambridge: Cambridge University Press, 1992.

Marx, Karl. *Capital: A Critique of Political Economy*. London: Penguin Books in association with New Left Review, 1981.

———. *Grundrisse*. London: Penguin, 1993.

Marx, Karl and Friedrich Engels. "The German Ideology by Marx and Engels: Saint Max." Accessed 26 June 2014. http://www.marxists.org/archive/marx/works/1845/german-ideology/ch03a.htm.

Mill, John Stuart. *On Liberty and Other Essays*. Oxford: Oxford University Press, 1998.

———. *Principles of Political Economy: And, Chapters on Socialism*. The World's Classics. Oxford: Oxford University Press, 1994.

Morris, William. *News from Nowhere and Other Writings*. London: Penguin Classics, 1994.

Say, Jean Baptiste. *A Treatise on Political Economy: Or, The Production, Distribution, and Consumption of Wealth*. Translated by Clement Cornell Biddle. Philadelphia: Grigg & Elliot, 1832.

# CHAPTER SIX

# Greed and the New Spiritualism

Work all angles that bring you added money, possessions, good things of life.
—Theodor Adorno, *The Stars down to Earth and
Other Essays on the Irrational in Culture*

We saw in the previous chapter how greed was deployed in a number of dominant fields in the early and mid nineteenth century. We turn now to a different set of questions, looking at how greed was also integrated into more subterranean—but no less significant—areas of intellectual life. We take up these issues by considering how greed was deployed in occult and magical thought in the latter part of the nineteenth century, looking especially at its inclusion in descriptions of magic, in weird and decadent fiction, and in new forms of spirituality like Theosophy.[1] We also consider the ways that greed informed cross-cultural analyses of religion by looking at Marcel Mauss and gift exchange as well as greed's deployment as a sign of irrational degeneracy by social scientists.

These sources together provide insight into two key problems: how greed functioned in the informal economy (both economic and spiritual) and the way that greed was relegated to the premodern by connecting it to the primitive, to the exotic, and to the irrational. By isolating the atavistic qualities of occult and premodern greed, nineteenth- and twentieth-century Europeans could begin to naturalize the emotion in novel ways, locating it in terms of prior historical forms and opening the door for new psychological and psychoanalytic dimensions of the emotion that seemed entirely different in their orientation than what had come before. One way to begin this analysis is to consider the place of the occult in modern economic logic and to investigate the ways that greed was deployed to mark the boundary between rational and irrational economic thinking.

Writing from the vantage point of the mid twentieth century, Theodor Adorno took up the question of the irrational in modern culture in two justly famous essays. His "Theses against Occultism" (1947) and "The Stars Down to

Earth: The *Los Angeles Times* Astrology Column" (written 1952–53) were a part of Adorno's larger attempt to diagnose the psychological and social symptoms of what he called "late capitalism," an economic structure characterized by a deadened and sleepless opulence, a system weighted down by the narcissistic impulses of a culture industry seeking to extend its narcotic tentacles into every area of human endeavor and liberty. In Adorno's estimation, the prognosis was not good. "The tendency to occultism," he argued in the first essay, "is a symptom of the regression in consciousness."[2]

Rather than functioning as a reaction to modernity, occultism—with its premodern cultural sensibilities—had been co-opted: "The occultist draws the ultimate conclusion from the fetish-character of commodities: menacingly objectified labor assails him on all sides from demonically grimacing objects."[3] Even worse than the lives of malevolent commodities attacking the occultist from all sides and drawing her or him into the web of modern economic relations was the effect it had on all sorts of thought systems: "By its regression to magic under late capitalism, thought is assimilated to late capitalist forms."[4] The final result of an occult assimilated into the capitalist order was fascism. "The hypnotic power exerted by things occult," Adorno argued, "resembles totalitarian terror: in present-day processes the two are merged."[5]

Adorno increased the scale of his argument when he took up the topic of astrology in his essay "The Stars down to Earth: The *Los Angeles Times* Astrology Column." The premise of the piece is an amusing one: what unstated dreams of Angelenos are on display in a daily newspaper column that promised to convey the astrological knowledge of the *Los Angeles Times*—a "conservative paper leaning far to the right wing of the Republican party" in Adorno's estimation—to the everyday citizens of the great American city that Adorno had called home between 1941 and 1949?[6] Again, the conclusions were worrisome ones: "In eras of decline of social systems, with the insecurity and anxiety widespread in such eras, paranoid tendencies in people are evinced and often channelized by institutions wishing to distract such tendencies from their objective reasons."[7]

Naturally money was a central concern, and Adorno understood the astrology column to be a forum within which anxieties about financial matters could be confronted; the problem was an analytical one. He argued at one point, "The old concept of unbridled acquisitiveness is so deeply embedded in a business culture that it cannot be discarded or entirely repressed by spurious pseudo-activity though the columnist is well aware that it is no longer adequate to present-day economy."[8] Even worse, the stage of late capitalism that Angelenos experienced in the early 1950s was already a sucker's game: a "propensity for irrational material gain seems to be contingent upon the shrinking chances of making big money as a pioneer or on a rational basis of calculation."[9] Greed, in other words, was irrational. Like other members of the Frankfurt School who sought a fusion of Marx and Freud, Adorno employed a psychoanalytically informed method of analysis: "One of the most important contributions psychiatry and psychoanalytically-oriented sociology can make in this respect is to reveal certain mechanisms which cannot be grasped either in terms of being sensible or in terms of delusions."[10] Adorno's approach to the existence of the occult in late capitalism led him to consider those cultural forms not only to be irrational but also historically anachronistic. Not only were irrational beliefs in magic, luck, astrology, and alchemy ill informed, but they also indicated the presence of a kind of widely felt paranoid fantasy: if success is a function not of work or intelligence or any of the other bourgeois attributes thought to predict success in liberal capitalism but of fortune, astrological alignment, and utilitarian magic, then one's individual failures are more easily comprehended and assimilated.

The central argument of this chapter is that greed has a prominent place in the new forms of spirituality that developed during the second half of the nineteenth century. These "new spiritualties" ranging from a rejuvenated interest in the occult, Theosophy (and its offshoots), and magic developing in Europe challenge us to rethink the intersections of spirit and the money economy at the end of the nineteenth century. When we consider magic, modernity, medicine, and money we are able to see more clearly the ways that pecuniary interest influenced the intellectual and cultural lives of many diverse disciplines. We investigate the ways that critics writing during this period framed "modern" greed—understood as an expression of secular, capitalist desire—in relation to the magical, the occult, and the premodern. We explore the emergence of notions of magical wealth as they were expressed in the heart of modern industrial Europe at the end of the nineteenth century.

Alchemical fantasies, Faustian bargains, satanic money cults, witches swimming in gold, dreams of a Hand of Glory, a philosopher's stone, a Mandrake root, or a monkey's paw leading one to riches: these visions did not indicate a dehistoricized desire for wealth but in fact suggest a richly imaginative counterpoint to the gray rationality of what Max Weber called the "tremendous cosmos of the modern economic order."[11] The chapter also indicates the ways that acquisition and desire were imagined during the fin-de-siècle through premodern mechanisms of wealth creation that stood in contrast to nineteenth-century values like thrift, hard work, ingenuity, and entrepreneurialism.[12] We consider, in other words, what it might have meant to get rich through magic rather than work during the heart of the bourgeois century.

These arguments raise the issue of the "secularization thesis," the idea that secular ethics replaced religious systems of morality in the eighteenth and nineteenth centuries, and its applicability to the question of avarice, desire, and greed. The turn of the twentieth century is commonly assumed to be overwhelmingly secular and industrial, a time when social relations were governed by class and industry, but there was also a counterpoint located in the occult and a fascination with medieval and Renaissance magic. While the secularization thesis has been subjected to wide-ranging criticism, and many scholars are unimpressed by the suggestion that Christianity was undermined in Europe and North America due to the Enlightenment, the evidence indicates a new way to understand the tensions between the secular and the profane. By the end of the nineteenth century, we see alchemy, Satanism, and the occult reappearing in European society as a conscious antithesis to rational modernity. In other words, greed was an area that was not entirely secularized, but it also did not retain Christian systems of morality.

The desire seen in the late nineteenth century for a type of alchemical "philosopher's stone" that would allow the user to become rich provides evidence for a valuable alternative narrative about the secular and scientific nineteenth century. That this fixation on magic and the occult was intimately tied up with notions of wealth, riches, and financial gain tells us much about the ways that greed was understood a century ago. When the Decadent author J.-K. Huysmans wrote about Parisian Satanism in the 1880s (in *Là-Bas* [The Damned], 1891), he referenced the alchemical tradition and the magical bodies of the possessed. When Sigmund Freud, as we will see in the following chapter, first showed an interest in the psychoanalytic basis for the desire for money in 1897 (in his letters to Wilhelm Fliess), he too framed his observations in terms of religious magic, alchemy, and the early modern tradition.

The goal of this chapter is to trace these links and to understand why novelists, astute social observers, and the leaders of these "new spiritualities" framed their assumptions about pecuniary desire through references to late medieval and early modern cultural customs. Research on fields as widely separated as anthropology, literature, and medicine indicate that one of the ways that greed was conceptualized in the late nineteenth and twentieth centuries was through an appropriation of the past at the same time that economists, anthropologists, and imperialists were locating greed in colonial spaces or as an example of "primitive accumulation." In other words, at a time when the rational was thought to be ascendant, there were many who promoted the prerational; that wealth and greed were central concerns is indicative of the tensions roiling the cultural, social, and intellectual worlds of people living in the nineteenth century.

Rather than seeing greed and covetousness as by-products of secularization and industrialization, the preliminary evidence indicates that greed was instead displaced into the prerational past or naturalized through association with people Europeans considered primitive. We will also take up the "secularization thesis" by considering the ways that industrialization in the nineteenth century helped to shape new understandings of covetousness, greed, and desire. We examine in this chapter how the new spirit of the late nineteenth century deployed greed as emotional and economic practice alike.

Theosophical and esoteric societies like the Order of the Golden Dawn carefully managed their public forms to avoid the charge that they were simply moneymaking operations. While acknowledging that "magic is about power," these new spiritualist groups had to contend with the claim that they employed occult means—or worse, faked occult knowledge—in order to secure earthly wealth.[13] The critique was a powerful one, in part because within the locus of late nineteenth century spiritualism, black magic was understood as the "the manipulation of natural forces, often for self-interested purposes."[14]

Theosophists like Helena Blavatsky argued that "Occultism is not magic" because occultism had the ostensibly higher goal of soulful self-awareness.[15] Magic, on the other hand, was more directly instrumental. Blavatsky and her followers hoped to depict occultism as being tied to the production of a range of esoteric knowledge. Historian Alex Owen points out that in response to the formation of the Order of the Golden Dawn, Blavatsky established the "Esoteric Section of the Theosophical Society (1888)," which was dedicated to the study of what was called "practical occultism," the instrumentalization of occult knowledge.[16] Responding to the critique that she used her occult powers to become rich, Blavatsky flatly denied the charge, writing,

> With regard to the suggestion that I attempted to promote the "financial prosperity" of the Theosophical Society by means of occult phenomena, I say that I have never at any time received, or attempted to obtain, from any person any money either for myself or for the Society by any such means. I defy anyone to come forward and prove the contrary. Such money as I have received has been earned by literary work of my own, and these earnings, and what remained of my inherited property when I went to India, have been devoted to the Theosophical Society. I am a poorer woman to-day than I was when, with others, I founded the Society.[17]

Despite these claims to the contrary the evidence suggests that other founders of the Theosophical Society were equally concerned with maintaining the image of the group even as they attempted to apply esoteric knowledge in ways that would produce wealth. Blavatsky's right-hand man, Henry Steel Olcott, relates two stories in his early history of the Theosophical Society, *Old Diary Leaves*, that illustrate this public relations dynamic and how financial desires were understood by the Theosophists. Blavatasky and Olcott traveled together to India in the 1870s to broaden their knowledge of South Asian esotericism, and they ultimately established the headquarters of the Society in India.

Olcott relates in *Old Diary Leaves* an episode of alchemical transformation he saw while in India conducted by a man named Mohammed Arif. Arif, Olcott suggests, had a "practical knowledge of occult chemistry, and, at our request, consented to try an [alchemical] experiment with my help."[18] The experiment consisted of making a fire with dried cow patties into which silver rupees had been stuck with some "dried vegetable products": "pounded cloves, ahindra bark, and bechums." The piles were burned, then burned again, then burned a third time. "It was expected that in the morning we should find the coins completely oxidized, the pure metal being changed into an oxide of the consistency of lime, and crumbing between the fingers. The experiment proved, however, only partly successful, the surface of the coins being oxidized but the interior left unchanged."[19] Arif asserted that he could do better in different conditions, and described a process by which a "diamond is by a certain process known to them, reduced to ashes, these ashes added to melted tin are capable of changing the latter into silver."[20]

Olcott was impressed, but critical of the practical applications of the process: "Practically," he wrote, "of course the experiment is commercially valueless, the transforming agent being more costly than the resultant product. But the thought is important in its suggestiveness, for if the ashes of one substance containing carbon, when obtained by a certain process will transmute tin into silver, it opens the inquiry whether a nearly-related ash form another carbonaceous substance might not give the same result under conditions."

Despite the limitations of the procedure, Olcott was intrigued by the possibility of making money through alchemical means. He questioned Arif about other ways of achieving alchemical transformations and reports that Arif knows that "the Indian alchemists have proved that they can harden tin by combining with it carbon; hence they cover a broader ground than modern chemists in the department of metallurgy."[21] Olcott was aware that these claims would be met with skepticism, but argues through Arif, "Alchemical science is dishonored ... by the neglect of the educated, and the trickery and base frauds of charlatans, but still it is a great Science. I believe—nay, I know—that the transmutation of metals is possible."[22]

Not only did alchemy remain scientifically valid—and, Olcott hoped, "commercially valuable"—but it was also considered to be a legitimate field of esoteric study by Theosophists. Other critics from the time were not convinced. The Austro-Hungarian social critic Max Nordau, for instance, considered occultism to be a mark of degeneracy, albeit one that responded to human desires to manipulate the environment. "Magic, sorcery, astrology, divination," as Nordau described in his 1895 text *Degeneration*, "all these ancient beliefs correspond to a need of human nature; that of being able easily to act upon the external world and the social world; that of possessing, by means relatively easy, the knowledge requisite to make this action possible and fruitful."[23] The link between mysticism and degeneracy were clear to Nordau, and those who embraced mystic explanations displayed "a principal characteristic of degeneration" through their beliefs.[24]

Mysticism and the occult provided "degenerates" with alternative explanations of events, but also allowed them to pursue manias that knew no end:

"The astronomer becomes an astrologist, the chemist an alchemist and a seeker of the philosopher's stone; the mathematician labours to square the circle, or to invent a system in which the notion of progress is expressed by a process of integration, the war of 1870 by an equation, and so on."[25] Nordau's references to alchemy as chemistry in declination linked specifically to the philosopher's stone indicates that illegitimate forms of wealth generation remained a topic of interest to critics in the fin-de-siècle.

Despite the practical limitations of applied occult knowledge, Olcott was quite concerned with displaying a set of motives that would not discredit the Theosophical Society by impugning a type of greed to the organization. Olcott tells the story of a healing session he conducts in which the moral state of the patient prevents a full cure. The patient suffers in his arm and leg from "hemiplegia," a type of muscular disfigurement that Olcott asserts may be cured through occult means. Olcott reports, "I began on his arm, making passes along the nerves and muscles, and occasionally breathing upon them. In less than half hour I had restored the arm to flexibility."[26]

Then Olcott learns that the patient was "an avaricious person, well known for his closeness," and therefore was an undesirable. "Now, of all things that are disgusting to the occultist, money-greed is one of the chief: it is so low and ignoble a passion. My feelings underwent an instant change towards the patient."[27] He later inquires about the "miser": "The reply surprised me very much: the arm, they said, remained cured, but *the leg had relapsed into the paralytic state.* Although I had read of no similar case in the books on Mesmerism, the reason suggested itself at once—I had felt no real sympathy for the man after hearing about his miserliness, and therefore my vital aura had not vibrated along his nerves."[28] Theosophy may have been about marshalling and instrumentalizing occult forces, but it was also about policing the moral status of practitioners and patients alike.

If morality and the careful management of financial desire were central components of occultism at the end of the nineteenth century, these practices may have stemmed from the social environment within which occultism developed historically. Alex Owen writes, "Fin-de-siècle occultism attracted an educated, usually middle-class clientele in search of answers to fundamental but nonetheless profound questions about the meaning of life and the spiritual dimensions of the universe."[29] She provides evidence to demonstrate the claim that "these organizations had a distinctly bourgeois tone that smacked of the gentleman's private club."[30]

Blavatsky died in 1891, and Olcott ceded his control of the Theosophical Society to followers like Annie Besant, Charles Leadbeater, and Rudolf Steiner beginning in 1895. A number of schisms destroyed the institutional unity of the Theosophical Society, and scandals plagued the group.[31] This institutional chaos allowed a wide latitude of theosophical belief and practice, but Steiner presents an example of the ways that greed and financial desire continued to surface within the movement. Steiner, an Austrian, attempted to keep Theosophy organized within the terms of European culture (other branches were more attracted to "Eastern" philosophy), and he was known for his work on Goethe and Nietzsche.[32] One of the more complex ways that greed appears in Steiner's work comes about through a discussion of how he believed souls were formed, attracted, and repelled one another.

Steiner opens the question in one text, *Theosophy: An Introduction to the Supersensible Knowledge of the World and the Destination of Man* (1910), by discussing the operation of the soul as it comes into contact with other souls. "It attracts other formations in its neighbourhood by means of the sympathy ruling in it; but besides the sympathy there is at the time present in it antipathy, through which it repels certain things in its surroundings"[33] These feelings of attraction and repulsion, of sympathy and antipathy, are significant because they are best understood as the action of greed. Steiner argues,

> From the outside such a formation appears to be endowed with the forces of antipathy ONLY. This, however, is not the case. There is sympathy and antipathy in it, but the latter predominates. It has the upper hand over the former. Such formations play a SELF-SEEKING role in the soul space. They repel much that is around them, and lovingly attract but little to themselves. They therefore move through the soul space as unchangeable forms. The force of sympathy which is in them appears GREEDY. This GREED appears as the same time insatiable, as if it could not be satisfied, because the predominating antipathy repels so much of what approaches, that no satisfaction is possible (Here we have to do with what is described in theosophical literature as the lowest part of the astral world.)."[34]

Even the disembodied soul, it seems, experienced a type of covetousness.

Steiner also worked on the study of auras. The aura thrown off by a person was a valuable indication of his or her interior state, and in particular the shade of the aura provided insight into a person's moral status. "One can see," Steiner writes, "in the first part of the aura of the undeveloped man of impulse, all shades from red to blue."[35] "With him these shades have a dull, dirty character. The obtrusive red shades point to the sensual desires, to the fleshly lusts, to the passion for the enjoyments of the palate and the stomach. Green shades appear to be found especially in those lower natures that incline to obtuseness and indifference, greedily giving themselves over to each enjoyment but nevertheless shunning the exertions necessary to satisfy them."[36] Greed appears here in color form, the explosion of auric colors indicating the moral status and unstated desires of the subject him- or herself. "Where the desires are passionately bent on any goal beyond the reach of the capacities already acquired," Steiner concludes, "brownish-green and yellowish-green colours appear. Certain modern modes of life actually breed this kind of aura."[37]

Aside from the study of a person's aura, Steiner—like Olcott—was excited by the possibility of alchemical processes yielding new avenues of wealth, but he was also careful to indicate that this interest was entirely honorable. In a lecture titled "Materialism and Occultism" presented in the Swiss town of Dornach on 10 October 1915, Steiner took up the question of alchemy, asserting first, "The alchemists were honorable and did not seek egotistic gain, still worked to some degree with the old inspirations and intuitions, applying and elaborating them."[38]

The vexing question of what Steiner delicately called "egotistic gain" is an important one in that it suggests that the old alchemists merely pursued knowledge, never wealth as they laboriously applied their tinctures in their attempts to transform base metals to noble ones. The reason these alchemists could succeed in the past but never in the present was due to the fact that "vestiges of the old clairvoyance still stirred within them, although no longer accompanied by any reliable knowledge. But the number of people in which these vestiges of ancient clairvoyance survived decreased steadily."[39]

Steiner invoked this point to make a historical argument: the level of esoteric knowledge has declined in inverse relation to the increase in what he called "materialistic tendencies," a development that reached its high point in the middle of the bourgeois century. "The nearer we come to our own period, the more we are faced with a decline of old soul forces and a growth of tendencies in the human soul toward observation of the outer, *material* world," Steiner argued in the lecture.[40] "After slow, gradual preparation, this tendency [toward degeneration of occult capabilities] reached its peak in the middle of the nineteenth century.... Materialistic tendencies had by then [the mid nineteenth century] developed their greatest strength."[41] For Steiner, this deeply entrenched materialism had succeeded only in masking an inner ability to access what he called the "spiritual world." Located in the "subconsciousness," but hampered in their ability to see, there were materialistic Europeans of the mid nineteenth century "who knew that there was a spiritual world, who knew that we are surrounded by a spiritual world just as we are surrounded by air."[42]

Steiner's language of the subconscious is important, and Owen argues that Theosophy was attuned to the developing language of psychology: "Besant readily acknowledged the seemingly parallel preoccupations of psychology and occultism, but equally asserted the critical distinction between the two."[43] The connections between Steiner's version of Theosophy and psychology that appear in another section of the text indicate the degree to which Steiner was groping for a new language of desire: one that would fuse theosophical theory to materialism. He began by identifying the planes upon which human agency could be enacted in order to fulfill wishes: "Just as spacial [sic] extension and spacial [sic] movement are peculiar to corporal formations, so are excitability and impelling desire peculiar to the things and being of the soul world. For this reason one describes the soul world as the world of desires or wishes, or as the world of longing."[44]

The soul world, in other words, was the plane upon which human desires unfolded; it was the spatial location of greed. "These expressions," Steiner continued, "are borrowed from the human soul world. One must therefore hold clearly in view that the things in those parts of the soul world which lie outside the human soul are just as different from the soul forces within it as the physical matter and forces of the external corporal world are different from the parts which compose the physical human body. (Impulse, wish, longing, are names for the material of the soul world.)"[45]

The interest in understanding money, desire, and materialism that surfaced in Theosophy, occultism, and the new forms of spiritualism growing in Europe between 1875 and 1925 were also reflected in the new academic disciplines of sociology, anthropology, religious studies, and psychology. The most obvious indication of this fascination is demonstrated in the work of Marcel Mauss. Mauss was famous for his analysis of the religious history of sacrifice (written with Henri Hubert in 1898), but his most influential work, of course, was *The Gift* (published in 1923–24).[46] This text, an analysis of potlatch and gift exchange in non-European societies, has much to say about value, desire, and accumulation.

Beginning with the claim that Scandinavian mythology holds that "the miser always fears presents," moving through the Hindu declaration that "avarice breaks the circle of the law; rewards and foods are perpetually reborn from one another," identifying the Native American position that "the Tsimshian blame avarice and tell how their main hero, Crow (the creator), was dismissed by his father because he was miserly," and calling attention to the Islamic principle that "he who is on his guard against his avarice will be happy," Mauss arrives at European society and the money economy, which he accepts as based on a system of self-interest.[47] "The very word 'interest' is itself recent," Mauss asserts,

> originally an accounting technique: the Latin word *interest* was written on account books against the sums of interest that had to be collected. In ancient systems of morality of the most epicurean kind it is the good and pleasurable that is sought after, and not material utility. The victory of rationalism and mercantilism was needed before the notions of profit and the individual, raised to the level of principles, were introduced. One can almost date—since Mandeville's *The Fable of the Bees*—the triumph of the notion of individual interest.[48]

The anthropology of greed, at least as it was formulated through social science in the 1920s, reveals its European provenance, and Mauss implicitly marked it as a modern phenomenon. Mauss was responding to a half century of European social science that produced a range of new knowledge about wealth and desire when he wrote *The Gift*, and we turn next to the ways that premodern—even occult—religion and financial desire were conceptualized in decadent and "weird" fiction from the time.

We begin with a familiar story of a magical colonial fetish that allows an instrumental use of magic to obtain riches, although with terrible consequences. "The Monkey's Paw," written by W.W. Jacobs and published in 1902, tells the story of a family—the Whites—who are given the shrunken paw of a monkey by their friend Sergeant-Major Morris, who has just returned to Europe from colonial service in India. The paw, which gives hints of colonial monstrosities that can dangerously affect the metropole, "had a spell put on it by an old fakir, ... a very holy man. He wanted to show that fate ruled people's lives, and that those who interfered with it do so to their sorrow."[49] The obvious solution to such a ridiculously superstitious claim of occult powers is destruction: "throw it on the fire ... like a sensible man," the new owner is urged.[50]

He does not and instead indulges his desires with a "wish for something sensible," a windfall of £200.[51] Such occult desires are unpalatable to the son, who worries about the instrumental use of magic and what it could mean in terms of the moral standing of his father: "I'm afraid it'll turn you into a mean, avaricious man, and we shall have to disown you."[52] The plot twists as expected: the wish is fulfilled when the son is killed at work and the firm gives the parents £200 in compensation; the mother in her grief wishes to bring her boy back to her and when the zombie returns home, the father, panicking in horror, wishes for it to disappear again. While the man's zombie progeny is not put to work in some hidden factory, toiling away to enrich his parents, the monkey's paw retains its magical powers. One fantasy about the generation of wealth, in other words, could be identified through the occultification of money and the "occult economy," even if such matters were rendered in cautionary ways.

Jacobs's 1902 story, now a standard text in the "weird fiction" canon, was published in a cultural context that since the 1850s had operated under the spell of decadent fiction from the Continent. Decadent fiction, which scandalized and titillated alike, celebrated the undercurrents of society and thereby represented an alternative to the mainstream. Owen explains that philosophers like Henri Bergson's influence on wider European culture benefitted in part from the close correspondence between decadence, vitalism, and occultism:

> These notions, in turn, were echoed around the end of the century in a literary "decadence" that featured Symbolist sensibilities. As Holbrook Jackson recognized, the literary "decadence" of the 1890s was intimately related to "spiritual desire" and the rise of "mysticism," as well as to notions of an aestheticized self constituted through direct sensorial apprehension of the world. British "decadence" was heavily influenced by a genre of French writing that emerged with Théophile Gautier and Charles Baudelaire and continued through Paul Verlaine, Arthur Rimbaud, Stephen Mallarmé, and J.-K. Huysmans.[53]

Texts like Jules Barbey d'Aurevilly's *Les Diaboliques* (1874), J.-K. Huysmans's *A Haven* (1886), and Octave Mirbeau's 1887 story "The Octogenarian" each indicate the integration of greed and the occult. Texts in the decadent tradition defined greed in different ways, but they do have common elements. In Barbey d'Aurevilly's *Les Diaboliques*, greed is future oriented: "I lived for tomorrow," one character says, "like a miser, and I understood the pious who settle on this earth the way one settles in a dangerous place where one will spend the night."[54] The emotion was also linked quite clearly to passions that are difficult to transform. Avarice is "that passion that rarely relaxes its cold grip on the heart it has seized."[55]

Greed was also linked to base activities like treasure hunting, although other feelings would detach greed's pull. Huysmans writes in one text, "Although Uncle Antoine was tempted by the prospect of treasure, he did not give in. His greed was vanquished by his fear, and he restricted himself to shaking his head and replying: No doubt, no doubt, refusing even to examine the entrance to the cellars."[56] While these texts give a brief introduction to some of the ways that greed appeared in the decadent tradition I want to consider two texts in particular that demonstrate the ways that the occult and the economy were intertwined in decadent thought: J.-K. Huysmans's *Against Nature* (1884) and *The Damned* (1891).[57]

Huysmans's *A Rebours* (the title is rendered *Against Nature* in English translations) was considered upon its publication in 1884 to be a kind textbook for decadence. The book appeared at a significant moment in French cultural history, and scholars like Alex Owen suggest that 1884 was almost the ground zero of European interest in the occult: not only was Paris visited by the Theosophist Madame Blavatsky, but also in that year both *Against Nature* and Joséphin Péladan's *La Vice supreme* were published.

*Against Nature* gives the story of an aristocrat, Des Esseintes, who finds modern living to be unbearable and who retreats into a type of aesthetically informed isolation in which he gives free rein to his impulses for antinatural living. The text is important for our purposes because Huysmans provides a description of ennui and oversensitivity caused by the complete satisfaction of all desires. Des Esseintes has reached the end point of greed.[58] Des Esseintes gathers an extensive collection of arcane and occult texts ("Archelaüs, Albertus Magnus, Raymond Lull, and Arnaud de Villanova, which dealt with the cabbala and the occult sciences"[59]), but his greatest admiration is reserved for the godfather of French literary decadence, Charles Baudelaire. Huysmans writes that Des Esseintes's

> admiration for this writer was boundless. In his opinion, literature had, until then, restricted itself to exploring the superficial areas of the soul, or searching into those of its subterranean depths which were accessible and well lit, now and

again pointing out the lodes of the seven deadly sins, studying their seams, their development, noting, as did Balzac, for example, the stratification of the soul that is possessed by a monomaniacal passion, by ambition, by avarice, by paternal infatuation, by senile lust.[60]

The passage is significant not just for references to Balzac and Eugénie Grandet but also for the ways in which the soul is described in both catholic and geological ways. Avarice appears in the significantly central spot in the list of degenerated and decadent sins. Des Esseintes also develops an interest in witchcraft and magic, and Huysmans describes his understanding of Satanism and his interest in the early modern witch-hunting text *Malleus Maleficarum*.[61] Decadence, the occult, and the modern stratified "soul" all come to revolve around the larger issue of avarice.

The authors of decadent works may have wished to attack greed, but they themselves were not immune to the charge. In his analysis of "degeneration" published in 1895, Max Nordau described these writers as those who "form … "a portion of that riff-raff of great towns who professionally cultivate immorality, and have chosen this trade with full responsibility, solely from horror of honest work and greed for lucre."[62] After all, Nordau proclaimed in the dedication to the book, "Degenerates are not always criminals, prostitutes, anarchists, and pronounced lunatics; they are often authors and artists."[63]

Des Esseintes provides a reflection of what could be called the "decadent self": consciously aesthetic, (over)refined, and dedicated to the careful collection of things and experiences. These types of object relations, however, also bear a resemblance to what Alex Owen describes as the "occult self." There was an "occult preoccupation with self," Owen argues, "that looked within for the means of transcending the phenomenal world and accessing the spiritualized manifestations of an occluded reality. The 'powers of the interior man' were conceived in purely psychologized terms. In its attention to interiority occultism echoed certain aspects of 'decadent' Romanticism, but, like the medical psychology of the day, it sought to elucidate a rationalized self-consciousness stripped of Romantic excess and interpreted according to the conventions of modern science."[64]

Huysmans further developed this constellation of ideas about the occult, decadence, and economic issues in his 1891 publication *La Bas* (The Damned). *The Damned* tells the story of a Parisian journalist, Durtal, who takes on an investigation of Satanism in contemporary Paris and then is shocked to discover the presence of satanic cults. A late nineteenth-century interest in Satanism was excited by the twin publication of Baudelaire's *Les Fleurs du mal* (1857, notable for much, but especially for the "litany to Satan") and Jules Michelet's 1862 text *La Sorciere* (published in English the following year as *Satanism and Witchcraft*) and then further enflamed by the elaborate hoax perpetrated through Léo Taxil's 1891 declaration of a link between Satanism and freemasonry.

*The Damned* provides twin narratives. One centers on Durtal and his growing awareness of Satanism in Paris; the other is Durtal's exploration of early
modern Satanism, particularly the alchemical and Satanic experiences of Gilles
de Rais, a sinister lord who sought through demonic assistance the esoteric
knowledge required to produce the philosopher's stone. There are a number
of passages in the text that center on the financial in late nineteenth-century
Europe. Durtal comments for instance on what he calls the "enigma of money."
He begins by suggesting that the "rules of money are precise and invariable.
Money attracts money, money seeks to accumulate in the same places, money
is naturally attracted to scoundrels and those who are entirely bereft of any
talent."[65] Money has a kind of occult nature on its own in this formulation, and
never really has any positive consequences. Durtal proclaims,

> When, by an exception which proves the rules, money finds its way into the
> hands of a man who, though wealthy, is neither a miser nor has any murderous
> proclivities, it stands idle, incapable of creating a force for good, incapable of
> even making its way into charitable hands who would know how to employ it.
> One might almost say that it takes revenge for its misdirection, that it undergoes
> a voluntary paralysis whenever it enters into the possession of someone who is
> neither a born swindler nor a complete and utter dotard.[66]

The situation of this man—neither a miser nor a murderer—is significant;
even when money finds its way to a person like this it is rendered impotent,
incapable of active generation.

But an even worse situation develops when money winds up in the pockets
of the poor. Durtal, in a long passage worth quoting in its entirety, argues,

> When, by some extraordinary chance, it strays into the home of a poor man,
> money behaves even more inexplicably. It defiles immediately what was clean,
> transforms even the chastest pauper into a monster of unbridled lust and, acting
> simultaneously on the body and the soul, instills in its possessor a base egoism,
> not to mention an overweening pride, which insists that he spends every penny
> on himself alone; it makes even the humblest arrogant, and turns the generous
> person into a skinflint. In one second, it changes every habit, upsets every idea,
> transforms the most deep-seated passions.[67]

Money inflames passions to an extent that even the author of decadent
fiction found extreme. The gravitational pull of riches warps the most basic
human sentiments even as it reaffirms the boundaries of the individual. Huysmans, like other decadent authors, privileged the ascetic qualities of poverty
and critiqued money as a bourgeois weakness. Money, then, is irredeemable
and the desire for money is not spiritually, but ethically dangerous. Durtal asserts in one section of the text, "Money is the greatest nutrient imaginable for
sins of the worst kind, which in a sense it aids and abets. If one of the custo-

dians of wealth so forgets himself as to bestow a boon or make a donation, it immediately gives rise to hatred in the breast of the recipient; by replacing avarice with ingratitude, the equilibrium is established again: a new sin is commissioned by every good deed which is committed."[68]

Huysmans incorporated a range of other comments on money and the desire for wealth into *The Damned*, and aspects of the text function in some ways like an extended meditation on the meaning and value of money itself. One passage, centered on the insidious work of "capital," invites close historical analysis. "But the real height of monstrosity," Huysmans writes, "is attained when money, hiding the splendour of its name under the dark veil of the word, calls itself capital."[69] This transformation of money into capital—the putting into use of money in order to make more money, masks the dangerous core of greed. Huysmans explains, "At that moment its action is no longer limited to individual incitations to theft and murder, but extends across the entire human race. With a single word capital grants monopolies, erects banks, corners markets, changes people's lives, is capable of causing millions to starve to death."[70] Published in 1891, as millions were indeed starving to death as they were incorporated into global financial systems, the text offers an unflinching critique of the money economy.[71]

Durtal assumes that money's consequences are diabolical in origin, thus linking in clear ways the money and the occult economies. Durtal says, "And all the while that it does this, money is feeding on itself, growing fat and breeding in a bank vault; and the Two Worlds worship it on bended knee, melting with desire before as before a God. That's it! Either money, the master of the soul, is diabolical, or else it is beyond explanation. And how many other mysteries, equally unintelligible, are there, how many other phenomena which should make the man of reflection tremble?"[72]

Huysmans is quite clear in his equation of the modern, rational economy that operated in esoteric, hermetic, and ultimately antidemocratic ways. Durtal, as he comes to more clearly understand the occult roots of the economy, seeks further knowledge of Gilles de Rais and that man's hope of finding the alchemical knowledge necessary for health and wealth. Alchemy, Durtal asserts, stemmed from diabolism: "It was Satan's will that they would discover this powder which would both provide them [de Rais and his assistants] with endless wealth and render them almost immortal, because at this time the philosopher's stone was reputed not only to be capable of the transmutation of base metals, such as tin, lead, copper into the noble metals such as silver and gold, but also of curing every illness and prolonging life, without infirmities, beyond the three score years and ten ascribed by the patriarchs."[73] And worse, diabolism stemmed from greed even as it wrought an uncomfortable social transition: the nobility "has replaced [carnage and rape] with a monomania for business, the passion for lucre."[74]

The new economy, despite its occult shadow, remained weak and blood-less—bourgeois—in comparison to earlier economic forms. Unleashing greed and incorporating it as a rational mechanism of the market had simply adulter-ated the entire thing. In one humorous passage Durtal offers a rousing critique of bourgeois "cupidity" and the undermining of the guild tradition, which had policed the quality of the goods and the functioning of the marketplace:

> This miserable century … has constructed nothing and destroyed everything.
> … The only thing this century has invented is the adulteration of foodstuffs and
> more sophisticated manufactured goods. In that, it has proved without equal. It
> has even gone so far as to adulterate excrement! Why, as recently as 1888, the
> two chambers had to pass a law designed to prevent the sale of fake manure!
> That really does take some beating.[75]

Like William Morris with his modern medievalism, Durtal longs for an in-vented past when value was clearly identifiable and greed remained discredited. Even the Satanic no longer held the key to overcome the market forces that led to the urge to manipulate the market in manure.

Huysmans's *The Damned*, with its blend of medieval and modern, alchemi-cal and chemical, Christian and satanic, demonstrates the ways that the magical and the modern economies could function as one. Value could be manipulated through conventional as well as occult methods, meaning that it is difficult to completely separate the "occult economy" from the "regular economy." Huys-mans's ostensible topic in *The Damned* is not the functioning of the money economy or an historical exposé of diabolical alchemy. Rather the topic of the text is the new forms of spirituality—Satanism most obviously—that could be witnessed in Paris in the last decade of the nineteenth century. The connection between fictional representations of these new understandings of wealth and money and the self-conscious declarations of the adherents to these new forms of spirituality remain significant. Greed—or at least its status as an unspoken element—was addressed in powerful new ways within these spiritualist move-ments of the late nineteenth and early twentieth centuries.

The preceding evidence demonstrates that the occult, magic, and other per-haps more mainstream religious movements like Theosophy took the problem of greed seriously and used it to enter into debates about the moral landscape of late nineteenth- and early twentieth-century European culture and society. We can see, in other words, how these new forms of spirituality wrestled with many of the same problems that more established traditions had.

When considering this problem, Adorno understood the occult as a past thought form. "People always wanted to learn from occult signs what to expect and do," he argued in "The Stars down to Earth." He then suggested, "In fact, superstition is largely a residue of animistic magical practices by which ancient humanity tried to influence or control the course of events."[76] The presence of the occult in the modern, Adorno suggests, is something of an atavistic appendage. When magic was employed to manipulate or to understand the economic forces and logic of late capitalism, something must be wrong. Adorno's arguments in these essays have been persuasive, but recent scholarship poses a different take on this problem. Rather than seeing an occult and irrational premodern as something historically antecedent to an enlightened and rational modern, we are becoming aware of the ways that magic and modernity helped constitute one another.

When thinkers made greed premodern, occult, and irrational, they also opened the door to claims that a different sort of emotional complexity governed the lives of modern Europeans. Attaching greed to the primitive, occult, and magical meant that greed could be posited as something no longer fully integrated into secular, rational modernity. The historical production of modernity, in other words, was crafted in part through a suppression (in some cases) and a naturalization (in others) of old emotional regimes that no longer served an obvious purpose. The religious, economic, and medical critiques of greed that dominated discourse between 1500 and 1850 fit this mold. But if we consider the repression of these old visions of greed as a move nominally concerned with the production of modernity, we must also consider the status of claims about the modern condition that were produced by that negation.

Anthropologists and sociologists have made the argument most forcefully that magic and modernity are not opposing forces, and their points of congruence come quite frequently around financial and political issues. Based on anthropological fieldwork that he has conducted in Cameroon since the early 1970s, anthropologist Peter Geschiere has been able to demonstrate that modernity and magic are overlapping entities. Noting that a belief in the occult was not diminished with electrification, Geschiere argues, "It is difficult to maintain that there is a self-evident opposition between witchcraft and modernity. On the contrary, rumors and practices related to the occult forces abound in the more modern sectors of society."[77]

Politics and economics were two areas in which magic and modernity were particularly closely integrated. Geschiere notes the existence of "all sorts of interventions of occult forces in modern politics," and he is quite explicit about the use of those with "esoteric knowledge" to control the political process and to remove power from the people.[78] Geschiere's evidence suggests that witchcraft and magic are intensely political, if antidemocratic in orientation, and therefore implicated in larger processes of modernity.

The political is one area that Geschiere believes demonstrates the close connections between modernity and magic. The economic is another. Geschiere posits a clear "relation between the occult and new forms of power and wealth," and his evidence indicates that the occult is understood to be a mechanism through which people may enrich themselves.[79] These depictions of the occult basis of wealth have important historical and remembered antecedents, and our evidence demonstrates that the integration of the occult into modernity was a process experienced not only in the periphery but also in the European metropole. Geschiere describes a belief in a "sorcery of success," or a "witchcraft of the whites," that Cameroonians feel mirrors the economic and power relations of the colonial period.

The instrumentalization of magic in the money economy is a central feature of Geschiere's anthropology, and again we are confronted with the clear application of the process in Europe in the same historical period. The exploitation of the labor power of a zombified slave population produces one avenue through which one could become rich. Oneiromancy is another; naturally the magical oneiromancy of the colonial periphery has a type of corollary seen in Freudian dream analysis in the metropole.[80] Geschiere's evidence indicates a belief that vivid dreams and oneiric travel provide clues that one could assay in order to discover new ways of becoming rich. Geschiere suggests, "in his dreams, [the dreamer] will see a land where money flows and many laborers work for him."[81] One consequence of economic expansion was to heighten the importance of witchcraft, and Geschiere asserts, these "economic changes reinforced witchcraft tensions."[82]

As economic conditions improved, accusations of occult knowledge were used to seize wealth; in periods of economic decline those same accusations were employed to explain economic contraction and often were linked to anxieties about the arrival of strangers who were perhaps ready to zombify a village and put them to work on the plantations of the rich. Geschiere concludes, a "common thread in all these stories is that they hardly correspond to the stereotype of witchcraft as a traditional barrier against change and innovation On the contrary, there is a constant proliferation of new forms of sorcery or witchcraft that seem, rather, to express determined efforts to appropriate new riches."[83]

Sociologists Briget Meyer and Peter Pels agree that magic and modernity are affines. Noting an older historiography that "acknowledged the existence of magic *in* modernity," Meyer and Pels argue for a theoretical position that allows us to "reflect ... on the ways in which magic *belongs to* modernity."[84] In the introduction to the volume Pels asserts that people like Adorno have wrongly located magic in the premodern and have "predominantly made [magic] to define an antithesis of modernity: a production of illusion and delusion that was thought to recede and disappear as rationalization and secularization spread throughout society."[85] Better, Pels believes, to theorize magic "as being explicitly of modernity" and "culturally at home in the institutions and practices we associate with the Occidental world."[86] This leads him to argue that magic and modernity supplement one another, forming the "*magic of modernity itself.*"[87]

Crucial to this argument is a deeper definition of "modernity"—that vexing term that always eludes easy definition. Working from Habermas and others,

Pels argues that scholars should begin "to take *modernity* to refer to the global (but not hegemonic) spread of a *consciousness of radical temporal rupture.*" Furthermore, he argues, magic is "crucial for the definition of something specifically 'new'" and its newness therefore forms a vital component of any experience of the modern.[88] The upshot of Pels's argument is that magic is a hidden foundation upon which modern relations are formulated.

Pels explores the problem by looking to Bruno Latour: "We might say that the radical distinction between magic and modernity is a form of modernist purification that is constantly being betrayed by the translations and mediations needed to relate the two. Thus, magic is reinvented in modernity, an 'invention of tradition' that does not create continuity with the past as much as it distances itself from it."[89] Because "invented traditions" are so important to any kind of modern experience, the human action of making meaning is also central to the problem. As Pels asserts, "*the modern study of magic is largely a study of human subjectivity.*"[90]

Pels's claim that magic is an important realm of human activity is borne out by the work of historian Alex Owen, who has written a clearly reasoned and fascinating account of occultists in late Victorian England. Her understanding of the occult in this period is characterized by a sensitivity to the agency of the people under discussion. Owen sees the new forms of spirituality that developed in the last third of the nineteenth century as a type of human agency. Writing about spiritualists, Owen indicates, "If they were in revolt, it was partly against what they saw as the dead hand of traditional religious observance and the scientism and materialism of Victorian culture."[91] The occult, in other words, was a form of resistance, but it was also modern: scientific and materialist.

Occultists, Owen shows, "sought to mobilize a reworked notion of science in the name of the religion of the ancients, and represented a paradigmatic shift in which the universe and the place of humankind within it were rationalized but brought back into sharply spiritual focus. Magic in particular played to the idea that magical powers can be clearly demonstrated, and occultism in general allied itself with the idea of scientific validation."[92] This marriage of the occult and the scientific method was embodied preeminently in the Society for Psychical Research, which used scientific methodologies to probe the unseen spirit world.[93] Owen argues ultimately, "Late-Victorian occultists were among those who self-consciously referred to themselves as modern, and these women and men were not unusual in feeling that they were living at the advent of new and exciting times."[94]

Owen's evidence indicates that occultism was a "thoroughly modern project—albeit one that sought to confound the modern distinction between reason and the irrational."[95] Magic and science, in other words, were not to be understood as divergent phenomena, but as convergent ones. The range of professional experiences that occultists had confirmed this attitude. Owen writes, "Fin-de-siècle occultists were not resistant to the idea that occult phenomena or magical powers represented a manifestation of the little-understood power of the mind."[96] Owen notes the centrality of science in the occultist's self-conception and marks the ways that "fin-de-siècle enchantment was committed to the guiding principle of reason and played to a formalized concept of rationality even as it contested a strictly secular rationalism."[97] Magic must be thought of as a part of the late nineteenth-century rationalizing moment, another way of expressing Enlightenment principles.

This unexpected confluence of reason and magic at the end of the nineteenth century leads Owen to argue, "The formulation of occult subjectivity was inseparable from the instrumental rationality that Weber argued is intrinsic to the complex social processes of a modern order. In particular, and in common with all magical traditions, fin-de-siècle occultism was characterized by the will to both know and control the natural world."[98] Owen's argument that "the often subtle ways in which the occult was itself intrinsic to the making of the modern" provides a useful indication of the ways that Enlightenment rationality remained but one of many ways of understanding behavior (economic and otherwise) at the turn of the century.[99] As Owen puts it, "Occultism was intimately bound up in the cultural configuration of the modern, [and] the modern was equally characterized by some of the very tensions that occult subjectivity sought to incorporate and enchantment to mediate."[100]

Owen does not directly deal with economic issues, but we need to take seriously her claim that magic and modernity were equally at home in the European fin-de-siècle, and we need to consider the ways that magic was assimilated into the fabric of European economic life. Anthropology and sociology again provide clues as to how this process operated. Pels considers the realm of economics through an analysis of Marx and the commodity fetish. While this is a valuable reminder of the "magic" inherent in modern economic relations, our interest in the relationship of the occult to financial desire requires that we return again to a more decisive account of how the two might have functioned together within the realm of "human subjectivity" and new forms of spiritual agency that developed during the time that we are considering.

Jean and John Comaroff have written any number of justly famous anthropologies of Africa. One in particular, "Occult Economies and the Violence of Abstraction: Notes from the South African Postcolony," is of interest to this account of money, magic, and financial desire. The essay analyzes magic and modern economic relations in South Africa soon after Mandela's victory, and it offers a brilliant account of what the Comaroffs call the "Age of Futilitarianism," a time of contracting economic possibilities and a period of heightened social and political tensions that are best understood by many South Africans through occult mechanisms. The Comaroffs identify what they call an "occult economy," which operates alongside and within the "regular" one. There are "symptoms of an occult economy waxing behind the civil surfaces of the 'new' South Africa," they write before arguing, "This economy is itself an integral feature of millennial capitalism—that odd fusion of the modern and the postmodern, of hope and hopelessness, of utility and futility, of promise and its perversions."[101]

The "black" market, like the instrumentalized forms of "black" magic populating the European imagination provide analytical insight into the ways magic and the economy might function together, and the Comaroffs argue that these fault lines are particularly apparent in times of radical economic change like that which Europeans experienced at the end of the nineteenth century.[102] While the Comaroffs focus on the transitions experienced in South Africa during the transition to a postapartheid order, the changes included a series of unleashed economic fantasies: "In South Africa ... the end of apartheid held out the prospect that everyone would be set free to speculate and accumulate, to consume, and to indulge repressed desires."[103] When these wishes proved difficult to fulfill, the explanatory function of the "occult economy" emerged.

Many South Africans, the Comaroffs argue, understood economic change as a set of esoteric and hidden relations: "That these not-quite-fathomable mechanisms—precisely because they are inscrutable, occult—have become the object of jealousy and envy and evil dealings; that arcane forces are intervening in the production of value, diverting its flow for selfish purposes."[104] This way of understanding economic relationships reflects what the Comaroffs call the "essential paradox of occult economies [, that is,] the fact that they operate on two inimical fronts at once. The first is the constant pursuit of new, magical means for otherwise unattainable ends. The second is the effort to eradicate people held to enrich themselves by those very means; through the illegitimate appropriation, that is, not just of the bodies and things of others, but also of the forces of production and reproduction themselves."[105] Magic could be powerfully entwined with the "real" economy, and producers and consumers, workers and capitalists (mis)aligned in hermetic systems thought knowable only to a privileged few.

Like the Cameroonians about whom Geschiere writes, the Comaroffs describe South Africans who consider the role of the living dead in the production of value. Not limited to what would be called in the United States a "zombie bank," wealth itself was produced by people without knowing it, on behalf of people of whom they would never be conscious. "The living dead exist only to serve their creators," the Comaroffs write, "bereft of tongues to give voice to their affliction, they are believed to work after dark, mainly in agriculture."[106] Others, "ghost workers," were "magically transported to urban centers; in fact, to any place where they might accrue riches for their owners."[107] And even contingent labor was not immune to the threat of zombification.

The Comaroffs explain the occult nature of the dawn of the dead with a phrase that will certainly sound familiar even to those with full-time employment: "In this era of increasingly impermanent employment, there are even 'part-time zombies': people who wake up exhausted in the morning, having served unwittingly in the nocturnal economy to feed the greed of a malign master."[108] As intriguing as the transnational dimensions of the zombie myth are, I wish to turn to a closer analysis of the magical and occult economy that existed in Europe around the turn of the twentieth century. Zombies play a role, as does a brand of instrumentalized magic that indicates the presence of the irrational at the hidden heart of the rational century of moneymaking. While the claim that the nineteenth century was the great age of rationality is perhaps overstated, the period does retain some aura of a rational sensibility.

Scholars like Brady Brower and Jay Winter indicate the extent to which interest in the occult—shaped in the late nineteenth century—continued to exert intellectual influence well into the twentieth.[109] A prominent aspect of this history of ideas is the confluence of ideas about the sacred and the profane in the late nineteenth and early twentieth centuries. The presumed secularization of European society and culture, theoretically demonstrated with the victory of Darwin's supporters in an early round of the culture wars, is often taken to demonstrate that the intellectual force of religion had lost its sway.[110] Within the context of these larger debates about rationalism, faith, and science we see develop an unexpected discourse on money projected through the lens of literature.

This chapter has presented material that bridges the occult and the rational, the scientific and the artistic, the academic and the ad hoc, but the evidence exposes the centrality of greed in the "occult economy" as it was incorporated into a range of new spiritualties at the end of the nineteenth century. The negation of prior understandings of greed that developed in late medieval and early modern Europe indicate the extent to which the emotional character of modern life was developed around an act of suppression.

Blavatsky and the Theosophists under her sway—Olcott, Leadbeater, and Steiner—as well as the no less hermetic Order of the Golden Dawn dabbled in a neomedieval understanding of natural philosophy that served to legitimize and extend their own form of novel spirituality. Exhibiting an interest in the occult, in zombification, in treasure hunting and divination, not to mention a self-promoting form of black magic not only indicates the presence of an "irrational" occultism at the heart of Europe's rational century but also allows us to see the vexed and conflicted desires at home in Theosophy. A syncretic blend of Eastern and Western mysticisms, Theosophy produced an ultimately colonialist, even Orientalist discourse, on magical money and the greedy desires that sustained it.

The Theosophists, so bejeweled and glittering in their language of the soul, were also afraid that the harmonic symphonies of coins ringing in their pockets would deaden their oracular sensitivities and render them dead to the astral world. More traditional constructions like Satanism, witchcraft, and the alchemical traditions of the European transformation into early modernity were no less mystic, even in their late nineteenth-century forms. As amusing as decadence is, the preoccupation of decadent authors with wealth, with the illicit and esoteric, and with the demonic are rendered neutered by their celebration of an occult economy that never fundamentally altered the basic conditions of desire but merely rewrote the terms by which it was to be understood.

As Theodor Adorno wrote in "The Stars down to Earth" (1953), greed assumes a peculiar place in the psychoanalytic understanding of economic exchange and meaning:

> Thus nineteenth-century liberalism with the idea of the small independent entrepreneur who accumulates wealth by saving has probably elicited character formations of the anal type more than, say, the eighteenth century, where the ego idea was more largely determined by the feudal characterological imagery which would be called in Freudian germs "genital"—although closer scrutiny would probably show that the aristocratic ego ideal hardly had so much basis in fact as romantic desires would have it be the case.[111]

We turn now to a consideration of the ways that greed was integrated into these new languages of psychology and psychoanalysis, looking closely at how the emotion was embodied anew amid new medical interventions at the end of the nineteenth and the beginning of the twentieth centuries.

## Notes

1. Portions of this chapter related to Rudolf Steiner also appear in Joanne Miyang Cho, Eric Kurlander, and Douglas T. McGetchin, eds., *Transcultural Encounters between Germany and India: Kindred Spirits in the Nineteenth and Twentieth Centuries*, Routledge Studies in the Modern History of Asia (Abingdon, Oxon: Routledge, 2013), 55–67.
2. Theodor W. Adorno, *Adorno: The Stars down to Earth and Other Essays on the Irrational in Culture*, Routledge Classics (London: Routledge, 2002), 128.
3. Ibid., 129.
4. Ibid.
5. Ibid.
6. Ibid., 41.
7. Ibid., 122; For Adorno's time in California, see Ehrhard Bahr, *Weimar on the Pacific: German Exile Culture in Los Angeles and the Crisis of Modernism* (Berkeley: University of California Press, 2007).
8. Adorno, *Adorno*, 85–86.
9. Ibid., 86.
10. Ibid., 35.
11. Max Weber, *The Protestant Ethic and the Spirit of Capitalism*, Routledge Classics (London: Routledge, 2001), 123.

12. Deborah M. Valenze, *The Social Life of Money in the English Past* (New York: Cambridge University Press, 2006), 145–78.
13. Alex Owen, *The Place of Enchantment: British Occultism and the Culture of the Modern* (Chicago: University of Chicago Press, 2007), 4.
14. Ibid., 19.
15. Ibid., 46.
16. Ibid.
17. "The Society for Psychical Research and the Theosophical Phenomena: The Report of the S.P.R. on Madame Blavatsky," accessed August 10, 2010, http://www.blavatskyar chives.com/sprhpb.htm.
18. Henry Steel Olcott, *Old Diary Leaves* (London: Theosophical Publ. Soc., 1900), 280.
19. Ibid., 281.
20. Ibid., 282.
21. Ibid., 282–83.
22. Ibid., 283.
23. Max Simon Nordau, *Degeneration* (New York: D. Appleton, 1895), 218.
24. Ibid., 45.
25. Ibid., 60.
26. Henry Steel Olcott, *Old Diary Leaves*, 384.
27. Ibid., 384.
28. Ibid., 385–86.
29. Owen, *Place of Enchantment*, 4–5.
30. Ibid., 5.
31. Owen describes one scandal in particular involving the accusation that Leadbeater had instructed young boys in his care about a range of what was delicately called "demoralizing personal practices" that were perhaps "reciprocal." See *Place of Enchantment*, 105.
32. For more on the historical development of Theosophy in German-speaking Europe, see Corinna Treitel, *A Science for the Soul: Occultism and the Genesis of the German Modern* (Baltimore: Johns Hopkins University Press, 2004), ch. 4; Helmut Zander, *Anthroposophie in Deutschland: Theosophische Weltanschauung und gesellschaftliche Praxis, 1884–1945* (Göttingen: Vandenhoeck & Ruprecht, 2007); Peter Staudenmaier, "Occultism, Race and Politics in German-Speaking Europe, 1880–1940: A Survey of the Historical Literature," *European History Quarterly* 39, no. 1 (2009): 47–70; Peter Staudenmaier, "Race and Redemption: Racial and Ethnic Evolution in Rudolf Steiner's Anthroposophy," *Nova Religio* 11, no. 3 (2008): 4–36.
33. Rudolf Steiner, *Theosophy: An Introduction to the Supersensible Knowledge of the World and the Destination of Man* (London: K. Paul, Trench, Trübner, 1910), 94–95.
34. Steiner, *Theosophy*, 95. Emphasis in original.
35. Ibid., 178.
36. Ibid.
37. Ibid.
38. Rudolf Steiner, *Spiritualism, Madame Blavatsky, & Theosophy: An Eyewitness View of Occult History* (Great Barrington, MA: Anthroposophic Press, 2001), 143.
39. Ibid.
40. Ibid., 144.
41. Ibid.
42. Ibid., 147.

43. Owen, *Place of Enchantment*, 126.
44. Steiner, *Theosophy*, 90.
45. Ibid., 90–91.
46. Marcel Mauss, *The Gift: The Form and Reason for Exchange in Archaic Societies*, 2nd ed. (London: Routledge, 2006); Henri Hubert and Marcel Mauss, *Sacrifice: Its Nature and Functions* (Chicago: University Of Chicago Press, 1981).
47. Mauss, *The Gift*, 3, 73, 143 fn 145, 99.
48. Ibid., 97.
49. W. W. Jacobs, *Selected Short Stories* (London: Bodley Head, 1975); See Jared Poley, *Decolonization in Germany: Weimar Narratives of Colonial Loss And Foreign Occupation*, Studies in Modern German Literature (Bern: Peter Lang Publishing, 2005), for more on colonial "monsters," 115–50.
50. Ibid., 34.
51. Ibid.
52. Ibid., 36.
53. Owen, *Place of Enchantment*, 139.
54. Asti Hustvedt, ed., *The Decadent Reader: Fiction, Fantasy, and Perversion from Fin-de-Siècle France* (New York: Zone Books, 1998), 56.
55. Ibid., 178.
56. Ibid., 463.
57. See Hustvedt, *Decadent Reader*.
58. J.-K. Huysmans, *Against Nature*, trans. Margaret Mauldon (Oxford: Oxford University Press, 1998), 7–8.
59. Ibid., 115.
60. Ibid., 117.
61. Ibid., 130–32.
62. Nordau, *Degeneration*, 506.
63. Ibid., vii.
64. Owen, *Place of Enchantment*, 114.
65. J.-K. Huysmans, *The Damned*, trans. T. J. Hale, Penguin Classics (London: Penguin Books, 2001), 12.
66. Ibid.
67. Ibid., 12–13.
68. Ibid., 13.
69. Ibid.
70. Ibid.
71. Mike Davis, *Late Victorian Holocausts: El Niño Famines and the Making of the Third World* (London: Verso, 2002).
72. Huysmans, *The Damned*, 13.
73. Ibid., 72.
74. Ibid., 103.
75. Ibid., 104–5.
76. Adorno, *Adorno*, 37.
77. Peter Geschiere, *The Modernity of Witchcraft: Politics and the Occult in Postcolonial Africa*, trans. Peter Geschiere and Janet Roitman (Charlottesville: University Press of Virginia, 1997), 3.
78. Ibid., 4.
79. Ibid., 166.

80. See Jared Poley, "Magic, Dreams, and Money," in *Everyday Magic in Early Modern Europe*, ed. Kathryn Edwards (Burlington, VT: Ashgate, 2015) for an exploration of these themes in the early modern period.
81. Geschiere, *Modernity of Witchcraft*, 152.
82. Ibid., 148.
83. Ibid., 166.
84. Birgit Meyer and Peter Pels, eds., *Magic and Modernity: Interfaces of Revelation and Concealment* (Stanford, CA: Stanford University Press, 2003), 3.
85. Ibid., 4.
86. Ibid.
87. Ibid., 5. Emphasis in original.
88. Ibid., 30.
89. Ibid., 32.
90. Ibid., 31.
91. Owen, *Place of Enchantment*, 8.
92. Ibid.
93. For the European context, see M. Brady Brower, *Unruly Spirits: The Science of Psychic Phenomena in Modern France* (Urbana: University of Illinois Press, 2010) and Corinna Treitel, *A Science for the Soul: Occultism and the Genesis of the German Modern* (Baltimore: Johns Hopkins University Press, 2004).
94. Owen, *Place of Enchantment*, 8–9.
95. Ibid., 255.
96. Ibid., 120–21.
97. Ibid., 12.
98. Ibid., 14.
99. Ibid., 237.
100. Ibid., 236–37.
101. Jean Comaroff and John L. Comaroff, "Occult Economies and the Violence of Abstraction: Notes from the South African Postcolony," *American Ethnologist* 26, no. 2 (1999): 283.
102. There were radical economic dislocations in both the 1870s and 1890s, when European and global economies alike suffered major declines.
103. Comaroff and Comaroff, "Occult Economies," 284.
104. Ibid.
105. Ibid.
106. Ibid., 289.
107. Ibid.
108. Ibid.
109. Matthew Brady Brower, "Re-Membering the Modern Subject: The Wounded Body and the Politics of Mourning, 1917–1937," MA Thesis, University of Colorado, 1996; Matthew Brady Brower, "The Fantasms of Science: Psychical Research in the French Third Republic, 1880–1935" (Ph.D. Diss., 2005); J. M. Winter, *Sites of Memory, Sites of Mourning: The Great War in European Cultural History*, Studies in the Social and Cultural History of Modern Warfare (Cambridge: Cambridge University Press, 1995).
110. Peter J. Bowler, *Evolution: The History of an Idea*, 3rd ed., completely rev. and expanded (Berkeley: University of California Press, 2003).
111. Adorno, *Adorno*, 122.

# Bibliography

Adorno, Theodor W. *Adorno: The Stars down to Earth and Other Essays on the Irrational in Culture.* Routledge Classics. London: Routledge, 2002.

Bahr, Ehrhard. *Weimar on the Pacific: German Exile Culture in Los Angeles and the Crisis of Modernism.* Berkeley: University of California Press, 2007.

Bowler, Peter J. *Evolution: The History of an Idea.* 3rd ed., completely rev. and expanded. Berkeley: University of California Press, 2003.

Brower, Matthew Brady. "The Fantasms of Science: Psychical Research in the French Third Republic, 1880—1935." Ph.D. dissertation. Rutgers University, 2005.

———. "Re-Membering the Modern Subject: The Wounded Body and the Politics of Mourning, 1917–1937." MA Thesis, U of Colorado, 1996.

Brower, M. Brady. *Unruly Spirits: The Science of Psychic Phenomena in Modern France.* Urbana: University of Illinois Press, 2010.

Cho, Joanne Miyang, Eric Kurlander, and Douglas T. McGetchin, eds. *Transcultural Encounters between Germany and India: Kindred Spirits in the Nineteenth and Twentieth Centuries.* Routledge Studies in the Modern History of Asia. Abingdon, Oxon: Routledge, 2013.

Comaroff, Jean, and John L. Comaroff. "Occult Economies and the Violence of Abstraction: Notes from the South African Postcolony." *American Ethnologist* 26, no. 2 (1999): 279–303.

Davis, Mike. *Late Victorian Holocausts: El Niño Famines and the Making of the Third World.* London: Verso, 2002.

Geschiere, Peter. *The Modernity of Witchcraft: Politics and the Occult in Postcolonial Africa.* Translated by Peter Geschiere and Janet Roitman. Charlottesville: University Press of Virginia, 1997.

Hubert, Henri and Marcel Mauss. *Sacrifice: Its Nature and Functions.* Chicago: University of Chicago Press, 1981.

Hustvedt, Asti, ed. *The Decadent Reader: Fiction, Fantasy, and Perversion from Fin-de-Siècle France.* New York: Zone Books, 1998.

Huysmans, J.-K. *Against Nature.* Translated by Margaret Mauldon. Oxford: Oxford University Press, 1998.

———. *The Damned.* Translated by T. J Hale. London: Penguin Classics, 2001.

Jacobs, W. W. *Selected Short Stories.* London: Bodley Head, 1975.

Mauss, Marcel. *The Gift: The Form and Reason for Exchange in Archaic Societies.* 2nd ed. London: Routledge, 2006.

Meyer, Birgit and Peter Pels, eds. *Magic and Modernity: Interfaces of Revelation and Concealment.* Stanford, CA: Stanford University Press, 2003.

Nordau, Max Simon. *Degeneration.* New York: D. Appleton, 1895.

Olcott, Henry Steel. *Old Diary Leaves.* London: Theosophical Publ. Soc., 1900.

Owen, Alex. *The Place of Enchantment: British Occultism and the Culture of the Modern.* Chicago: University of Chicago Press, 2007.

Poley, Jared. *Decolonization in Germany: Weimar Narratives of Colonial Loss and Foreign Occupation.* Studies in Modern German Literature. Bern: Peter Lang Publishing, 2005.

———. "Magic, Dreams, and Money." In *Everyday Magic in Early Modern Europe.* Edited by Kathryn Edwards. Burlington, VT: Ashgate, 2015.

Staudenmaier, Peter. "Occultism, Race and Politics in German-Speaking Europe, 1880–1940: A Survey of the Historical Literature." *European History Quarterly* 39, no. 1 (2009): 47–70.

———. "Race and Redemption: Racial and Ethnic Evolution in Rudolf Steiner's Anthroposophy." *Nova Religio* 11, no. 3 (2008): 4–36.

Steiner, Rudolf. *Spiritualism, Madame Blavatsky, & Theosophy: An Eyewitness View of Occult History.* Great Barrington, MA: Anthroposophic Press, 2001.

———. *Theosophy: An Introduction to the Supersensible Knowledge of the World and the Destination of Man.* London: K. Paul, Trench, Trübner, 1910.

"The Society for Psychical Research and the Theosophical Phenomena: The Report of the S.P.R. on Madame Blavatsky." Accessed August 10, 2010. http://www.blavatskyarchives.com/sprhpb.htm.

Treitel, Corinna. *A Science for the Soul: Occultism and the Genesis of the German Modern.* Baltimore: Johns Hopkins University Press, 2004.

Valenze, Deborah M. *The Social Life of Money in the English Past.* New York: Cambridge University Press, 2006.

Weber, Max. *The Protestant Ethic and the Spirit of Capitalism.* Routledge Classics. London: Routledge, 2001.

Winter, J. M. *Sites of Memory, Sites of Mourning: The Great War in European Cultural History.* Studies in the Social and Cultural History of Modern Warfare. Cambridge: Cambridge University Press, 1995.

Zander, Helmut. *Anthroposophie in Deutschland: Theosophische Weltanschauung und gesellschaftliche Praxis, 1884–1945.* Göttingen: Vandenhoeck & Ruprecht, 2007.

# CHAPTER SEVEN

# The Psychology and Psychoanalysis of Greed

The previous chapter traced the inclusion of greed in new forms of spirituality that some Europeans experienced at the end of the nineteenth century. We saw in the course of Chapter Six the ways that greed—typically thought to be a foundation of modern capitalist economic logic—was also a holdover from the premodern that haunted the dreams of Europeans when they envisioned a dark past or imagined an authentic colonial spirit. That evidence suggested, among many things, that greed continued to exist as a fraught emotion, even by people for whom the rational and instrumental use of magic remained possible. This chapter considers an allied problem: the incorporation of greed into a range of social sciences at the end of the nineteenth and early twentieth centuries. We consider its integration into psychology and sociology, examine how greed was incorporated into psychoanalytic discourse, and contemplate the ways that greed was "embodied" in new ways by these novel medical approaches. In short, the chapter considers the ways greed was understood as a medical and psychological pathology beginning at the end of the nineteenth century.

William Morris, as we saw in Chapter Five, was convinced that he was living through a declination. Other cultural critics of the 1880s and 1890s had similar convictions but offered a different set of explanations for the decline. Max Nordau complained, "Contempt for traditional views of custom and morality" characterized the fin-de-siècle.[1] "To the voluptuary," Nordau sniffed, "this means unbridled lewdness, the unchaining of the beast in man; to the withered heart of the egoist, disdain of all consideration for his fellow men, the trampling under foot of all barriers which enclose brutal greed of lucre and lust of pleasure."[2]

To Nordau's mind, the social values that had once preserved a type of purity in consumption had dissolved, and a "brutal greed" could be found in its place. But an even worse catastrophe lurked. In his discussion of French psychologist Valentin Magnan's *Recherches sur la centre nerveux* (1893), Nordau notes the "irresistible desire among the degenerate to accumulate useless trifles," the outward symptoms of an insidious nervous condition "'oniomania,' or 'buying craze.'"[3] Nordau reports that the oniomaniac "neither buys enormous quantities of one and the same thing, nor is the price a matter of indifference to him.... He is simply unable to pass by any lumber without feeling an impulse to acquire it."[4] The trembling oniomaniac, incapable of passing up a sale, feverishly acquires, piling needless possession upon unwanted object upon passionless matter.

Nordau's degenerate, a person who "is ever supplying new recruits to the army of ... seekers for the philosopher's stone, the squaring of the circle and perpetual motion," was also subject to the wildfires of desire.[5] Nordau suggests that Magnan's work provides a key to understanding the manias of the fin-de-siècle: "The present rage for collecting, the piling up, in dwellings, of aimless bric-a-brac which does not become any more useful or beautiful by being fondly called *bibelots*, appear to us in a completely new light when we know that Magnan has established the existence of an irresistible desire among the degenerate to accumulate useless trifles."[6]

Nordau, despite his cultural conservatism and his overdetermined medicalism, did recognize the key differences between accumulation and retention: "This [oniomania] is not to be confounded with the desire for buying, which possesses those who are in the first stage of general paralysis. The purchases of these persons are due to their delusion as to their own greatness. They lay in great supplies because they fancy themselves millionaires."[7] Nordau's claims about the medical and criminological conditions of degeneracy had a wide readership, and his psychologization of desire remains an important marker of the ways that psychology—and the psychology of desire in particular—provided new ways of discussing behaviors that in previous periods remained under the sway of morality and ethics.

Max Nordau's *Degeneration* was published in 1895, and the text indicates some of the ways that greed surfaced in medical and criminological thinking at the time. We see surfacing in that book one of the central concerns of social critics around the turn of the twentieth century: how do we understand desire, especially when it is manifested in behaviors that seem outside the bounds of normal society? We see in sociology the development of another field of inquiry whose central intellectuals provided intricate analyses of greed and avarice in the last decade of the nineteenth century and the first decade of the twentieth. While Max Weber was undergoing his nervous breakdown (and preparing his return to intellectual life by writing *The Protestant Ethic and the Spirit of Capitalism*), his colleague Georg Simmel was writing his great analysis of value, *The Philosophy of Money*, which was published in a first edition in 1900 and in a second enlarged form in 1907.[8]

Simmel's 1889 article "On the Psychology of Money" opened up this topic for him, and it was in this piece that Simmel was first attracted to the problems of greed and avarice.[9] In *Philosophy of Money* Simmel takes his readers on an extended interior voyage into the mental territory occupied by money, and he probes in the text the close connections between the mental actions that the money economy requires and human behaviors. There is much in the text that we cannot consider in this discussion, but Simmel does produce at a number of spots a thoughtful analysis of greed and avarice, which he understands in fundamentally psychological ways: "If the character of money as an ultimate purpose oversteps that intensity for an individual in which it is the appropriate expression of the economic culture of his circle, then greed and avarice emerge."[10] Greed in particular is a "hypertrophied category" dependent on local and very specific economic and cultural conditions.[11]

Greed and avarice are represented by Simmel as differing responses to economic conditions: one centers on acquiring, the other on retaining money. "Generally speaking," he writes, "the threshold for the beginning of a real greed for money will be relatively high in a developed and lively money economy, but relatively low at primitive economic levels, whereas the reverse is true for avarice."[12] "Greed and avarice are not identical phenomena although they have a common basis in the evaluation of money as an absolute purpose."[13]

One recent critic of Simmel's book, Gianfranco Poggi, asserts that this section of the argument is particularly significant: "On this account, Simmel considers the two parallel and contrasting vices of avarice and greed (the first focused on storing and retaining, the second focused on acquiring, as much money as possible) as phenomena that, whatever their significance, deny rather than affirm money's very nature."[14] The dual nature of this emotional desire is a critical insight of Simmel's. Like the critics from the early modern period that we considered in previous chapters, Simmel oriented the problems of avarice and greed around a set of cultural concerns that circulated around the appropriate use of wealth. The problem was understood in terms of feelings that have "overstepped the boundary of the normal."[15] Simmel pointedly argues, "Greed and avarice, although they appear in most cases in unison, must none the less be precisely distinguished both conceptually as well as psychologically."[16]

Because one "cannot deny a proportionate relationship between the speed of acquisition and the speed of expenditure," Simmel demanded a balanced view of retention and acquisition.[17] Greed and avarice are merely emotional deflections or insertions into a longer process of assessing value and normalizing behaviors within a particular social context. It is in this regard that Simmel took up the issue that so vexed Nordau: oniomania. Simmel took up the problem and offered an unflattering comparison that resonates with a current critique of hoarders and "pack rats": "Some people's most remarkable psychological mania for accumulation, a trait that often leads people to compare them to hamsters: such people pile up precious collections of any kind without getting any satisfaction from the objects themselves, frequently without even caring about them."[18] Simmel argued that value is irrelevant for the oniomaniac, but the fact of possession is paramount: "Merely having these things in their possession is valuable for such people."[19]

The process was linked in importantly psychological ways to the expression of individual aims and desires: "It is usually interpreted as egoism since it shares with it the negative side of the common form of egoism—the exclusion of all others from ownership."[20] While attracted to psychological explanations, Simmel does not get into the question of motivations but does argue, "It is, in any case, a psychological fact which only enters into a variety of combinations with the sequence of purposes of a personal nature. The collector who shuts away his valuables from everyone else and who does not even enjoy them himself, yet watches most jealously over them, colours his egoism with an admixture of supra-subjective valuation."[21]

An implication of this line of argumentation centers on the process of how one assigns value to material objects, and therefore Simmel moves into an analysis of how money provides a conduit through which behaviors and objects could be joined. Avarice and greed are significant factors in the process of valuation because of the ways that they deflect the emotional currents of desire in pathological ways. For the person who experiences greed or avarice, money is no longer a means to an end but has reached the point of what Simmel called "final purpose," the point at which one possesses money for itself and not for what it could be used. Calling avarice and greed "pathological deformations of the interest in money," Simmel argued that money itself took on immense psychological and emotional importance in the money economy, not just for the greedy or the avaricious but also as a consequence of its seductive power over the dream life of individuals.

"Money that has become an ultimate purpose," Simmel argues, "does not tolerate the coordinated definite values even of those goods that are of a noneconomic nature. Money is not content with being just another final purpose of life alongside wisdom and art, personal significance and strength, beauty and love; but in so far as money does adopt this position it gains the power to reduce other purposes to the level of means."[22] Anticipating a Freudian language of wish and fulfillment accomplished through money, Simmel identifies greed as the point of oversatisfaction: "The greatest discrepancy between wish and fulfillment exists, the exact reverse takes place if the psychological character of money as a final purpose has become permanently solidified and greed, too, has become a chronic condition."[23]

The end point of Simmel's psychology of greed is a transformed relationship to all objects (but especially money): "The abstract character of money, its remoteness from any specific enjoyment in and for itself, supports an objective delight in money [for those 'greedy for money'], in the awareness of a value that extends far beyond all individual and personal enjoyment of its benefits."[24] The issue was acutely obvious when considering misers, who experience a transformed relationship to money conditioned by its abstract qualities. For misers,

> Money is kept outside of this personal sphere which is taboo to him. To him, money is an object of timid respect. The miser loves money as one loves a highly admired person who makes us happy simply by his existence and by our knowing him and being with him, without our relation to him as an individual taking the form of concrete enjoyment. In so far as, from the outset, the miser consciously forgoes the use of money as a means towards any specific enjoyment, he places money at an unbridgeable distance from his subjectivity, a distance that he nevertheless constantly attempts to overcome through the awareness of his ownership.[25]

When Simmel dwelled specifically on the psychological mechanisms of avarice, he objectified money and considered the emotional connections that misers formed between themselves and their love objects. "Money builds a bridge between people and objects," Simmel claims.[26] "In crossing this bridge, the mind experiences the attraction of their possession even if it does in fact not attain it."[27] Misers experience a peculiar relationship to unspent money: their "sense of power must be more profound and more valuable than any control over specific things could ever be."[28] Money has a kind of "potential value"— what you could buy with it—and a "kinetic" value (to borrow from the mechanical language of physics).

Avarice and greed operate at different ends of the spectrum. Poggi too is struck by the way Simmel identifies a "final cluster of properties of money" that centers on "its 'potentiality.'"[29] Avarice deflects appropriate emotional connection to things. For the miser, objects resist what Simmel calls "passionate ownership" and produce deep feelings of dissatisfaction.[30] Money subverts this emotional endgame, because money's fungibility allows us to own it "completely and without reservations; it is only money that merges completely into the function we assign to it. The miser's pleasures must be aesthetically similar to this."[31] Greed for money, an emotion that in Simmel's estimation may "discharge ... itself quite formlessly and with a growing intensity," develops a curious cathectic diffuseness because it remains unattached to specific entities or objects.[32]

Acceding to the idea that in some conditions "possession equals freedom" in the sense that ownership allows one to exploit an object's use value, Simmel nonetheless recognizes in greed and avarice a perversion of this principle.[33] When greed "pass[es] beyond" the point of recognizing and enjoying the use of an object, problems arise: "It reveals its absurdity both in the lack of satisfaction that is part of its own fulfillment, and in the occasional constraint and restriction with which an excess of possessions turns into the opposite of their original character and goal."[34]

Simmel's *Philosophy of Money* produces a rich and exciting way of understanding greed and avarice around the turn of the twentieth century. His candid assessment of greed and avarice as socially and culturally defined behaviors, the point at which a person transcends the permeable boundaries of acceptable behavior, not only produces a valuable theoretical insight into the problem of greed, but it also engenders a valuable historical insight as well. Simmel wrote his text at the high point of the European social sciences, a period during which Europeans assumed that they could learn and know everything if only they applied scientific methods to the project of producing knowledge.

Simmel provides an effective pre-Freudian psychology of money in this text, and he is comfortable discussing the "personality's direct relationship to money" as well as "psychological states" in the *Philosophy of Money*.[35] His reliance on concepts that Freud would popularize and the way this text is laden with terms that anticipate psychoanalytic ones (psychology, wish, desire, etc.) allows us to connect Simmel's rationalist discourse on greed with the psychoanalytic ones that were produced just before the first edition of *Philosophy of Money* was published in 1900 and concurrent with the production of the second edition in 1907.

In a letter written to Wilhelm Fliess in January 1897, the year following the publication of Simmel's first papers on the philosophy of money, Sigmund Freud situated his emerging understanding of modern greed alongside powerfully magical figures of the sixteenth century, reinforcing once again the idea that the modern and the magical were not necessarily antitheses of one another. Freud wrote on 24 January 1897 about an idea, a way of understanding money and its symbolic valences, and he did this by tracing various connections back in time to the sixteenth century and before: "The idea of bringing in witches is gaining strength," Freud writes,

> I think it is also appropriate. Details are beginning to abound. Their "flying" is explained; the broomstick they ride probably is the great Lord Penis.... I read one day that the gold the devil gives his victims regularly turns into excrement; and the next day Mr. E., who reports that his nurse had money deliria, suddenly told me (by way of Cagliostro—alchemist—*Dukatenscheisser* [the shitter of ducats]) that Louise's money always was excrement. So in the witch stories it is merely transformed back into the substance from which it arose.

He goes on: "If only I knew why the devil's semen is always described as 'cold' in the witches' confessions. I have ordered the *Malleus maleficarum*, and now that I have put the final touch on the infantile paralyses I shall study it diligently. The story of the devil, the vocabulary of popular swear words, the songs and customs of the nursery—all these are now gaining significance for me."[36]

Freud's interpretations of greed and avarice proved to be tremendously influential in the first part of the twentieth century, when psychoanalytic categories appeared to offer a new way of understanding and interpreting behavior. We turn now to consider the suite of associations that developed in Freud's thinking about greed.

Freud's conclusions about the psychosexual origins of greed and the way he approached the issue from the standpoint of health and development provide a key to understanding twentieth-century approaches to greed. It is important to see how Freud's theories—oriented first around a discussion of individual traits but then broadened into "characterological" ones that could be applied to entire populations of people—were embraced over the course of the first half of the twentieth century. One characteristic element of twentieth-century greed, then, was its inclusion in medical discourses that reframed older questions about religion, morality, and behavior as something that could be apprehended through medicine.

If psychoanalysis was to succeed as a legitimate field of inquiry, its practitioners had to assume a position of scientific authority, its professional borders rigorously policed, and references to the occult tradition banished. Freud adopted psychology and psychoanalysis, rather than psychical research, in his attempt to understand the medical basis of greed, a project that unfolded over the course of the first decade of the twentieth century.[37] In *The Interpretation of Dreams* (1900), he elaborated further on the connections between money and dirt that he had proposed earlier in the letter to Fliess. Writing about a patient who has difficulty paying for her treatments, Freud suggests that the thought of paying for the analyst's time was "avaricious or *filthy*. (Uncleanliness in childhood is often replaced in dreams by avariciousness for money; the link between the two is the word 'filthy.')"[38]

The topic surfaced again in Freud's "Psychopathology of Everyday Life" (1901) in which he notes his own tendency to avoid paying bills, concluding that greed and acquisitive desire may be the root cause: "It may perhaps be generally true that the primitive greed of the suckling, who wants to take possession of every object (in order to put it into his mouth), has only been incompletely overcome by civilization and upbringing."[39] These brief descriptions of retention and acquisition appeared early in Freud's thinking about avarice and greed.

While Freud's attention was dedicated to the production of self-knowledge in the first part of the 1900s, his attention was drawn more insistently to the psychodynamics of greed beginning in 1907. In the process of his work with patients in the first decade of the twentieth century, Freud developed an entire theory of emotional development, and he located the etiology of greedy behavior in the ways children experienced relationships with certain areas of their bodies. For Freud, greed developed in people due to a flaw in psychosexual development associated with control over excretion.

In the last months of 1907 Freud participated in the analysis of a patient since known as the "Rat Man," due to the significance of rats in his instance. The case, finally published in 1909 as "Notes upon a Case of Obsessional Neurosis," centered on a man who had a number of different difficulties but whose vexed relationships with family members, especially his father, were expressed through a series of fantastical scenarios in which rats, collected in a sack, would be attached to his exposed posterior. The rats, he feared, would attack his anus, chewing their way painfully into his interior. The "Notes" as well as the notebooks Freud produced during the analysis and published later as "Process Notes for the Case History" provide evidence for the ways that Freud began to attach greed and miserly behavior more and more insistently to the anal zone. In October 1907 Freud notes that his patient "is beginning to act like a miser, though he has no such inclination."[40]

On 26 November Freud described a series of what he calls "anal phantasies" expressed by his patient, which, for Freud, were crucially linked to retention. He argues after hearing a particularly descriptive fantasy of his patient having sex with Freud's daughter "by means of a stool hanging from his anus" that "he [the patient] was probably one of those infants who retain their faeces."[41] Three days later, rats and money came to be connected in the case, in part through a complex German homophone that linked rats (*Ratten*) and financial installments (*Raten*). Freud reported in the case notes, "He [the patient] has a great deal of annoyance over money matters with his friends (giving security, etc.). He would dislike it very much if the situation turned in the direction of money. Rats have a special connection with money.... He now pays in rats.—Rat currency."[42]

Two weeks later the issue resurfaced in the analysis, and the patient connected sex, rats, incest, and money, which "shows that rats are something which is payable."[43] Finally Freud felt he had cracked open the case by understanding the psychoanalytic processes at work in the production of his patient's miserliness. On 19 December Freud wrote, "His miserliness is now explained" and could be chalked up to the pecuniary interest his father had taken in his bride-to-be's dowry, and this "made him [the patient] detest the poverty which drives people into such crimes."[44] In the end the Rat Man's treatment was declared a success, his obsessions diminished, and the treatment was concluded in January 1908. The ability to track this particular patient was frustrated by the patient's death in the Great War.

Freud's treatment of the Rat Man at the end of 1907 established a constellation of theoretical insights into avarice and greed for Freud that he collected and published in March 1908 as an essay titled "Character and Anal Eroticism." The essay, short as it is, has proven to be an enduring and influential piece. Freud argues in the essay that the origin of character traits—adult behaviors— may be discovered in psychosexual development, and he notes in particular those people who display "a regular combination of the three following characteristics. They are especially *orderly* [*Ordentlich*], *parsimonious* [*Sparsam*] and *obstinate* [*Eigensinnig*]."⁴⁵ He defined parsimony as an exaggerated form of avarice [*Geize*]."⁴⁶ These adult behaviors, Freud believed, could be traced to specific events in the development of the child that were most acutely demonstrated during the period of time in which the child developed control over his or her bowels.

Potty training, in other words, had profound implications for the ways people later responded psychologically to money and behaved socially toward it. Freud believed by examining case studies that people who demonstrated that suite of characteristics that came to be known as the "anal personality type" successfully completed toilet training later than typical, and as children Freud reports that they "derive[d] a subsidiary pleasure from defecaeting; for they tell us that even in somewhat later years they enjoyed holding back their stool, and they remembered—though more readily about their brothers and sisters than about themselves—doing all sorts of unseemly things with the faeces that had been passed."⁴⁷ Freud concludes from these case studies that "such people are born with a sexual constitution in which the erotogenicity of the anal zone is exceptionally strong."⁴⁸

Freud believed that this strong anality is sublimated in the course of development through shaming mechanisms, feelings of (self-)disgust, and so on. The resulting deformations of development result in certain specific behaviors: "It is therefore plausible to suppose that these character traits of orderliness, parsimony and obstinacy, which are so often prominent in people who were formerly anal erotics, are to be regarded as the first and most constant results of the sublimation of anal eroticism."⁴⁹ These connections remain deeply entrenched in a person's psyche, Freud thought, and they linger powerfully over the course of a lifetime even though the connections between the "complexes of interest in money and of defaecation ... seem so dissimilar."⁵⁰

In terms of a larger trajectory of development over the course of a lifetime, the pathway was obvious to Freud: "The original erotic interest in defaecation is, as we know, destined to be extinguished in later years. In those years the interest in money makes its appearance as a new interest which had been absent in childhood. This makes it easier for the earlier impulsion, which is in process of losing its aim, to be carried over to the newly emerging aim."⁵¹ One ramification of the Rat Man's course of treatment was to produce for Freud a set of ideas about the psychodynamic implications of different parts of the anatomy. The anus, because of the powerful connections between that part of the body, money, and excrement, helped determine a person's later relationship to financial issues. Offering a judgment about human development quite different from the psychological dimensions that Simmel perceived in a person's relationship to money, Freud nonetheless offered a way to trace the effects of the body on a person's later behaviors.

"Character and Anal Eroticism" was a blockbuster, a stunning proclamation of how the hidden transformations of childhood haunted the lives of adults. The Vienna Psychoanalytic Society naturally followed Freud's lead in the matter, and its members pushed Freud's analysis further, seeking other bodily origins of greedy behaviors. The minutes of the meeting of the Society held on 13 May 1908 indicate the ways Freud's ideas about the anal personality type and the anus's relationship to money were received by his disciples. Alfred Adler "recounts the case of a woman who suffers in springtime from early morning vomiting and ructation. After some interviews it became evident that this was a case of avarice; thus, avarice can sometimes hide behind vomiting."[52] Otto Rank, the minutes note, "remarks that some time ago he already had had the opportunity to observe a case showing the connection between avarice and vomiting. He is inclined to postulate such a connection for all excretory functions; he knows cases in which the passing of urine or semen was connected with avarice."[53]

Over the course of the following year the ideas continued to be worked out, but the basic premise remained intact: avarice stemmed from, and could be symptomized by, the actions of a part of the body. Rank reported in a meeting of the group on 7 April 1909, "In *avarice*, we find a curious analogue to the character of the masturbator—specifically in frugality, which includes the passion to collect. Indeed, the link with money is by no means characteristic of the anal zone alone."[54] Adler countered in June 1909 with the report that avarice could be linked "back to sensitivity. On the other hand, this sensitivity is strengthened by the causes for the development of an anal character. Ultimately, sensitivity goes back to a fear of soiling, which in the earliest childhood years surely represents a phenomenon of civilization, and goes directly back to the anal character."[55]

Sándor Ferenczi, another colleague of Freud's, took the principle seriously as well, arguing in his essay "Introjection and Transference" (1909) "that the money complex, transferred to the treatment, is often only the cover for more deeply hidden impulses [avarice, ruthless selfishness, ignoble covetousness] Freud has established in a masterly characterological study ('Charakter und Analerotik')."[56] Secure in the support of his colleagues, Freud sought further examples of the principle that the anus, avarice, and a fear of filth were connected. In his 1910 essay "Leonardo da Vinci and a Memory of His Childhood," Freud wonders if the "forms of expression in which Leonardo's repressed libido was allowed to show itself—circumstantially and concern over money—are among the traits of character which result from anal eroticism."[57]

Freud undertook a longer discussion of the central thesis of "Character and Anal Eroticism" in his 1914 essay "Anal Eroticism and the Castration Complex" (publication was delayed until 1918 as a result of the Great War). The patient in this case, known popularly as the "Wolf Man" because of the content of a dream that Freud analyzes in the course of his treatment, suffers a range of problems, including constipation and, Freud decides later, an oedipal disorder. The Wolf Man was under Freud's care from the summer of 1910 to the outbreak of the war. Our interest in the case focuses in the issue of money and avarice and how Freud discusses these issues in relation to the Wolf Man and his treatment.

Freud writes, referencing his 1908 essay, "We are accustomed to trace back interest in money, in so far as it is of a libidinal and not of a rational character, to excretory pleasure, and we expect normal people to keep their relations to money entirely free from libidinal influences and regulate them according to the demands of reality."[58] Freud notes the Wolf Man's relationship with money, and labels him a "miser" and "spendthrift" but is unsure which term is most appropriate.[59] The interesting section of Freud's report for our purposes centers on the way that Freud reinforced the links he perceived between adult behaviors and childhood development. Ruminating on the psychosexual development of the Wolf Man, Freud connected gift and gift giving with the excremental process.

The Wolf Man, Freud writes, made "use of the content of the intestines in one of its earliest and most primitive meanings. Faeces are the child's first *gift*, the first sacrifice on behalf of his affections, a portion of his own body which he is ready to part with, but only for the sake of some one he loves."[60] Following a series of symbolic chains that develop out of his analysis of the Wolf Man Freud produces two sets of triple connections. The first links money, feces, and babies: "Money can take over the meaning of baby and can thus become the means of expressing feminine (homosexual) satisfaction."[61] The second connection—feces, babies, and the penis—allows Freud to take up the problem of castration.

In each of these cases, however, money and avarice retain significant and powerful positions as markers or symptoms of more deeply experienced feelings about the anus. The logic of this second set of connections form a section of the analysis that Freud produces in his 1915 essay "On the Transformations of Instinct as Exemplified in Anal Eroticism," in which he again argues that the three qualities of avarice, pedantry, and obstinacy "spring from anal-erotic sources."[62] He argues in the essay that both excrement and babies are perceived as a "gift" or a "sacrifice" given to loved ones. Freud writes, "The interest in faeces is continued partly as interest in money, partly as a wish for a baby, in which latter an anal-erotic and a genital impulse ('envy for a penis') converge."[63] Many of the central pillars of Freudianism—anal eroticism, Oedipus, castration anxiety, penis envy—can be usefully examined within the context of Freud's changing understanding of the bodily origins of financial desire.

As Freud began to issue the summary statements of his career in the 1920s— texts like *The Future of an Illusion* (1927) and *Civilization and its Discontents*

(1930)—he continued to advance the basic thesis that there were powerful connections between behavior (and financial behavior specifically) and the ways that the body was cathected over the course an individual's psychosexual development. While avarice might be interpreted by Freud as antisocial behavior that may be successfully repressed among "civilized peoples," others "do not deny themselves the satisfaction of their avarice, their aggressive urges or their sexual lusts, and … do not hesitate to injure other people by lies, fraud and calumny, so long as they can remain unpunished for it; and this, no doubt, has always been so through many ages of civilization."[64] In *Civilization and Its Discontents*, Freud takes up the question of understanding what he calls "the economic task of our lives," which he traces to "the anal eroticism of young human beings."[65]

Reproducing his argument from 1908, Freud argues, "Their [young human beings] original interest in the excretory function, its organs and products, is changed in the course of their growth into a group of traits which are familiar to us as parsimony, a sense of order and cleanliness—qualities which, though valuable and welcome in themselves, may be intensified till they become markedly dominant and produce what is called the anal character."[66] In another remarkable passage Freud contrasts the money economy with one based on differentiated material possessions. "Aggressiveness was not created by property," Freud argues.[67] "It reigned almost without limit in primitive times, when property was still very scanty, and it already shows itself in the nursery almost before property has given up its primal, anal form; it forms the basis of every relation of affection and love among people (with the single exception, perhaps, of the mother's relation to her male child."[68]

One of the ways that Freud demonstrated the validity of his ideas about the equation of excrement and wealth was through a frequent recitation of psychomythological statements. The link between gold and excrement was "supported by copious evidence from social anthropology," Freud suggests in *Interpretation of Dreams*, citing work from Otto Rank ("Die Sybolischichtung im Wecktraum und ihre Wiederkehr im mythischen Denken"), Ernst Dattner ("Gold und Kot"), and Theodor Reik ("Gold und Kot") to support the claim.[69] Because the connection between excrement and money was perhaps an outrageous one, Freud carefully identified the multiple ways that the two terms had been linked in the past.

"Wherever archaic modes of thought have predominated or persist," Freud writes in the essay, "in the ancient civilization, in myths, fairy tales and superstitions, in unconscious thinking, in dreams and in neuroses—money is brought into the most intimate relationship with dirt."[70] Demonomania appears in the passage, as do occult treasure hunting and the "shitter of ducats" (*Dukatenscheisser*). "Indeed," Freud concludes, "even according to ancient Babylonian doctrine gold is the 'the faeces of Hell' (Mammon = ilu manman)."[71] Freud's work with

David Oppenheim in what could be called comparative psychomythology was also drawn, again and again, to peasant life and the presumably early modern sensibilities that nineteenth-century central European peasants displayed.

One essay titled "Dreams in Folklore," probably composed in 1911 with Oppenheim (but lost and published only in 1958), is built upon source material drawn from Friedrich Krauss's *Anthropophyteia* (4 volumes) that included contributions from Franz Boas and Ernst Bloch. The essay proposes to uncover the age-old cultural belief that "gold, according to ancient oriental mythology, is the excrement of hell."[72] And "In dreams in folklore gold is seen in the most unambiguous way to be a symbol of faeces," a conclusion that Freud certainly felt supported his larger claims about the "anal character" of the greedy. If the connection between money and excrement was a timeless and universal one, then perhaps so too were the claims about the development of character traits from the psychosexual development of children.

Freud's interest in the psychomythological connections between past cultural forms and present displays of financial behavior that had been powerfully conditioned by the ways an individual experienced his or her body in development remained limited in their effectiveness because he never explained fully how the symbolic connections between excrement and money were reproduced over time. His disciple Sándor Ferenczi filled this lacuna with an influential essay first published in 1914 titled "The Ontogenesis of the Interest in Money." Ferenczi set out in the essay "to examine the question of whether, and to what extent, individual experience favours the transformation of anal-erotic interest into interest in money."[73]

Ferenczi accepted the basic premise of Freud's 1908 essay, and he attempts to isolate the connections between money and excrement as a culturally encoded set of symbols going far back into the past. Specifically Ferenczi identifies a set of symbolic relationships about money, excrement, and value and then considers how those symbols come to be embodied. His argument begins with an image of the self-constipated child: "The excrementa thus held back are really the first 'savings' of the growing being, and as such remain in a constant, unconscious inter-relationship with every bodily activity or mental striving that has anything to do with collecting, hoarding, and saving."[74]

As the child begins to learn to walk he or she transfers this interest in excrement to an interest in mud, which Ferenczi notes bears a similar smell and texture but has been rendered less disgusting because repressive forms have not been established in such a strong way. As mud becomes objectionable through a refined sense of cleanliness, the child forms an interest in sand— filth is "dehydrated." Sand becomes a problem and instead Ferenczi argues that the child forms an interest in rocks and pebbles. "After stones," Ferenczi writes, "comes the turn of artificial products, and with these the detachment of the interest from earth is complete. Glass marbles, buttons, fruit pips, are eagerly collected—this time no longer only for the sake of their intrinsic value, but as measures of value, so to speak as primitive coins, converting the previous barter exchange of children into an enthusiastic money exchange."[75]

From the "first savings" collected by the anal-erotic toddler to the child collector, the supple transformation of excrement into money was complete in the capitalist money economy. "The character of capitalism, however, not purely practical and utilitarian, but libidinous and irrational, is betrayed in this stage also: the child decidedly enjoys the collecting in itself."[76] Max Weber's essays on the "spirit" of capitalism (which were published ten years before Ferenczi's essay) located the origins of twentieth-century economic behavior in early modern theology, specifically Calvin's doctrines. Ferenczi attacked the problem by medicalizing the "character" of capitalism, locating its origins in psychosexual development.

Ferenczi completed the characterological sequence by suggesting that stones could not for long suffice to entertain the collecting and bartering practices of children. "Even stones begin to wound the child's feeling of cleanliness—he longs for something purer—and this is offered to him in the shining pieces of money, the high appreciation of which is naturally also in part due to the respect in which they are held by adults, as well as to the seductive possibilities of obtaining through them everything that the child's heart can desire."[77]

The final station for this remarkable train of thought is that "pleasure in the intestinal contents becomes enjoyment of money, which, however, after what has been said is seen to be nothing other than odourless, dehydrated filth that has been made to shine."[78] Money itself is revealed to be coded excrement: "But whatever form may be assumed by money, the enjoyment at possessing it has its deepest and amplest source in coprophilia."[79] Satisfied with his argument, Ferenczi reproduced aspects of it in further essays such as "The Psychic Consequences of a 'Castration' in Childhood" (1916/17)[80] and "Composite Formations of Erotic and Character Traits" (1916/17), in which he "could confirm a marked avarice [in a series of case studies] ... (avarice—anal character + filth—anal eroticism)"[81]

Two case studies from 1917 further confirmed for Ferenczi the close connections between miserly behavior, excrement, and money that Freud identified. In "Pecunia Olet" Ferenczi relates the case of a man who is engaged to a wealthy woman but is tempted to break off the engagement when he kisses his fiancée and experiences an unpleasant odor. Ferenczi notes, "an evidently insignificant odour from the lady's mouth became associated with the patient's primitive anal eroticism from which was derived his love of money; he was nigh owning to himself that he was about to marry for money; he wished to escape from this possibility as anxiously as he did from his own badly repressed anal erotic impulses."[82]

The second case concerned a woman who jilted one fiancé in order to marry a richer man. When she meets the first man by chance, he kisses her hand, but she has just come from the bathroom and is intensely anxious that her hands will smell. Ferenczi's conclusion is that the "sentence, money does *not* smell, is a euphemistic reversal. In the unconscious it is certainly: *pecunia olet*, that is money = filth."[83]

Reflecting in a 1926 essay "Present-Day Problems in Psychoanalysis," Ferenczi remarked on the development of characterology, noting in particular the ways that psychoanalysts had seen greed and avarice as emotions produced by different libidinal forces. In ways that Freud never directly commented, Ferenczi identifies in the essay the differing psychological dimensions of greed and avarice. Like Simmel before him, Ferenczi indicates greed and avarice as having distinct etiologies. Greed reflects a disorder of the oral phase, avarice one of the anal one.

Accumulation and retention stem from different psychological principles. Ferenczi argues in this essay that the "resolving of anal-eroticism, for instance, results in the development of quite distinct anal character traits: cleanliness, avarice, obstinacy, pedantry, ceremoniousness. From the oral-libidinal phase develops, on the one hand, the character trait of greed, perhaps also jealousy, and probably also a need for tenderness, whereas the anal character traits remain connected in their primary amalgamation with hate and sadism."[84]

Freud was held in high esteem, and his ideas have held undeniable sway for the past century. Still, it remains to be seen how Freud's ideas about the avaricious character were incorporated into larger intellectual systems in the first half of the twentieth century. We can gauge aspects of this story by examining how the psycho- and characterological analysis of greed appeared in the work of three of Freud's fellow travelers: Ernest Jones, Erich Fromm, and Joan Riviere. Ernest Jones was responsible for importing Freud into the British intellectual scene, and he and Freud remained friends after 1914 despite the ways that the Great War disrupted intellectual networks in Europe. Jones took up the question of the persistence of economic irrationality in his 1918 essay "Anal-Erotic Character Traits," arguing, "All collectors are anal erotics, and the objects collected are nearly always topical copro-symbols."[85]

Jones also provides a long list of practices demonstrating the psychopathology of everyday life in relationship to miserliness: people who collect money or books, people who hoard food, people who cannot bear to part with coins; people who refuse to do their laundry or who ritually re-use their underwear. Jones asserts that in his view, "When such people are compelled to part with more than they are willing to, they display the reaction of annoyance and resentment discussed earlier in this paper: thus, when money is stolen from them, and particularly when it is stolen by their being given 'bad'—i.e., 'rotten'—money—

that is, when they are made to excrete against their will."[86] With Jones we may see a tighter description of miserly behaviors in the first part of the twentieth century. Divorced from the strange fantasies of the Rat and Wolf Men, different from Ferenczi's meticulous account of the transformation of excrement into money, Jones provided an assessment of greed that included the more or less hidden behaviors of the anal-erotic's fruitless quest to retain his or her money.

The basic social unit for Freud, Ferenczi, and Jones was the individual. Erich Fromm broadened his characterological study of the financial implications of anal eroticism to include bourgeois society as a whole. In an essay published in the Frankfurt School's *Zeitschrift für Sozialforschung* in 1932, Fromm noted the anal character traits first identified by Freud in 1908 of "orderliness, parsimony, and obstinacy" and attempted to similarly apply these insights in order to understand society as a whole. Fromm sought to uncover which traits were privileged in modern mass capitalist society. Like other intellectuals associated with the Frankfurt School, Fromm attempts a fusion of Marxist and Freudian social analysis. Such a method, it was thought, would use psychoanalysis to understand the broader historical development and maturation of base/superstructure relationships.

The basic thrust of the essay is Fromm's insight that anal eroticism was peculiarly connected to and displayed in bourgeois society. Both as consumers and as workers, the development of a society of anal erotics was equally productive of and produced by modern capitalism. The character of an ideal worker ("orderliness, punctuality, cleanliness, and stinginess") was produced through anal eroticism, as was a type of ideal consumer: the "continuation of the original love for feces, which finds expression primarily in love for possessions."[87]

Indeed, the "acquisitive personality" not only was linked to anal eroticism but also found its economic corollary in modern capitalism. As Fromm wrote, "The problem of the 'spirit'—i.e., the psychic basis—of capitalism seems to be a particularly suitable example for two reasons. First, because the most relevant part of psychoanalytic characterology for an understanding of the bourgeois spirit—the theory about the anal character—happens to be the most developed part of psychoanalytic characterology."[88] Referencing Isador Isaak Sadger, Fromm claims, "'Anything that is not Me is dirt.' Such people enjoy a possession only if no one else has anything like it. They are inclined to regard everything in life as property and to protect everything that is 'private' from outside invasions. This attitude does not apply to money and possessions only; it also applies to human beings, feelings, memories, and experiences."[89]

Since capitalism is often understood as the larger operational working out of a sequence of individual decisions, Fromm's insight into the larger economic ramification of a society of anal erotics is a significant attempt to come to terms with the larger machinery of capitalism. The "anal function [is the] most important productive activity," Fromm explains, and then he asserts, "Earning money, accumulating possessions, amassing bits and pieces of knowledge without transforming them into something productive—all these are expressions of this attitude."[90] The implications for a capitalist economy and society are profound: "In marked cases of anal character formation, almost all the relationships of life are viewed in terms of having (keeping) and giving; i.e., in terms of possessions."[91]

Possessions were only one aspect of the problem for Fromm, however, and he also argued, "Parsimony and avarice do not relate solely to money and monetary values. Time and energy are treated in a similar way, and such people abhor any waste of either."[92] The trajectory of the argument was clear: "If we compare these character traits with the typical traits of the anal character ..., we can readily see that there seems to be a wide spectrum of agreement and correspondence ... the typical libidinal structure of bourgeois man is characterized by an intensification of the anal libido."[93] Fromm is unclear whether the capitalist economy produced anal eroticism or anal eroticism produced a capitalist economy, and he advocated further research into the problem.

Fromm picked up the thread he started in 1932 with an essay titled "Psychoanalytic Characterology and Its Application to the Understanding of Culture" that was published in 1949 as part of the *Culture and Personality* volume edited by psychologists S. Stansfeld Sargent and Marian W. Smith. Fromm begins by reasserting the basic premise of Freud's 1908 text and argues that it represented a significant shift in our understanding of behavior because "in order to understand and to cure a symptom one has to understand the total character structure."[94] Elevated from a mere symptom to a character type, the miserly anal-erotic developed an identifiable relationship to the people and things that he or she confronted in life. Fromm suggests, "What Freud called the anal character can be understood as a particular kind of relatedness to the world."[95] Autarchic, even paranoid, the anal character was embodied by a "person withdrawn, living in a fortified position, whose aim is to ward off all outside influences and to avoid letting anything from this entrenched position be carried into the outside world."[96] The anal personality type is most deeply experienced through a condition of absolute alienation because "isolation spells security ... [and] stinginess is an attempt to fortify this person's isolated position, to make it as strong as possible, and not to let anything go out of this entrenched position."[97] We have seen how the embellishment and refinement of Freud's understanding of the origins of greed that was carried out over the first part of the twentieth century focused on the anal zone and the ways it governed behavior. However, the views of other psychoanalysts, especially those of women, provide a usefully diverse range of opinion on the matter.

Joan Riviere was one of Freud's interlocutors, and she translated a number of his texts into English. She was colleagues with Ernest Jones and an early supporter of and collaborator with Melanie Klein. Her work with Klein is especially important to our discussion, particularly a public lecture that Riviere gave in 1937 titled "Greed, Hate, and Aggression" that was then published alongside Klein's work "Love, Hate, and Reparation."[98] The essay is framed by the analysis of greed, and in this sense Riviere offered a different, if not necessarily more finely tuned, set of insights from Freud's. Like her mentor, Riviere accepted the idea that economic desires and decisions stemmed from psychosexual development. Unfulfilled desires, she argues, are met with a sense of loss and aggression. Unsatisfied desires, she believed, could be experienced as an attack. Importantly this "human reaction has a real bearing on economic questions; it is well known that a lack of the means of subsistence in peoples and classes rouses their aggression, unless they are in a condition of hopeless apathy, despair and inertia."[99] These deeply felt emotions, however, did not stem from toilet training, but progressed from an earlier moment in development. Greed, she felt, stemmed from the original relationship with the mother. When feeding goes badly, the baby erupts in rage and aggression because of the demonstrated position of dependence and helplessness. For Klein and Riviere alike, it is important to note the central position of the breast and the nipple rather than the anus or genitals as prime locations of psychic energy. While not necessarily feminist in orientation, Riviere's argument that the psychic origins of greed could be found in the access to or denial of the breast remains innovative. The implications are clear: "The hate and aggression, envy, jealousy and greed felt and expressed by grown-up people are all derivatives, and usually extremely complicated derivatives, both of this primary experience [frustrated suckling] and of the necessity to master it if we are to survive and secure any pleasure at all in life."[100] Avarice and retention, then, have little to do with the anus in Riviere's estimation but exist as inward forms of greed. Miserliness stems from frustration derived by the denial of the breast. "In the miser and the recluse," she argues, "we see that a dissatisfaction with the source of life has almost poisoned life itself for them, as they turned from it; and their vindictive disappointment often vents itself in the few relations with the rest of the world that they cannot avoid."[101]

Acquisition remains the key category and psychic drive; retention is subsidiary. Greed may operate, in fact, as a defense against "disintegration within [and the] connection of greed and acquisitiveness with *security* is in any case evident."[102] For Riviere, this means that greed is in some ways a consequence of being human. "Some measure of greed exists unconsciously in everyone," she writes. "It represents an aspect of the desire to live, which mingled and fused at the outset of life with the impulse to turn aggression and destructiveness outside ourselves against others, and as such it persists unconsciously throughout life. By its very nature it is endless and never assuaged; and being a form of the impulse to live, it ceases only with death."[103]

Acquisition is a curiously powerful drive that encapsulated for Riviere a suite of positive attributes. She offers first a wide-ranging definition of greed: "The longing or greed for good things can relate to any and every imaginable kind of good—material possessions, bodily or mental gifts, advantages and privileges."[104] The satisfaction of these desires culminates as "proofs to us, if we get them, that we are ourselves good, and full of good, and so are worthy of love, or respect and honour, in return. Thus they serve as proofs and insurances against our fears of the emptiness inside ourselves, or of our evil impulses which make us feel bad and full of badness to ourselves and others. They also defend us against our fear of the retaliation, punishment or retribution which may be carried out against us by others, whether in material or in moral ways, or in our affections and love-relations."[105] Greed is ultimately life affirming, a confirmation that our mothers do indeed love us.

Riviere's promotion of the breast/mouth symbiosis as the psychic mechanism by which acquisitive and greedy emotions are generated will remind many readers of *Anti-Oedipus*, published in France in 1972. While Gilles Deleuze and Felix Guattari ignore Riviere in favor of Melanie Klein and Wilhelm Reich in the writing of their book, the similarities in their arguments remain striking. "Desire," according to Deleuze and Guattari, is the "abject fear of lacking something."[106] This insight allows the pair to imagine how the psychodynamics of capitalist interaction might proceed, and their famous analysis of schizoid "desiring-machines" remains a popular critical assessment of the psychological ramifications of capitalism.

Deleuze and Guattari were explicit in their rejection of many aspects of Freudian orthodoxy (most obviously in their rejection of Oedipus), but they also questioned the premise of Freud's 1908 essay "Character and Anal Eroticism." "As long as we are content," they write, "to establish a perfect parallel between money, gold, capital, and the capitalist triangle on the one hand, and the libido, the anus, the phallus, and the family triangle on the other, we are engaging in an enjoyable pastime."[107] "The Marx-Freud parallelism between the two remains utterly sterile and insignificant as long as it is expressed in terms that make them introjections or projections of each other without ceasing to be utterly alien to each other, as in the famous equation money = shit."[108]

The solution to understanding the psychology of capitalism, and the answer to the question of whether capitalism produced anal erotics or if it was the other way around, was located in the historical production of desires. "We maintain that the social field is immediately invested by desire, that it is the historically determined product of desire, and that libido has no need of any mediation or sublimation, any psychic operation, any transformation, in order to invade and invest the productive forces and the relations of production. *There is only desire and the social, and nothing else.*"[109]

The previous chapter opened with Adorno's dismay at the presence of the occult in the modern economy, and this one finishes with Deleuze and Guattari's attempt to reenvision the inner logic of capitalism through a schizoanalysis that consciously avoids Freud's and Fromm's conclusions about the psychic energies of capitalism being generated by the anal zone. We may see a number of forces collide and diverge between 1875, when Blavatsky founded the Theosophical Society and unleashed a torrent of esoteric and instrumental magic that at least pretended not to wish for wealth, and 1972, when Deleuze and Guattari unleashed a torrent of esoteric and instrumental theory that also pretended to critique capitalism.

The charge that decadent writers were a collection of degenerates is nothing new, of course, and Nordau should hardly be seen as a friend of anyone but the most repressive, but to his credit he did—in his conservative way—address a central component of the modern capitalist system: greed and the oniomaniac, whose urge to buy useless things makes him or her a figure of pity. Georg Simmel's *Philosophy of Money* represented a point of radical transition in the nineteenth- and twentieth-century's understanding of financial desire. His insight that greed and avarice were competing psychological mechanisms that were understood best in social and cultural context represents a significant departure, even from those like Nordau, who relied on psychological descriptions to make his arguments. Although still fixed on the individual as the key social unit that experiences the emotion, Simmel produced an analysis of financial desire that allowed contemporary and succeeding critics to envision greed in ways that were simultaneously psychological and social.

When Freud produced a psychoanalytic description of greed, he first associated it with the occult but over time saw anal eroticism—and the avarice that developed from it—as a key to understanding several of the basic behaviors of modern Europeans. The elevation of the symptom to the level of a character indicates another significant transformation in the ways that greed was understood, even within the ambit of Freudian thought. After 1908, avarice would be positioned irretrievably alongside the anus. Erich Fromm, like other Frankfurt School intellectuals, broadened Freud's argument considerably, likening the anal character to the bourgeois character. Joan Riviere, like Deleuze and Guattari, rejected to some degree the emphasis on the anus implicit in these formulations but merely substituted the always-seeking maw of the hungry infant as the key orifice productive of greedy feelings.

Looking closely at these psychological and psychoanalytic theories about the origin and constitution of greed lets us see the ways that greed and avarice were integrated into medical discourse in the twentieth century. The connections between mind, body, health, and behavior that these thinkers identified were also a part of a larger search for the origins of the modern self. Greed—locating its causes and consequences—was the vehicle through which European intellectuals could glimpse the underlying foundations of their own world. Determining the ways greed helped produce the "spirit" or the "character" of modern capitalism along with the object relations, psychological outlooks, and desires upon which it depended was a primary thrust of European intellectual life in the twentieth century. Those understandings of greed, perhaps bizarre at times, constitute a history of the body and of behavior that continue to inform the core elements of Western modernity.

## Notes

1. Max Simon Nordau, *Degeneration* (New York: D. Appleton, 1895), 5.
2. Ibid.
3. Ibid., 27.
4. Ibid.
5. Ibid., 21.
6. Ibid., 27.
7. Ibid.
8. Georg Simmel, *The Philosophy of Money*, 3rd enlarged ed. (London: Routledge, 2004); Max Weber, *The Protestant Ethic and the Spirit of Capitalism*, Routledge Classics (London: Routledge, 2001).
9. Simmel, *Philosophy of Money*, 514.
10. Ibid., 238.
11. Ibid.
12. Ibid.
13. Ibid.
14. Gianfranco Poggi, *Money and the Modern Mind: George Simmel's Philosophy of Money* (Berkeley: University of California Press, 1993), 148.
15. Simmel, *Philosophy of Money*, 258.
16. Ibid.
17. Ibid.
18. Ibid., 239.
19. Ibid.
20. Ibid.
21. Ibid., 239–40.
22. Ibid., 241.
23. Ibid., 243.
24. Ibid., 241.
25. Ibid., 242.
26. Ibid., 327.
27. Ibid.
28. Ibid.
29. Poggi, *Money and the Modern Mind*, 144.
30. Simmel, *Philosophy of Money*, 327.
31. Ibid., 328.
32. Ibid., 249.
33. Ibid., 329.

34. Ibid., 329–30.
35. Ibid., 310, 328.
36. Sigmund Freud, *The Complete Letters of Sigmund Freud to Wilhelm Fliess, 1887–1904* (Cambridge, MA: Belknap Press of Harvard University Press, 1985).
37. Alex Owen, *The Place of Enchantment: British Occultism and the Culture of the Modern* (Chicago: University of Chicago Press, 2007), 6, 142.
38. Sigmund Freud, *The Standard Edition of the Complete Psychological Works of Sigmund Freud* (London: Hogarth Press, 1953–1974), 4: 200.
39. Ibid., 16: 158.
40. Sigmund Freud, *The Freud Reader*, ed. Peter Gay (New York: Norton, 1995), 317.
41. Ibid., 330.
42. Ibid., 331.
43. Ibid., 336.
44. Ibid., 336–37.
45. Freud, *Standard Edition*, 9: 169.
46. Ibid.
47. Ibid., 9: 170.
48. Ibid.
49. Ibid., 9: 171.
50. Ibid., 9: 173.
51. Ibid., 9: 175.
52. Wiener Psychoanalytische Vereinigung, *Minutes of the Vienna Psychoanalytic Society* (New York: International Universities Press, 1962), I: 399.
53. Ibid., I: 400.
54. Ibid., II: 199.
55. Ibid., II: 262.
56. Sándor Ferenczi, *Selected Papers* (New York: Basic Books, 1950), I: 45.
57. Freud, *Standard Edition*, 11: 106.
58. Ibid., 17: 172.
59. Ibid., 17: 173.
60. Ibid., 17: 81.
61. Ibid., 17: 83.
62. Ibid., 17: 127.
63. Ibid., 17: 131.
64. Ibid., 21: 12.
65. Ibid., 21: 96.
66. Ibid.
67. Ibid., 21: 113.
68. Ibid.
69. Ibid., 5: 403.
70. Ibid., 9: 174.
71. Ibid.
72. Freud, "Dreams in Folklore," 187.
73. Sándor Ferenczi, *Sex in Psycho-Analysis*, Contributions to Psycho-Analysis (New York: Dover, 1960), 270.
74. Ibid., 271.
75. Ibid., 275.
76. Ibid.

77. Ibid., 275–76.
78. Ibid., 276.
79. Ibid.
80. Ferenczi, *Selected Papers*, II: 248.
81. Ibid., II: 257.
82. Ibid., II: 362–63.
83. Ibid., II: 364.
84. Ibid., III: 33.
85. Ernest Jones, *Papers on Psycho-Analysis*, 5th ed (Boston: Beacon Press, 1961), 430.
86. Ibid., 429–30.
87. Erich Fromm, *The Crisis of Psychoanalysis* (New York: Holt, Rinehart, Winston, 1970), 142.
88. Ibid., 149.
89. Ibid., 143–44.
90. Ibid., 144.
91. Ibid.
92. Ibid., 146.
93. Ibid., 155.
94. S. Sargent and Marian Wesley Smith, eds., *Culture and Personality*, 25th anniversary ed. (New York: Cooper Square, 1974), 1.
95. Sargent and Smith, *Culture and Personality*, 8.
96. Ibid.
97. Ibid.
98. Melanie Klein and Joan Riviere, *Love, Hate and Reparation* (New York: Norton, 1964).
99. Ibid., 6–7.
100. Ibid., 10.
101. Ibid., 19.
102. Ibid., 26.
103. Ibid., 26–27.
104. Ibid., 27.
105. Ibid.
106. Gilles Deleuze and Félix Guattari, *Anti-Oedipus: Capitalism and Schizophrenia* (Minneapolis: University of Minnesota Press, 1983), 27.
107. Ibid., 28.
108. Ibid., 28–29.
109. Ibid., *Anti-Oedipus*, 29.

# Bibliography

Deleuze, Gilles and Félix Guattari. *Anti-Oedipus: Capitalism and Schizophrenia*. Minneapolis: University of Minnesota Press, 1983.

Ferenczi, Sándor. *Selected Papers*. New York: Basic Books, 1950.

———. *Sex in Psycho-Analysis*. Contributions to Psycho-Analysis. New York: Dover, 1960.

Freud, Sigmund. *The Complete Letters of Sigmund Freud to Wilhelm Fliess, 1887–1904*. Cambridge: Belknap Press of Harvard University Press, 1985.

———. *The Freud Reader*. Edited by Peter Gay. New York: Norton, 1995.

————. *The Standard Edition of the Complete Psychological Works of Sigmund Freud. London.* London: Hogarth, 1953–1974.

Fromm, Erich. *The Crisis of Psychoanalysis.* New York: Holt, Rinehart, Winston, 1970.

Jones, Ernest. *Papers on Psycho-Analysis.* 5th ed. Boston: Beacon Press, 1961.

Klein, Melanie and Joan Riviere. *Love, Hate and Reparation.* New York: Norton, 1964.

Nordau, Max Simon. *Degeneration.* New York: D. Appleton, 1895.

Owen, Alex. *The Place of Enchantment: British Occultism and the Culture of the Modern.* Chicago: University of Chicago Press, 2007.

Poggi, Gianfranco. *Money and the Modern Mind: George Simmel's Philosophy of Money.* Berkeley: University of California Press, 1993.

Sargent, S. and Marian Wesley Smith, eds. *Culture and Personality.* 25th anniversary ed. New York: Cooper Square, 1974.

Simmel, Georg. *The Philosophy of Money.* 3rd enlarged ed. London: Routledge, 2004.

Weber, Max. *The Protestant Ethic and the Spirit of Capitalism.* Routledge Classics. London, Routledge, 2001.

Wiener Psychoanalytische Vereinigung. *Minutes of the Vienna Psychoanalytic Society.* New York: International Universities Press, 1962.

# Conclusions
## Greed and History

Speaking on his "Theory of Symbolism" in the middle of WWI, Ernest Jones applied his psychoanalytic insight to the ways the British were financing the war effort: "Modern economists," he wrote later in the *British Journal of Psychology*,

> know that the idea of wealth means simply "a lien on future labour," and that any counters on earth could be used as a convenient emblem for it just as well as a "gold standard." Metal coins however, and particularly gold, are unconscious symbols of excrement, the material from which most of our sense of possession, in infantile times, was derived. The ideas of possession and wealth, therefore, obstinately adhere to the ideas of "money" and gold for definite psychological reasons, and people simply will not give up the "economist's fallacy" of confounding money with wealth. This superstitious attitude will cost England in particularly many sacrifices after the War, when efforts will probably be made at all costs to reintroduce a gold standard.[1]

Five years later, John Maynard Keynes made a similar point:

> Dr. Freud relates that there are peculiar reasons deep in our subconsciousness why gold in particular should satisfy strong instincts and serve as a symbol. The magical properties with which Egyptian priestrcraft anciently imbued the yellow metal, it has never altogether lost… Of late years the *auri sacra fames* has sought to envelop itself in a garment of respectability as densely respectable as was ever met with, even in the realms of sex or religion. Whether this was first put on as a necessary armour to win the hard-won fight against bimetallism and is still worn, as the gold-advocates allege, because gold is the sole prophylactic against the plague of fiat moneys, or whether it is a furtive Freudian cloak, we need not be curious to inquire.[2]

Jones and Keynes came to the topic of money from very different disciplinary positions, yet each of them connected in their statements the three themes that have animated this book: religion, economics, and health. Arguably, greed is the point of connection, the nexus around which these ideas swirled chaotically.

Greed—occult, degenerate, embodied, psychologized, socialized—remains an operative element of the modern capitalist order but also of its critique. If we take the fields of inquiry that we have considered over the course of this book as distinct avenues of intellectual inquiry—religion, economics, and health— we can ascertain the critical role that criticism of greed and avarice played in the generation of our culture. When we consider the cultural work that greed has performed over the past half millennium, we should be struck by the diverse terrain upon which people saw it displayed. We see greed as part of commercial life, a determinant of one's honor, and a fact of spiritual life. Greed was invoked in legal settings, in international disputes, and as a focus of social relations. Greed was used to distinguish the perfect from the imperfect, the good from the bad, the healthy from the sick; it provided ways to understand the complexities of heaven and hell, appropriate and inappropriate behaviors, balance and chaos.

It is important to note that the ways that greed was presented and discussed over the period of time under consideration in this book did not remain static. If anything, this book challenges the idea of the existence of a single form of greed, one that went from "bad" in the religiously dominated early modern period to "good" in the secular age of "Homo economicus." There was no single story of a vice transformed magically into virtue through the alchemical power of free markets and liberal democracy. Instead of one single historical transformation by which greed became good, a story that everyone claims to know but that is almost certainly wrong, this book has addressed three other prisms through which to view the history of greed.

In our discussions of religion, we saw how greed was used first as a critique of the Christian hierarchy by reformers and then how reformers like Martin Luther and Jean Calvin produced novel theological understandings of desire. While limited to a discussion of various Christian sects, that discussion allowed us to see how religious, social, and cultural changes were intertwined. Greed simply did not operate in the same fashion after it underwent a process of confessionalization; the category worked differently in different confessional contexts. We also traced how greed operated in light of other heterodox spiritualties that perhaps sought to recreate an occult tradition in the age of science and enlightenment. That greed—instable, transmutable—is a topic of interest to reform theologians and new age theosophists alike is a potent indication of its cultural power and significance.

Greed's potency is illuminated from a different angle when we turn our attention to economics and the applied effort to manage resources. For much of the period under consideration greed—and the profit motive more generally—imperiled one's financial honor. When considering state expenditures, a state's unwillingness to spend (and the avarice of its functionaries) undermined the economic well-being of an entire nation. Indeed, it is helpful to see that

those who collectively invented the foundations of our modern economic system—Adam Smith, but not alone—continued to employ a language of morality to describe its workings. It seems that only the Austrian economists of the
twentieth century—and their many fellow travelers—are comfortable with the
erection of a firewall between economic behavior and moral considerations.
When we take the long view of economic thinking—using greed and avarice
as the connecting point—we see that economic discourse was really only lifted
out of a language of morality in the early twentieth century, and this secularized
economics (which mocked the inclusion of moral considerations in economic
calculations as an atavism from the medieval period) did not assume its position as orthodoxy in the discipline until after WWII.[3]

The increasing attention to the psychology of desire by economic thinkers
who used greed and avarice as a way into a larger framework for understanding
economic behaviors is an equally striking historical trajectory. When we think
about how the history of greed and the history of health and medicine have intersected, we see a broad transformation from alchemy to psychoanalysis. Each
approach was interested in figuring out how inordinate desire shaped behavior
and health, and each recognized the centrality of the body in seeing the symptoms of the disease. Greed, it was widely seen, was something that made one
ill, and that illness was manifested not only in the body but also in the web of
social connections that joined individuals into a community.

While Poggio may have intuited aspects of the subsequent development of
the category in his 1429 dialogue, that story was much more intricate than
what we see in that text. Modern greed looks, feels, and operates differently
from prior incarnations of the vice. It challenged thinkers to imagine new possibilities for treatment, to probe its meanings with novel theologies, and to understand the economic ramifications of new forms of desire in different ways
and with different analytical tools. Greed is perhaps the emotion that makes
us most human and that, therefore, seems the most natural, or unchanged, or
outside of history. The central argument of this book has been that greed has
a history, one shaped in peculiar ways by the shared human experience of modernity, and this book has offered a collection of ways to view those changes
over time.

Greed not only obscures, but it also illuminates aspects of our shared history. Viewing historical change through the lens of a feeling and the ideas that
were generated to apprehend the ways it functioned allow us to understand
in new ways the foundations upon which our culture and society have been
built. Greed is uniquely positioned to allow us to view these changes—and the
deployments of power that facilitate the creation of our modern world—with
fresh insight. Understanding greed's history allows us to understand better our
world and the ways it works.

## Notes

1. Ernest Jones, *Papers on Psycho-Analysis*, 5th ed. (Boston: Beacon Press, 1961), 129; Ernest Jones, "The Theory of Symbolism," *British Journal of Psychology, 1904–1920* 9, no. 2 (1918): 181–229.
2. John Maynard Keynes, "Auri Sacra Fames," in *Essays in Persuasion* (New York: Harcourt, Brace, 1932), 182–83.
3. See, for instance, Ramon Diaz, "The Political Economy of Nostalgia," in *Toward Liberty: Essays in Honor of Ludwig von Mises on the Occasion of His 90th Birthday*, ed. F.A. von Hayek et al., vol. II, 2 vols. (Menlo Park: Institute for Humane Studies, 1971), 441–54.

## Bibliography

Diaz, Ramon. "The Political Economy of Nostalgia." In *Toward Liberty: Essays in Honor of Ludwig von Mises on the Occasion of His 90th Birthday*, edited by F.A. von Hayek, Henry Hazlitt, Leonard Read, Gustavo Velasco, and F.A. Harper, II:441–54. Menlo Park: Institute for Humane Studies, 1971.

Jones, Ernest. *Papers on Psycho-Analysis*. 5th ed. Boston: Beacon Press, 1961.

———. "The Theory of Symbolism." *British Journal of Psychology, 1904–1920* 9, no. 2 (1918): 181–229.

Keynes, John Maynard. "Auri Sacra Fames." In *Essays in Persuasion*, 181–85. New York: Harcourt, Brace, 1932.

# ~: INDEX :~

CPSIA information can be obtained
at www.ICGtesting.com
Printed in the USA
LVOW10*1715070217

523502LV00009B/201/P